Hugh Tyndale-Biscoe is an acclaimed marsupial biologist, who served latterly as Chief Research Scientist at the Commonwealth Scientific and Industrial Research Organisation's Division of Wildlife and Rangelands Research. Born in Kashmir, India in 1929, he attended the school his parents ran in Kashmir, then finished school in England. He was awarded a BSc from the University of New Zealand (then called Canterbury University College) in 1951. After a year of working at the Department of Scientific and Industrial Research, he returned to study at the University of New Zealand, receiving a MSc Hons. In 1955 Tyndale-Biscoe moved to Pakistan where he taught biology in a college. He later returned to Australia to study marsupial reproduction at the University of Western Australia. He finished his PhD in 1962 and took up a lectureship at the Australian National University in Canberra before moving to the CSIRO in 1976.

Since 1990 he and his wife Marina have lived in the solar-powered, rammed earth house they built by the Mongarlowe River in New South Wales, filled it with Kashmiri memorabilia and he wrote this book. In 2018 he was made a Member of the Order of Australia.

T0347821

'This is an engaging narrative of missionary work in Kashmir, based on diaries, correspondence and school records. Much to the disappointment of the Church Missionary Society, Cecil Tyndale-Biscoe was not concerned to convert Kashimiris to Christianity, but by his example to reveal an active Christian life to the six boys' and one girls' schools he founded. Many of his pupils came to govern Kashmir in the second half of the twentieth century; and he became a legend. The text is crammed with much fascinating incidental detail.' – **Francis Robinson, Professor of the History of South Asia, Royal Holloway, University of London**

'An absorbing, balanced and informative record of unrelenting Imperial proselytism, personal moral certitude and ineradicable, uncompromising courage in an outpost of the British Empire – Kashmir. The Victorian missionary Cecil Earle Tyndale Biscoe was an Anglican of conviction, compassion and obduracy who took the Christian Gospel of his God and the Games Gospel of his English Public School to Srinagar determined to "make men": caring and considerate "Biscoe Boys". His Honours Board recorded only his pupils' "plucky and noble deeds". Biscoe was a Christian Crusader in an "Unholy Land" – as he perceived it, fighting civil corruption, human cruelty and permitted paedophilia. He was a promoter of Christian manliness but unconcerned about Christian conversion; a preux chevalier of his western Deity. He personified the exigent virtues and vices of religious passion and of confident imperialism.

The Missionary and the Maharajahs is a story of a man on an egregious, ethnocentric mission; eudemonistical not ecumenical; yet a galvanic reformer who transformed social and educational mores in one colonial context. The author and publisher are to be congratulated on producing an enthralling record of a man who was on a mission!' – **Professor J.A. Mangan, author of *The Games Ethic and Imperialism: Aspects of the Diffusion of an Ideal* and editor of *Making Imperial Mentalities: Socialisation and British Imperialism* and *The Cultural Bond: Sport, Empire and Society***

The Missionary and the Maharajas

Cecil Tyndale-Biscoe
and the Making of Modern Kashmir

Hugh Tyndale-Biscoe

BLOOMSBURY ACADEMIC
LONDON · NEW YORK · OXFORD · NEW DELHI · SYDNEY

BLOOMSBURY ACADEMIC
Bloomsbury Publishing Plc
50 Bedford Square, London, WC1B 3DP, UK
1385 Broadway, New York, NY 10018, USA
29 Earlsfort Terrace, Dublin 2, Ireland

BLOOMSBURY, BLOOMSBURY ACADEMIC and the Diana logo
are trademarks of Bloomsbury Publishing Plc

First published by I.B. Tauris & Co. Ltd 2019
This paperback edition published by Bloomsbury Academic 2022

A catalogue record for this book is available from the British Library.

A catalog record for this book is available from the Library of Congress.

ISBN: HB: 978-1-7883-1479-4
PB: 978-1-3503-4581-2
ePDF: 978-1-7867-3544-7
ePUB: 978-1-7867-2544-8

To find out more about our authors and books visit
www.bloomsbury.com and sign up for our newsletters.

Contents

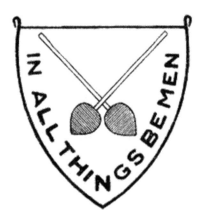

Crest and Motto
of the
Mission School, Srinagar from 1900

List of Maps

List of Illustrations

Images are the author's own, unless stated otherwise.

Preface

One morning in September 1980 during a holiday in Kashmir, three of us stepped into a taxi for a day trip into the hills. As we were about to leave, the driver leant out of his door and fell to the ground unconscious. We carried him to the pavement and began to apply mouth to mouth resuscitation and chest massage but to little effect. Other taxi drivers then carried him to a nearby surgery where the doctor attempted to revive him but soon declared him dead. He then said to me that the man had died in my care and that he was obliged to inform the police. I was much dismayed as he phoned the police and asked me my name. 'Biscoe?' he said. 'Are you related to Canon Biscoe?' 'Yes, he was my grandfather.' 'Oh, he was a great man, your grandfather. He taught us to help other people. Have a good holiday.' 'But what about the police report?' 'Don't worry about that.'

So, although by then my grandfather had been dead more than 30 years, his name was still potent in the land he had spent 57 years in. Indeed, we were in Kashmir to celebrate the centenary of the schools that he had run and which now bear his name.

I grew up in Kashmir and knew my grandparents as kindly old people living in the house next door. My childhood was spent in the company of many of my grandfather's Kashmiri colleagues, so I was aware of the story of his life. But all that was in a bygone age before India became independent and the last trumpet sounded the end of Empire; and the old imperialists – of which my grandfather was certainly one – had been consigned to revisionist ignominy. Yet here in Kashmir his name for some reason was still apparently revered. What was it about his life that made it memorable?

I began to think it would be interesting to revisit the story but here I came up against a stumbling block: while he had kept a diary throughout his adult life it was no longer extant. In his last years he had laboriously transcribed excerpts from the original diaries into six exercise books and then destroyed all the originals! Why did he do it? Were there things in the original diaries he did not want to be known, was he too outspoken in his opinions of his fellow missionaries or colleagues or did he just think he was leaving a tidier record of his life? Unfortunately the copied version is unreliable because he was already over 70 years old when he set himself to the task and he makes frequent mistakes in dates, as well as interpolating comments about related matters that happened years later. Where the original diaries would have been an invaluable record of his life the copied version is a poor and unreliable substitute. So for contemporary records I have had to rely on the 51 Annual School Logs; treasured scraps of letters held by the families of his colleagues and letters he wrote to his own family; and the archives of the Church Missionary Society (CMS) at the University of Birmingham; annual reports and publications of the CMS held at the United Theological College, Bangalore and the India Office Records at the British Library, London.

With these quite full records and other contemporary books and articles I have been able to fill out Cecil Tyndale-Biscoe's life and character. In doing so I have discovered that, while his work was generally regarded favourably by the British authorities in India, it was never supported particularly well by the Church Missionary Society that employed him, either in India or in the head office in London. The problem, from the Society's perspective, was that he was not interested in making converts so much as opening the eyes of his pupils to social injustice and preparing them to do something about it when they left school; in the annual logs there were no long lists of converts and 'enquirers', which were the purpose for which people in Britain gave their money to the missions, but rather stories about Hindu and Muslim boys putting out fires in the city, rescuing people from drowning and taking hospital patients for trips on the lake. Indeed, the number of converts to the Christian faith that he was responsible for were fewer than 20 and not many of these retained their faith.

As a result financial support from the Church Missionary Society was always insufficient and he had to rely on raising the shortfall from other sources. Because the State schools in Kashmir were free the State Government was reluctant to support a rival school with regular grants and, for the same reason, he could not charge fees to cover costs. So he largely relied on private donations from supporters in Kashmir, India and Britain, which entailed an enormous correspondence that occupied him every evening after the school day was over.

The other constant in his story was his poor health. As a child he had meningitis, which, without antibiotics, was a prolonged and debilitating disease that left him small and weak. He was sent to Kashmir because it had a benign climate but his health was seldom robust and in his third year he almost died from typhoid, surviving only because of the nursing care of his young wife and the missionary nurses.

He was supported throughout his life by his wife, Blanche, but there is very little in the written record about her. For most of the time he also had an English assistant. Initially his predecessor, Hilton Knowles, helped him especially when he was ill; then for several years his younger brother George supported him. From 1905 until 1921 Frank Lucey was his staunch assistant, and thereafter Eric, his youngest son, assumed the role until 1940.

In Kashmir the efforts of the foreign missionaries had mixed success: the evangelists were singularly unsuccessful in converting either Hindus or Muslims in Kashmir proper and had little effect on Muslims in Baltistan or Buddhists in Ladakh; the medical missions were well respected at the time and well supported by the State but have had little long-term effect; the educational missionaries had to put up with much greater resistance at the time from the State and only survived because of tacit support from the

British Resident but have had a far greater long-term impact on Kashmir society and political development.

The School and its tradition of social service continues to flourish in the present troubled times and Cecil Tyndale-Biscoe has become a legend around which many stories gather.

Acknowledgements

In researching and writing this book I have been helped by many people, many of whom are no longer alive. First among these was my late sister, Ann Barnes, who, in 1998, encouraged me to embark on the task when we spent a month together searching the archives of the Church Missionary Society at the University of Birmingham, and in 2000 when we searched the Kashmir papers in the India Office Records of the British Library in London, and in 2009 when we transcribed the whole correspondence which had been conducted weekly during 1934–35 between our grandfather and father. These provided the essential contemporary evidence on which the story could be built and she also provided her own insights into our shared experience of our grandfather's life.

Marina, my wife, accompanied me on four visits to Kashmir and India and helped me search the CMS archives in Bangalore. In 1980 we were helped in Kashmir by the then principal, John Ray and his wife Catherine and in subsequent visits by their successors Parwez Samuel Koul and Joyce Koul the current Principals of the Tyndale-Biscoe and Mallinson Schools, when we met many of the current staff and students. In Srinagar we also met Munshi Ghulam Hassan who showed us the diary of his grandfather, Munshi Hassan Ali, one of the first teachers in the Mission School. In Jammu we were enlightened by five retired senior teachers of the Schools: Sat Lal Razdan, Arjan Nath Mujoo, Balbadar Sapru, Prithvi Nath Razdan and Amar Nath Mattoo; and in Delhi by Dwarka Nath Koul and Madan Mehta. I also thank my cousin Stephen

Tyndale-Biscoe, who materially helped by lending me a precious diary and letters of his grandfather George, describing his time in Kashmir in 1895.

I have also received professional help from several people who it is a pleasure to acknowledge. The University Archivist at the University of Birmingham, Christine Penney, was most helpful to Ann and me during our month's search of the Church Missionary Society Archive. The Principal of the United Theological College, Bangalore, Dr Ghana Robinson, extended hospitality and professional help as did the staff at the India Office Records in London. I am much indebted to Christine Payne who drew the two maps for me, and I have been much helped with computer matters by Karen Mobbs. When I began to write I was greatly helped by the New Zealand writer, Kath Beattie who reviewed the first chapters and endeavoured to lighten my style; later my daughter Nicola and my sons Simon and Paul read and commented on several chapters and Marina read the whole thing and has been a constant encouragement as the years have passed.

Finally, I wish to thank Lester Crook who decided it is worth publishing and the team at I.B.Tauris who are making it happen.

Canberra, June 2018

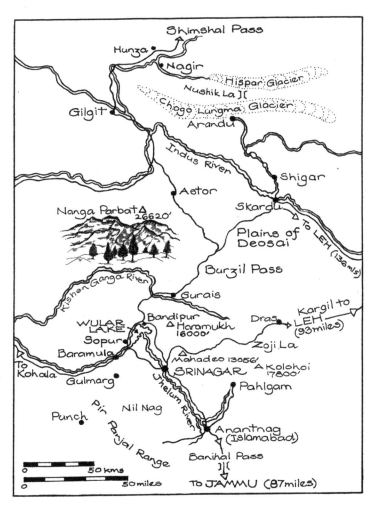

The Vale of Kashmir and the northern regions of Baltistan and Gilgit

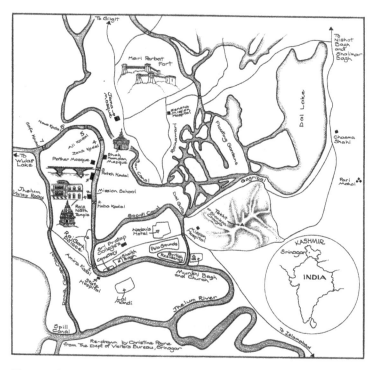

The city of Srinagar and its environs in the 1930s

1

Breaking Up and Building, 1890–95

Shahbash! The smell of your good deeds in our city has
reached to Kabul and nearly to London.
                    Boatmen after the Srinagar fire of 1892[1]

The first thing one noticed was his bent nose; and the
laughing blue eyes. The blue eyes he got from his mother
and the bent nose from boxing but the laughter was all his
own. He was short and slight and, at 27, full of confidence and zest
for all the experiences of his new life as a member of the Church
Missionary Society (CMS) of London 'going out to the field'. On
the voyage to India he offered the Captain his services as chaplain
but was not averse to pranks; Clara Warren,[2] another young
missionary, thought him a nice little man but hoped he would not
frighten her again by climbing the mast beyond where the leaders
are and there losing his new imperial hat, the solar topi. For this he
was punished by being tied to a spar.

For the past two years Cecil Biscoe had been working as a curate
in the slum districts of London, developing unorthodox methods
to help the most disadvantaged people in English society, before
being accepted as a missionary to go to Kashmir. He knew so
little about it that he had to visit the Royal Geographic Society

Figure 1 Cecil Tyndale-Biscoe aged 38 years

library to find out where it was, but he was confident that he would manage.

India was utterly different from England – the diversity of people, the strange noises, and the dust[3] – yet he felt at ease as he was passed from one English person to another. In Lahore he met a young subaltern who asked him why a fellow like him from a public school and Cambridge would want to waste his life as a missionary. In Amritsar he attended the induction of the new Colonel of the 3rd and 4th Gurkha Regiments, where he met an old boy of his public school, before meeting the missionaries at the home of Robert and Elizabeth Clark. The Clarks had been in India for 40 years and were the Head of the Mission in the Punjab and Kashmir. They were a formidable pair: he had been a mathematical wrangler at Cambridge and she could speak several European languages and read Sanskrit before she even went to India. Mrs Clark kept the younger missionaries under strict control; the men dared not speak to the women or offer them coffee. However, after the prayer meeting Biscoe ignored the protocol, surprising Mrs Clark by his forwardness.

Biscoe had three advantages in the new society he was entering: having been born into the English upper class, he moved easily among the senior civilians and military men; he subscribed to the prevailing beliefs in the superiority of British ways and the importance of their rule in India – the White Man's Burden; and his rowing prowess at Cambridge and Henley only six years before had given him a new confidence and brought him that special respect that elite sportsmen receive from other men.

In the missionary circle he was entering, however, these attributes were not appreciated. He was too independent for the senior missionaries and insufficiently pious for the others; when asked by one of them if he was among the 40,000 'saved souls' he said he very much hoped not as he didn't want to keep anyone else out. This tension would dog him in all he tried to do in Kashmir. While his work was admired by the British civilian and military men, it was never well supported by the CMS for whom he worked.

Medieval Kashmir

Biscoe left Amritsar for Rawalpindi at the beginning of December 1890 by *ekka*, a horse drawn country cart and a very bumpy ride; then the final journey into Kashmir in a slightly more comfortable tonga with sprung wheels, on the new cart road that had been completed earlier that year, winding its way along the cliffs above the thundering roar of the Jhelum River. After three days in the tonga driven by Jehu the Pathan, negotiating land slips and changing ponies, they reached the wide valley itself at Baramula. Wheeled traffic went no further; indeed, wheels were still unknown in Kashmir.[4] For everyone the 32 miles to the capital, Srinagar, was either by boat or pony.

Arriving at Baramula at midnight they were surrounded by crowds of men with flaring torches of resinous pine, eager for Biscoe's custom. His luggage was seized and he, thinking he had been robbed, lashed out with Jehu joining in. One man in a dirty nightgown was holding out a letter for him but Jehu knocked him to the ground. The letter was from a fellow missionary, Arthur

Neve, saying that he had sent this man with a boat to bring him to Srinagar – if Jehu had a different plan it was now thwarted, the messenger placated and the luggage and young sahib taken to Iqbal's waiting *doonga*. This was a long flat-bottomed craft made of sweet-scented deodar,[5] with a low, thatched roof and sides of bull-rush matting; a room at the front was furnished with floor rugs for the passenger and a room at the back for the crew of three. The latter included a mud-plastered fireplace for cooking, the smoke from which, mingled with the pungent scent of tobacco from the boatmen's hookah, pervaded the whole boat. For many young Englishmen coming on leave to Kashmir, the *doonga* owner would provide young Kashmiri women to ease the tedium of the three day trip to Srinagar; Biscoe was not offered this service but two years later his brother was; and was properly outraged. But for those who accepted, the price of the trip rose from 4 rupees to as much as 500, particularly if the sahib was sufficiently senior and anxious for discretion.

They set off in the morning, two men towing from the bank and the wife steering in the stern. At Sopor, where the river widens into the Wular Lake, they stopped; the crew would not cross in the afternoon because sudden squalls, known as the Nag Kawn, can blow up easily swamping a *doonga*. As Biscoe was trying to continue, the headmaster of the local school, Pandit Amar Chand, who could speak English appeared[6] and explained the danger to him but then helped him persuade the crew to continue. This was his first encounter with an educated Kashmiri and one who would later join his staff and be a great help to him. For now they parted and he with Iqbal continued in the *doonga* across the lake, putting up thousands of wild duck and geese in the process, and safely tied up before dark.

On a later trip across the lake his *doonga* was actually caught in the Nag Kawn.[7] The matting sides flapped; the water lapped against the sides as the wind whipped up the waves; the boatman shouted to his wife and she shouted back words that Biscoe could not understand; the waves splashed more violently and began slopping in over the sides. Then the boatman put down his paddle and rushed towards his wife and infant and, taking off his turban,

Figure 2 Sketch of the Mission School at the Third Bridge, drawn by Biscoe in 1892 for first log

started to tie them all together. When Biscoe asked him what he was doing, he said that this way they would all drown together. 'Please, can't you spare part of your turban for me as well?' The boatman was so taken aback that he burst out laughing at the idea of a 'lord sahib' begging from him and lost his fear. He took up his paddle in the bow and Biscoe took another in the stern and they got the boat facing up into the wind instead of broadside on.

But back to his first journey, the next day it was snowing and bitterly cold as the *doonga* was slowly towed up the now placid Jhelum River. Debris of the city floated by, dirty foam, floating straw and bloated carcases on which vultures perched, and their rancid smell and the smoke from the kitchen drove him out to run along the bank with the men. On the third day they smelt the city before they reached it: spices and cooking onions, riverside latrines and more rotting carcases. Passing under Safah Kadal, the seventh bridge, the sounds of the city joined their senses. Under the bridge of great deodar timbers hundreds of starlings flew about, creening kites[8] wheeled overhead or swooped down to snatch a morsel from the river, bells rang out from Hindu temples, vendors called their produce, boatwomen quarrelled loudly from their moored *kutchus* – the great barges of commerce on the river – and pi-dogs yelped as they were driven off. They passed under Nawa Kadal, Ali Kadal and Zana Kadal, the sixth, fifth and fourth bridges and, as an accomplished waterman himself, Biscoe admired the boatmen's skill in navigating the *doonga* between the piles and against the current, taking advantage of every swirl and eddy, using every crack and hole to pole the boat forward. Now on the right bank they passed the great Shah-i-Hamdan Mosque that commemorates Mir Sayeed Ali Hamdani, who in 1380 brought Islam to Kashmir from Persia; the mosque was originally built in 1392 over a Hindu temple to the goddess Kali, it was twice destroyed by fire and last rebuilt of deodar in 1732. On the opposite bank they passed the Pathar Masjid Mosque built by the Mughal Queen Nur Jehan in 1620; not used as a mosque, because it was raised by a woman, but very useful as a granary.

Lining both banks of the river and rising from plinths of ancient carved stone were three and four storey timber houses with intricate lattice windows and roofs of earth on birch bark; these were interspersed with broad stone steps leading down to the water's edge. Here people were washing, collecting water in large earthen pots, gossiping or stepping into *shikaras*, the water taxis of the city. Just above Fateh Kadal, the third or Gallows Bridge, they passed some tall buildings on the left bank one of which, though Biscoe didn't then know it, would be at the centre of his life for 50 years. Some of the boys, curious to glimpse their new teacher were astonished to see a fair-haired youth standing on the prow of the *doonga*.

Near it on the same bank was the Rago Nath Temple with its high dome of silvery shining metal. Headquarters of the Hindu Dharam Sabha or High Council where important religious matters were decided, it would also figure largely in Biscoe's life. The stretch of river between Habba Kadal, the Bridge of Air, or gossip and rumour, and the King's Bridge, Amira Kadal, was the preserve of Maharaja Pratap Singh: the left bank was almost wholly occupied by his palace and the *Zenana* or women's palace, and by the opposite bank were moored the royal barges with seats for 60 paddlers, the smaller 30-paddle *parindas*, or birds, and the fine steam launch given to his father, the late Maharaja Ranbir Singh by Queen Victoria in 1875.[9] A century on it now rests in the Museum garden across the river.

Upstream of the palace the river makes a sharp bend and here the city opened out with large gardens on the left bank and the British resident's garden on the right bank. Upstream of this on the same bank was the Munshi Bagh, a large park shaded by giant chenar or plane trees, which the previous Maharaja set aside as one of the two places where British people could stay. There were bungalows for the missionaries and the few foreigners employed by the State, known as the Barracks, and sites where summer visitors could set up their tents.

Here Biscoe's journey ended as he was greeted by his fellow missionaries, Hinton Knowles the padre, and the doctors Arthur and Ernest Neve, with whom he would stay because Mrs Knowles was ill with typhoid. The Knowles had been in Kashmir for seven years preaching the Gospel in the villages and, against strong opposition from the State, running a Mission School for Hindu boys in the city. Knowles was a scholarly man; he was a Fellow of the Royal Geographical Society of London, had recently written a book on Kashmiri folktales[10] and was currently translating the Bible into Kashmiri. He was 36 and had been pleading with the Society to relieve him of the school so that he could concentrate on other activities. The Neve brothers were 31 and 29 respectively but unlike Biscoe, were tall, solemn men with military moustaches. Both had graduated with high honours from Edinburgh Medical School and come out to Kashmir within a year of graduation. Arthur had been in Kashmir for eight years and his brother for four. Neither was married and would not be so for many years; both were deeply engaged with running the Mission Hospital and were already fluent in Kashmiri and Urdu. Their recreation was exploration of the mountainous country to the north and east of Kashmir. Arthur had already made two quite extensive expeditions to Baltistan in the north and was at the time trying to persuade the Society to let him make a trip to Kafiristan that lies between Afghanistan and Chitral to the west of Kashmir.[11] Ostensibly his purpose was to bring the Gospel to the non-Muslim animists, known as Kafirs, but there was a large element of adventure in his proposal and he was frustrated by the lack of support he was getting from Lahore. In the view of the British Resident in Kashmir, 'Neve is a clever fellow but extremely conceited and greedy of power and influence.'[12] Ernest had not yet made any expeditions on his own but in a few years would visit Leh with Biscoe and be the first to climb many of the surrounding peaks, including the 17,000 feet Mount Kolahoi, and much later was a foundation member of the Himalayan Club.

Ernest believed that:

> Medical mission work is completely in accordance with the spirit of the East. The medical missionary, as healer and evangelist, goes forth on a very distinct mission, and one with the highest Scriptural and humanitarian sanctions. His ideals are the highest. His failures are due to inherent weakness or unfavourable environment and not to low aim. His life is a peculiarly happy one, spent as it is in daily ministering to the needs of those who are in pain and sorrow, and pointing at the same time, as he does, to the Source of all comfort.[13]

On that first winter afternoon of Biscoe's arrival in Srinagar, the Neve brothers took Biscoe for a pony ride up the nearby Shankra Charya hill to show him the view of the Dal Lake to the north, lying below Mount Mahadeo on the right and the Hari Parbat Fort to the left. Far away in the south and west, the snow-covered peaks of the Pir Panjal Range formed a backdrop to the broad windings of the Jhelum River with the medieval city spread along both banks. At the top of the spur overlooking the lake they met the missionary nurses, Elizabeth Hull and Elizabeth Newman, who had ridden out for a breather after their day's work; they had been in Kashmir for two years working in the city with Kashmiri women, particularly the boatwomen. Elizabeth Newman would become a strong ally of Biscoe's during the next 30 years, going where he as a man could not go.

When Knowles and Biscoe walked the five miles through the city to the Mission School near Fateh Kadal the next morning he really got to see what the city was like; and it was far worse than anything he had seen in the slums of London. It was the stench and utter filth of the narrow streets where rubbish and slops from the houses on either side were dumped and where people eased themselves. Packs of maimed and scurvy pi-dogs and starving donkeys and cows tried to get a living from the filth, while men picked their way carefully around it on wooden clogs; at that time of the day there were no women to be seen. The timber framed houses, plastered with mud and roofed with thatch or a thick layer of earth were mostly off the straight, leaning against each other like old friends. Later in the winter another hazard was added to walking in the streets as wet snow often slipped off the roofs onto the street below. No house had a chimney and the small lattice windows were covered with oiled paper, for glass was unknown. People kept warm inside, each with a small *kangri*, or charcoal brazier, held against the body under the single voluminous gown, called a *pheran*.

Knowles had begun the school for boys in 1883, the year he arrived and, within a year, he had attracted 60 pupils, and reported that 'some of them are very nice intelligent lads'. He found the Kashmiri Hindu pupils very quick at learning and many of them had a great desire to study English as they saw this as a route to a lucrative job with the State. All Hindus in Kashmir belonged to the Brahmin caste and those that were educated were given the honorific title of Pandit. Knowles and his wife taught scripture in the school every day, the pupils learning passages by heart. He thought their progress in the subjects they had been studying so good that some of the upper boys should soon be able to go in for the Entrance examination of the Punjab University. Earlier in the year he had managed to rent the much larger house at Fateh Kadal so that the school could now accommodate over 330 pupils,[14] which he was about to introduce to Biscoe.

As they reached the third floor Biscoe reeled at the smell and sight of the 200 senior pupils sitting on the floor and pinched himself to make sure he was not having a nightmare. Every boy was wrapped in a *pheran* with a *kangri* underneath; none had washed during the cold months; and the hot air passed through the outer clothes damp from snow or rain. Many of the faces turned up to him had full beards, for many of the pupils were married men. Being Brahmins, all wore white turbans tied as tightly as a bandage to their heads, red paint smeared from their foreheads down the bridge of their noses, on the lobes of their ears and their throats. Many wore heavy gold ear-rings, which had to be supported by string over their heads because their ears were so stretched. As he looked into their eyes he got another shock: he was transported back to the terror of his English public school when, as a small boy he was about to be raped by the school bullies. Then he had learnt to box to defend himself – and in the process got his bent nose. Here they were again but now he had the power.

When he was asked to speak to the class he suggested that they might like a holiday to mark his arrival and was astonished by the response: a groan and the complaint that they had come to school to learn English and didn't want to waste a day. Well, Kashmiri boys must be very different from English boys! Perhaps he was wrong about their eyes. He asked Knowles how he punished such pupils and was astonished to learn that there was no need for punishment as a word of caution was sufficient. In his diary he wrote, 'I marvelled! And saw that I had much to learn'. Later he thought, Knowles had not been a boarder in an English public school and therefore did not recognise a sexual predator as he did. He determined to hold his ideas to himself until Knowles went on leave when he would be able to act.

Back at Munshi Bagh in the last days of 1890, Biscoe was introduced to the small English community in Srinagar. General Thatcher, a veteran of the 1857 Mutiny and the owner of the first houseboat to be built in Kashmir, would stand at the club on cold days and offer everyone cherry brandy. Colonel Neville Chamberlain, son of another veteran of the mutiny was adviser to the Maharaja's army. Another was Walter Lawrence, the Land Commissioner appointed two years before by the British government to establish an equitable settlement of the cultivated land in the Kashmir Valley. Biscoe also met the Governor, Sirdar Roop Singh, who kept him waiting a long time to show his importance. The Governor's importance was further enhanced by his owning the only house in the city that had glass in the windows. On Boxing Day, according to custom, they went to old Mrs Johnson's house for cake and wine. Her husband had worked for Maharaja Ranbir Singh as a surveyor in 1865–68 and later as Wazir of Ladakh where in 1883 he was murdered. In recognition of his service she was given a house free of rent.[15]

The missionaries joined each evening for a service in the chapel at the hospital and then walked home to the Munshi Bagh. When Biscoe escorted the women home, Ernest Neve objected and explained to him that the natives would not understand his intentions. However well meant, this advice did not please Biscoe, who had worked in the slums of Whitechapel during the time of Jack the Ripper, and was disregarded. So his relationship with Ernest was cool, whereas Arthur Neve and Biscoe developed a friendship from the first. Arthur took home leave in the new year and travelled overland through Persia by camel, returning in November with his niece, Nora, to help in the hospital.

As Biscoe digested these first impressions he pondered on his fitness for the task he had been given; his colleagues were scholars in their chosen fields and each had adapted to the strange customs of the country and could speak in the vernacular. By contrast he knew he was no scholar and had never been able to learn foreign languages. How could he teach these clever Hindu boys, all of whom belonged to the scholar caste of Brahmin and were taught from an early age to believe in their spiritual superiority to the majority of Kashmiris, who were Muslims? When at his home in England he had received his orders to go to Kashmir to teach in a boys' school his family had burst into laughter at the idea of Cecil teaching anyone anything, let alone in a foreign language!

One thing at least he knew he could do in this city built on a river and surrounded by lakes and that was boating. Before the year's end he had bought a canoe from Mrs Losach, one of the English residents and had it converted into a rowing skiff. This gave him his own means to travel about the city and out to the Dal Lake. This was timely because by January the whole country was under snow and the roads were impassable in the city. He was soon elected Captain of the sahib's boat club and was asked to build

Figure 3 The first crew of Kashmiri teachers to row an English boat, 1892

rowing boats and to organise a regatta when the weather warmed up. He had never built a boat before but borrowed plans from a French trader in the city and had a four-oared clinker boat with a crew of missionaries on the water by May.

But when he tried to get a school crew together he came slap up against Kashmiri custom; only low class Muslim boatmen did that, certainly no Pandit or educated person could possibly row a boat. And although everyone travelled in boats no one in Srinagar could swim, so every year many people drowned. Here was something where his experience and interest could be useful and he set out to get a nucleus of young teachers ready to learn to row and swim. On the first occasion he arrived at the school in the new rowing boat he invited two of the more promising young teachers to join him for a row and so set an example to the others. 'I cannot do so because I shall get muscles on my arms and shall be like a coolie', answered Mahanand Razdan, but a moment later he and Hari Ram were both in the boat with Biscoe, drifting down the river towards Fateh Kadal Bridge. They had to use the oars or be washed under the bridge. With their example three other teachers followed and so the first crew was formed. It comprised a Muslim Cox, Din Mohammad, a Christian as stroke, Bejoy Sircar, the two Brahmins, Hari Ram and M. Razdan and a Jammu Dogra of the Hindu soldier caste called Poonoo.[16] By the next summer they were competing in the regattas against the missionary crew and the English visitors.

In September that year (1891) the British Viceroy, Lord Lansdowne came to Kashmir to oversee developments in the northern regions of Gilgit where a border skirmish was brewing, and he shot a large markhor with horns 58.5 inches long.[17] He visited the school overlooking the river and mindful of his host's rowing prowess, expressed the hope that the boys would soon be racing in eight-oared boats, like Oxford and Cambridge for the 'Head of the River', against other schools in Srinagar. Some hope, thought Biscoe; but at least it was more encouraging than the opinion of another British visitor who said, 'so you think you will get these lazy Brahmins to row, do you? You might as well try to change a leopard's spots. The best you can do is to pack up your bags and go back to England. There are plenty of people to convert there.'[18]

But the speed with which he persuaded the younger teachers to break publicly with their customs showed that this pessimistic view of Kashmiris was wrong: when offered the opportunity and given leadership, there were many who would follow him, and by the next spring there were several crews eager to row to the Wular Lake. One of these young men was Munshi Hassan Ali. As a young Muslim in Srinagar he decided, against the advice of the mullahs, that he wanted to learn English; he adopted English dress and about seven years before had come to an arrangement with Knowles to teach him Kashmiri if Knowles would teach him English. He joined the staff of the Mission School in 1884 and, after it moved to Fateh Kadal he became the head *Munshi*, or Bursar, and later administered the Waifs and Strays Fund. He served on the staff for the rest of his working life. He also kept a diary in Urdu, which has passed to his grandson in Srinagar, Munshi Ghulam Hassan, and gives a perspective different from Biscoe's of those formative times.

First Journeys into the Countryside

As winter gave way to spring Kashmir came alive; almond trees blossomed, wild tulips and irises opened and strange, lovely birds – golden orioles, paradise flycatchers and hoopoes – arrived from the plains of India to nest in the gardens. Knowles took Biscoe into the countryside where Biscoe sketched and broadened his understanding of the school and local society. Their first trip was 30 miles up river to the second town in Kashmir, known by Hindus as Anantnag and by Muslims as Islamabad. Here the mission had a small hospital and a second school. They travelled in a *doonga* belonging to Naraian Das, who told Biscoe of the difficulties that he and two other Hindu friends, Anand Koul and Tara Chand Kachroo, had encountered during the time of Maharaja Ranbir Singh seven years before because they had attended the Mission School. They were by then studying Law in the State School when a government official, Pandit Dhar, discovered that they could pronounce English correctly and therefore must have attended the Mission School. All three were visited at their homes by the police and held in the lock-up for two days until released through the representations of Arthur Neve. Since the death of Maharaja Ranbir Singh in 1885, however, such overt opposition to the Mission School had declined. Naraian Das did not pursue law but, unusually for a Pandit, developed a business, building boats for hire to summer visitors. He built the first houseboat with timber sides instead of matting[19] and in 1892 Biscoe commissioned him to build one with a rooftop deck, which he called *Shotover*, in honour of the person who gave him £25 as a wedding present. Tara Chand, like Hassan Ali, joined the staff of the Mission School. On their return to Srinagar, Biscoe wrote to the Society in London:

> We have been up to Islamabad to see our school there and are returning. This morning we had a grand little congregation at Bijbehara outside a shrine. The people are really most attentive and quiet. You can of course get a huge crowd who will listen most eagerly at any place in this country and Knowles says that they think over and repeat what they hear. The Islamabad

school is certainly going ahead under the able supervision of Luke and a native Christian. And our school in Srinagar is growing week by week. I find the school work most interesting. The boys seem to be almost too keen to learn, so very different to the ordinary English school boy. They receive plenty of scripture teaching, and they are gradually dropping their family superstitions and accepting the truth.[20]

A month later Knowles and Biscoe were off on another trip to the countryside, this time down river to the Wular and across to Sopor with Mrs Knowles (now recovered from typhoid) and the Knowles' two young children. In this first written account of his impressions Biscoe wrote:

Another Hindu festival having arrived on the scene has obliged us to shut our school for a week. We have taken this opportunity of diving into the country. We were meditating where to go, when an old Christian of 40 years standing, named Kadra Baksh (said to be 103 years old) arrived with his daughter at Knowles' house, having come from the village of Woogra, two marches from Srinagar. He had come to ask Knowles to go to his village, as there was much interest manifesting itself in Christianity, and in consequence the Muslims were persecuting the inquirers by endeavouring to confiscate their land. This news made us determined to go to Woogra and to make use of the waterways as much as possible. General Thatcher gladly lent us his houseboat, which was large enough for our party; it is divided into three rooms. We also took a native *doonga*, which we used for our kitchen, and which the servants, boatmen and Kadra Baksh used. We stowed on board the dandy (a boxed seat for Mrs Knowles, carried by four men), 3 tents and the usual camp furniture and started directly after school; gliding down the swift current (the River is very full at this season). We passed under five of the picturesque pile bridges and between two lines of the quaint wooden houses stretching along the river banks for two miles below the school. At nightfall we tied up to the bank and were serenaded for most of the night by the jackals, which were assembling from their several lairs, for the enjoyment of their nightly repast in the village. Until quite late the old Christian's voice could be heard from the servants' boat, preaching to the boatmen. One Muslim was contradicting him and saying that Adam had two sons, one a Hindu and the other a Muslim. Kadr Baksh was heard to answer, 'how could there have been Muslims before that Mohammed was born?' This was certainly a score for KB. Before daybreak we were on the move, as the boatmen are always anxious to cross the lake before the sun rises on account of the frequent mid day squalls. When we awoke we found ourselves on the Wular Lake, which washes the bases of many glorious mountains. The lake was quite calm and the sun was bathing everybody and everything with warmth and light. My morning tub was an easy matter, just one plunge through the window and I was in the lake swimming by the side of the boat, and Knowles very soon joined me. There are a great many fishing eagles[21] in these parts, beautiful birds and not very shy. We saw very few duck as they migrated some weeks ago to the far north to the arctic regions. At mid day we sighted Sopor, a town on the south side of the lake, where we had to hire coolies for the march to Woogra [...] Whilst the coolies were fixing up their loads the old Christian did not lose his chance of preaching to them, in fact as he did to everyone he met on the road, his pony being his pulpit. After a pleasant walk of eight miles we arrived at Woogra and pitched our tents outside the village between two snow fed torrents. Knowles saw three of the inquirers and advised them and others as regards their baptism, also about the matter of the land.[22]

At Sopor, where Biscoe had met Pandit Amar Chand four months before, Knowles was keen to meet a young Muslim, Munshi Abdul Kadir, who had attended the Mission School and wished to become a Christian. Arthur Neve had sent him to the Punjab where he had been baptised, much against the wishes of his family. On his return to Kashmir his father shut him up in their house until he outwardly reverted to Islam. Having done so his parents were happy to give Knowles and Biscoe a great feast, which they served in the boat. Nevertheless, Biscoe felt sorry for Abdul Kadir in his predicament and when they returned to Srinagar he engaged him to teach him Urdu.

These early encounters with young Kashmiris who aspired to become Christians and for it were cast out of their homes, made a deep impression on Biscoe, and in his annual report two year's later he wrote:

> It brought before one the great responsibility of teaching these boys Christianity, and therefore taking away their ancient religion. A man with no religion is far worse off than a man with one and in taking away their Hinduism one puts these boys in a very dangerous position, unless one can induce them to face persecution and accept Christianity, in which they profess their belief. But this dangerous step none yet dare to take.[23]

He was moving to the position he would adopt henceforth of attracting young teachers who supported his ideas on social change through the school, but not asking them to change their religion. Good deeds were to him far more important than formal professions of belief.

Knowles and Biscoe were developing a strong friendship and each wrote to the London Secretary of the Society. Knowles thanked him for sending them such a congenial, godly fellow helper and formally handed over the school to Biscoe and reverted to pastoral work and his translation of the Bible into Kashmiri. Biscoe wrote:

> We are a very pleasant party here, and get on capitally together. The English people here are very friendly personally, but are I fear opposed to missionary enterprise, which is I believe almost entirely due to their ignorance of the matter. But we hope by degrees to break down their prejudices and make them alive to their responsibilities.[24]

He then raised the delicate matter of his marriage. The rule in the CMS was that a missionary could not marry until he had passed the language test and Biscoe was having great difficulty with this and feared that his betrothed in England might have to wait several years. So he used another tack: he pointed out that when the Knowles went on leave the following year there would be no married missionary in Kashmir and he suggested that if the language requirement were to be waived he and his wife would provide the necessary respectability to prevent scandal arising when missionaries met for public reading and other gatherings. He went on to say:

> The country so far suits me splendidly, so that I have not been more fit since my college days; this country is very healthy and in every way fit for ladies; and Dr Arthur Neve will be returning here about November next and could escort Miss Burges out. I hope you may see fit to consider this question and come to the same conclusion as the missionary party here have done.[25]

Knowles lent his support, and it worked; his marriage was approved and he could look forward to Blanche coming out with Arthur and Nora Neve and being with him by the end of the year.

They had first met more than five years before when she was just 18. He had been on a summer mission from Cambridge University to children at Llandudno beach where her three brothers were among the boys attracted to the mission. They invited him to their home in Birmingham where their father was the Rector of a large but impoverished city parish. Blanche was the youngest of seven sisters and her three younger brothers received most of their parent's attention. Cecil was attracted to her because she seemed to be neglected by the rest of the large family. How that first meeting developed in the coming years is not related anywhere. He went back to Cambridge to complete his degree, study for ordination and then serve as a Curate in Bradfield and later in Whitechapel. What Blanche did in those intervening years is not recorded but she did not qualify for any profession and probably followed the prevailing practice of helping at home and in her father's large parish. After Biscoe was accepted by the CMS in July 1890 they became engaged and his mother invited her to visit his home at Holton. That was it; he left for India in November and she prepared to wait until he was permitted to marry. Again, there is no evidence that she prepared for a future life in Kashmir by learning Hindustani or training for a missionary life.

Walter Lawrence's Friendship and Influence on Biscoe's Thinking

An equally important influence on Biscoe's thinking in the first half of 1891 was his developing friendship with Walter Lawrence, who by the summer of that year had taken very much to Biscoe and his ideas. Walter Lawrence was six years older than Biscoe but they had similar backgrounds; both had been to public schools and both had rowed at university, Biscoe at Jesus College, Cambridge, Lawrence at Balliol, Oxford. While at Oxford Lawrence had made friends with a detective from Scotland Yard, who took him about in Whitechapel, where for the first time he crossed the frontier of middle class life and came to know the Victorian wilderness of metropolitan poverty,[26] just as Biscoe had before he came to Kashmir. Lawrence had entered the Indian Civil Service in 1879 at 22, already prepared by a knowledge of Hindustani learnt at Oxford, and was posted to Lahore which he reached on a cold December morning 'without a friend and without a blanket, shivering in my flimsy garments and with a purse as cold as my body'.[27] Ten years later and with much experience in British India he had been offered the position of Settlement Officer to the Kashmir Government. His task was to develop a just system of taxation for the farmers of the valley. Now in 1891 he was spending much of his time in the countryside assessing the land and hearing the appeals of farmers and local officials against his assessments. He would invite English friends to accompany him on these tours. In May he had been accompanied by E.F. Knight, who wrote a vivid description of the trip in his book *Where Three Empires Meet*,[28] and in June Biscoe went with him to Islamabad and thence rode into the hills around Pahalgam. Although he has not left an account like Knight's it is most likely that he had a similar experience. Having arrived in Kashmir wholly ignorant of its history and people, this was a wonderful opportunity to learn of the problems of the cultivators and villagers firsthand, and of the recent history of the State that had led to Lawrence's appointment. As they travelled the now familiar river trip, Lawrence would have outlined the recent history of Dogra rule in Kashmir.

The previous Maharaja Ranbir Singh was a man of noble presence and good intentions but he was more interested in religion than in the affairs of State, which he grievously neglected. Through the Amritsar Treaty of 1846 between his father, Gulab Singh, and the British East India Company the Maharaja owned all the land in the country and the cultivators were obliged to give him two-thirds of all they produced in kind. The collection of this revenue was managed through a three-tiered system; the village headman or *Lambadar* was required to deliver the goods to the district chief, or *Tehsildar* who in turn delivered it to the State Governor. Each step in the process was open to rampant corruption, particularly as the officials were paid very little. By far the majority of the cultivators were Muslims whereas the higher officials were Hindu Pandits, who lived in Srinagar and, being clever men, plundered the villagers for the benefit of the city. It was most convenient to these officials that the Maharaja remained ignorant of the real situation in his lands and busied himself with religious matters.

This inequitable system, and its dire consequences for the country people, had been brought to the attention of the British Government as long ago as 1870 by Robert Thorp, a young man whose mother was Kashmiri and his father English. He visited Kashmir for the first time in 1868 and was horrified by what he found;[29] he wrote a pamphlet entitled *Cashmere Misgovernment*[30] but was poisoned in Srinagar before it was published. Although his pamphlet raised the issue in the House of Commons, the British Government did not respond; but seven years later the situation became acute when there was a terrible famine in Kashmir. It began with a poor harvest in 1877 but the 1878 crop was good and should have made up for it. While it stood in the fields waiting for city officials to assess it, heavy and continuous rain began to fall in October and it was beaten to the ground, and even that which had been cut rotted in the fields. When it was realised that there would be no maize or rice for food, the traders hoarded the remaining stocks and officials raided the villages for seed. The villagers desperately hid their remaining stocks in the ground where it was lost. Through the winter draught animals died and so in spring the fields could not be ploughed, and there was no seed for planting the new crop. The starving people ate the fruit before it was ripe and they even ate the bark of trees so that by summer famine was raging. But the starving people were forbidden to leave Kashmir so that utter demoralisation set in and the dead were left unburied for pi-dogs to scavenge. More than half the people in the valley died and by far the majority of these were the Muslim country folk. Hindus did not suffer heavily in the famine because they wielded the power to seize all available grain. The great loss of life of farmers and their draught animals in 1878 meant that few crops were planted and tended in 1879, so the famine continued. The State appealed to the Punjab for grain but when it was brought in, it was seized for the city folk again. And so the famine continued into 1880.

The only foreigners in the city at this time were three missionaries, Rev Wade and Dr and Mrs Downes. They tried to help as best they could, taking in many orphan children and starting a school for them. So began the Mission School in Kashmir. When the British Officer on Special Duty, Captain Henvey, returned in the spring of 1880 he wrote a detailed report on the situation, from his own observations and those of the missionaries who had been there through the winter.[31] He excoriated the Pandit officials and urged the Indian Government to intervene and appoint a Resident with wide powers to oversee the Maharaja, establish an equitable land settlement and appoint properly paid tax collectors who would not exploit the cultivators. The Viceroy and the Indian Government accepted his findings but deferred action until the death of the Maharaja, which was imminent.

The Maharaja had three sons and custom dictated that the eldest should succeed to the Gadi, or throne. However, Henvey's successor, Colonel Oliver St John had a very low opinion of the eldest son, writing in 1884:

> The Maharaja has occasionally had serious thoughts of setting aside his two eldest sons Pratap Singh and Ram Singh in favour of his third son Amar Singh. Mian Pratap Singh the eldest is about 30 years of age and has besotted an intellect, never very strong, by habitual indulgence in the most degrading vices. The Maharaja has attempted from time to time to associate him with himself in the administration of the country, and on his recent visit to Kashmir entrusted him with certain powers which he at once abused. It is certain that he would be a very weak, if not bad ruler. The third son, Amar Singh, a very good-looking lad of 18 is a general favourite and is at least superior in ability to his elder brothers.[32]

He recommended that Amar Singh be preferred as the next Maharaja but was overruled by the Viceroy, Lord Ripon, so after the Maharaja's death in 1885, Pratab Singh was installed as the third Maharaja of Jammu and Kashmir. He succeeded to a corrupt administration and, although he wished to carry out reforms, he had none to help and many to hinder him. St John and his successor Plowden despised the young Maharaja; the Pandits had the power and the army enforced it against the villagers. The Viceroy further humiliated the Maharaja by changing the status of the British representative to a Resident who would oversee the affairs of State. This was ameliorated by the appointment of Colonel Parry Nisbet, who was much friendlier than his predecessors.

But within three years the Kashmir State was bankrupt and in March 1889 the Maharaja was stripped of his power but allowed to retain his title, and Parry Nisbet became the de facto ruler overseeing a Council of Regency, with Raja Amar Singh as its president. Key positions in the management of the State were filled with British men and public works were begun, such as the Jhelum Valley road, and an equitable Land Revenue Settlement initiated.

Lawrence was offered the post of Settlement Officer in 1889 but when he arrived in the beautiful valley, he noticed that his welcome was chilly, for, though the Maharaja wished for a settlement, the officials had decided that there should be no settlement which might interfere with their privileged hold on the produce of the country. Not only was Lawrence rebuffed by the Hindu officials, he also had no success with the villagers.

One incident changed their attitude. He discovered the unrest in one village was caused by a Dogra officer, Colonel Natha, forcing men to leave their land and be taken as unpaid porters for the army of Gilgit, a system known as *begar*, which they greatly feared because so few men ever returned and because the crops could not be managed in their absence. Colonel Natha had just torn off half the beard of one man who resisted him and he had no time for the strange Englishman who came upon him. Lawrence was appalled by what he saw and realised that the imposition of *begar* directly thwarted his work. He promised the villagers that he would stop *begar* and get rid of Colonel Natha, neither of which promises did the villagers expect to see fulfilled. But within a few weeks Lawrence had accomplished both, and from that time his fame spread across the valley and he received the cooperation of the country people in all his work. He wrote:

> When I went back to the villages, the very children talked to me, and the sudden change from grim silence to glad loquacity was astonishing and even embarrassing. Under the plane trees and the walnuts, on the green banks over the grey-green stream, they would talk for hours and I would listen. Or, better still, as the nights grew colder, they would sit in a circle round the camp-fire of cedar wood, taking snuff in birch-bark packets, and telling me curious stories.[33]

Hearing Lawrence's stories during their two-day boat journey to Islamabad Biscoe became much better informed about the recent history of Kashmir and ready to see how Lawrence set about his task. They camped in a pleasant orchard outside the town where the people again gathered to meet Lawrence, the man they called the Bandobast Wallah – chief person for official business – and hear what level of taxation he had determined for their lands.

As usual the *Lambadar* of the village came up to disparage the condition of the land, despite the excellent crops to be seen around; hoping thereby to obtain a reduction in the assessment. While he spoke the other cultivators ranged themselves in a melancholy chorus of pitiable weeping at the terrible state of their land. But as soon as Lawrence showed that he saw through their performance they good-humouredly accepted the assessment. Then it was on to the next village with the spear-bearing *chowkidars* – watchmen – in gay uniforms leading the way, several officials accompanied them and behind toiled the coolies carrying the tents and baggage. The cultivators of the first district walked with them to the boundary of their land where they left them to be escorted by those of the next district.

As they travelled Lawrence pointed out to Biscoe how to recognise a Hindu from a Muslim by subtle points of dress and behaviour: a Hindu wears the tuck of his turban on the right, the Muslim on the left; the Hindu has long narrow sleeves and fastens his *pheran* on the left, the Muslim has short full sleeves and fastens his *pheran* on the right; the Hindu has tight trousers the Muslim loose ones; the Hindu mounts a pony on the near side, the Muslim on the off side; the Hindu begins his ablutions with the left leg, the Muslim invariably with the right.

As well as learning from Lawrence about the social customs of the people, Biscoe also got a better appreciation during this tour of the injustices of the rigid class system that prevailed, especially in the city where the students who attended the Mission School came from: these young men were the sons of the officials who resisted the land assessment that Lawrence was charged to do, and who so ruthlessly exploited the Muslim village cultivators. While explaining to Biscoe the oppression and cruelties then practised, Lawrence stopped and looking him straight in the face said, 'Now mark my words, Biscoe, the time is coming when the pendulum will swing and you will see the Muslims persecuting the Hindus in the city as the Hindus do now the Muslims.'[34] One hundred years later, all the Hindus were driven from Kashmir and their houses burnt down.

The impressions of the students Biscoe had on his first day at the Mission School were now reinforced by this trip into the country and encouraged his resolve to change the way the Mission School operated when he assumed full charge: bookwork would be subordinated to social service. He wanted to make these sons of high officials aware of the plight of the people for whom they would later in life be responsible, and teach them to be honest in their dealings.

Accompanying Lawrence and Biscoe was the new headmaster for the branch Mission School at Islamabad and, on their return to Srinagar, Biscoe wrote to London:

> I went up to Islamabad last week to take up our new headmaster, Secundra Ali, an Afghan by tribe who converted to Christianity about three years ago. He was brought up in the Amritsar Mission School. He bears the good qualities of his race, plus a cheerful disposition; all the boys have taken a great fancy to him and hang round him all day. I found the school flourishing in every way. The boys there, besides being keen students are also very keen on sports, so I got some capital games of cricket and swims in the Jhelum with them. They appear to be altogether more manly than the boys at our school in Srinagar, and therefore will make better Christians.[35]

The favourable assessment of Secundra Ali was premature for a few weeks later Biscoe got letters from some parents reporting that Secundra Ali was taking boys to his lodging at night to read the Bible and there committing sodomy. Biscoe called him to Srinagar and, when the charge was confirmed, dismissed him. Secundra Ali rose from his chair and said, 'Don't you know that I am a Pathan and can use my knife?' To which Biscoe replied, 'I am a Britisher and have fists so out of the door with you'. The Pathan departed but Biscoe does not relate how his action was viewed by the Punjab Secretary of the CMS, Robert Clark, who had supported Secundra Ali's appointment.

The Hunza-Nagir Campaign of 1891–92

In September, when the Viceroy visited Kashmir, preparations for the forthcoming action in Gilgit were begun. The purpose was to reinforce the Kashmir troops engaged in controlling the trade route to Central Asia that was regularly raided by men from Hunza and Nagir. Two of the British officers, Lt Manners-Smith and Lt Aylmer, who would both earn the Victoria Cross before year's end, passed through Srinagar, as well as E.F. Knight, who was to accompany the force as the correspondent for *The Times of London*. Biscoe took a special church service for them and was invited to accompany the expedition as chaplain but had to decline as he was about to go to Bombay to meet his fiancé, Blanche.

In Bombay Cecil's brother Albert joined him and together they went onto the ship to meet Blanche. The next day Cecil and Blanche were married in the Girgaum Church. Arthur Neve and his niece, Nora, who had come out to work with her uncles in the hospital, left for Kashmir and Albert returned to his artillery regiment in Peshawar. Cecil and Blanche travelled from Bombay to Agra, Delhi, Amritsar, Rawalpindi and thence by tonga to Srinagar. General Thatcher lent them his houseboat for the journey to Srinagar and they settled in the Barracks at Munshi Bagh. There is no record of Blanche's impressions of her new life; she was 24 and in photos of the missionaries she looks very young and frightened, unlike Nora Neve who appears smiling and confident.

Meanwhile in Gilgit, British and Kashmiri troops, led by Algernon Durand, moved up the Hunza river and soon engaged Hunza and Nagir forces below the hamlet of Nilt, who were well entrenched in the Nilt Fort; the battle to capture the fort lasted for almost three weeks, during which time Durand was wounded and evacuated to Gilgit. The turning point for the invading forces came when a few of the most daring Kashmiri soldiers found a route up the cliffs, which could not be hit by guns from the fort, and overpowered the defenders from above. The Hunza leader Safdar Ali fled to Central Asia with some of his followers and his brother was installed as Mir of Hunza, but the Nagir leader Uzrar Khan, who also fled was taken prisoner and brought to the Hari Parbat Fort in Srinagar with two young sons. These two boys were sent to the Mission School. Biscoe described his first encounter with one who was extolling the courage of his father, who had the ambition to be Mir. The boy said:

> My father was helping his brother, my uncle onto a horse and shot him dead as he was doing so; and on another occasion my father went into the *Zenana* – women's quarter – where his old mother was sitting and asked her to look out of the window whereupon he shot her also. But you see my grandmother was only an old woman and had no teeth, Sahib. Oh my father was a very brave man![36]

Biscoe admitted that he was never able to tame this boy or teach him to honour old women who have no teeth.[37] Uzrar Khan had deposed his father so, after the conflict the old father was restored to the Mirship and the sole surviving brother, Sikander Khan, who had sided with the British, became the regent and eventually the Mir. His six sons were later sent to the Mission School where they excelled in sports and mountaineering, later returning to Nagir and Gilgit as honourable men who did respect old women with no teeth.

With the imprisonment of Uzrar Khan in the fort on Hari Parbat there was a passing fear that the Kashmir army might mutiny and murder all Europeans in Srinagar, so Walter Lawrence called together all British men in Ram Munshi Bagh. There they were out of danger from the guns on Hari Parbat Fort. Geoffrey Millais, a British photographer living in Kashmir, and Biscoe decided to reconnoitre the fort; they walked past the first sentry post where the three sentries were asleep and then, as they tiptoed past the second sentry post, the sentries awoke, rushed for their rifles and raised the alarm. As the two ran to the third post the commanding officer (CO) emerged to stop them with his hands up. Biscoe punched him and when the CO recovered his breath he became angry and said he would report them to the Maharaja. But Biscoe said he would report the CO for allowing his sentries to be asleep on guard duty, so he gave up and showed them around the fort. Biscoe's unprovoked assault on the CO was only possible because of the privileged position of British people in Kashmir. He was not reprimanded by the Resident or Lawrence because they were all supremely secure in their sense of superiority and manifest destiny. Knight expressed it in the last words of his book:

> I was also fortunate enough to acquire the friendship of many of those soldiers and civilians of our own race who in the Far East maintain the glory of our Empire, working bravely and loyally. There one seems to live in a purer atmosphere, and old-fashioned patriotism takes the place of parochial-politics squabbling. It is in Asia, perhaps that one realizes best what Great Britain is, and there one sees the pick of her sons living the larger and nobler life that men should live.[38]

Biscoe Assumes Full Charge of the Mission Schools

In March 1892 the Knowles left Srinagar on furlough and Biscoe assumed full control of the four schools: the Central School at Fateh Kadal, the high school at Islamabad, and two junior schools in Srinagar at Habba Kadal and the suburb of Rainawari. Biscoe had been in Kashmir for just over a year and had travelled into the country on three occasions and learnt much about the customs and the history of the place. He still had not mastered either the Kashmiri language or Urdu and had to communicate through the English-speaking staff of the schools. By now some of these men were beginning to understand his unconventional ideas about education. He changed the direction of the school from accommodating to prevailing customs, as Knowles had done, to establishing new rules of cleanliness, compulsory Christian teaching, compulsory games, swimming and corporal punishment for misbehaviour – as thunder follows lightening so punishment must follow misdemeanour.

The first punishment was meted out at Rainawari School.[39] Biscoe had learnt that the headmaster Pandit Sundri Koul was letting a young Pandit friend, Vishnu Koul, procure boys in the school for sex. Taking along with him a large Muslim boatman, Ishmailia, and a rope he whipped Vishnu Koul in front of the assembled school and then summarily dismissed the headmaster.

So it was not only Pathan Christians that had to be disciplined but Pandits too. Pandit Amar Chand from Sopor replaced him.

Introducing Football to Kashmiri Boys

In her luggage Blanche had brought a football from England and early in the new year Biscoe introduced the game to the Hindu boys. To them leather was unclean and not to be touched; none of them wore leather shoes for this reason but only wooden clogs. The first game was described many times in Biscoe's subsequent writings and was clearly a transforming experience. Here is the version written 30 years later:

> I remember well the pleasure with which I brought that first football to the school, and the vision that I had of the boys' eagerness to learn this new game from the West. Well, I arrived at the school, and at a fitting time held up the ball to their view, but alas, it aroused no such interest or pleasure as I had expected.
> 'What is this?' said they.
> 'A football,' said I.
> 'What is the use of it?'
> 'For playing with. It is an excellent game and will help to make you strong.'
> 'Shall we gain any rupees by playing it?'
> 'No.'
> 'Then we do not wish to play the game. What is it made of?'
> 'Leather.'
> 'Then we cannot play; we cannot touch it. Take it away, for it is unholy to our touch.'
> 'All right,' said I. 'Rupees or no rupees, holy or unholy, you are going to play football this afternoon at three-thirty, so you had better learn the rules at once.'
> And immediately, with the help of the blackboard, I was able to instruct them as to their places on the field, and the chief points and rules of the game. Before the end of school I perceived that there would be trouble, so I called the teachers together and

explained to them my plans for the afternoon. They were to arm themselves with single-sticks, picket the streets leading from the school to the playground, and prevent any of the boys escaping en route. Everything was ready, so at three o'clock the porter had orders to open the school gate. The boys poured forth, and I brought up the rear with a hunting-crop. Then came the trouble; for once outside the school compound they thought they were going to escape; but they were mistaken. We shooed them down the streets like sheep on their way to the butcher's. Such a dirty, smelling, cowardly crew you never saw. All were clothed in the long nightgown sort of garment I have described before, each boy carrying a fire-pot under his garment and so next to his body. This heating apparatus has from time immemorial taken the place of healthy exercise.

We dared not drive them too fast for fear of their tripping up (as several of them were wearing clogs) and falling with their fire-pots, which would have prevented their playing football for many days to come.

At length we are safely through the city with a goodly crowd following and arrive at the playground. Sides are made up, the ground is cleared and ready, the ball is in the centre, and all that remains is for the whistle to start the game.

The whistle is blown, but the ball does not move.

Thinking that the boys had not understood my order, I tell them again to kick off the ball immediately after hearing the whistle. I blow again, but with no result. I notice that the boys are looking at one another and at the crowd of spectators with unmistakable signs of fear and bewilderment on their faces.

On my asking them the cause, they say: 'We cannot kick this ball, for it is an unholy ball and we are holy Brahmans.' I answer them by taking out my watch and giving them five minutes to think over the situation: at the expiration of the time, I tell them, something will happen if the ball does not move. We all wait in silence, an ominous silence. The masters armed with their single sticks are at their places behind the goals.

Time is just up, and I call out: 'Five seconds left, four–three–two–one. Kick!' The ball remains stationary! My last card had now to be played, and I shout towards the right and left goals: 'Sticks!'

Sticks won the day, for as soon as the boys see the sticks coming the ball bounds in the air, the spell is broken, and all is confusion. Puggarees are seen streaming yards behind the players, entangling their legs; their shoes and clogs leave their feet as they vainly try to kick the ball, and turn round and round in the air like Catherine wheels descending on any and everybody's head. The onlookers who have followed us from the city are wildly excited, for they have never in their lives before seen anything like it – holy Kashmiri Brahman boys (in dirty nightgowns) tumbling over one another, using hands and legs freely to get a kick at a leather ball.

Well, as I said before, all was noise and excitement, when all of a sudden the storm is succeeded by a dead calm: the game ceases, the Brahmans, both players and onlookers, are all sucking their fingers for all they are worth (a Kashmiri way of showing amazement), and all eyes are turned towards one of the players who is a picture of misery. And no wonder, for this unholy piece of leather had bounded straight into this holy one's face, had actually kissed his lips. He had never before in his life felt the smack of a football, and certainly never dreamed of such a catastrophe. He thought all his front teeth were knocked out and that his nose was gone for ever. He would touch his mangled (?) features, but he dared not. Once or twice he essayed to do so, but his heart failed him. His face was defiled, so that he could not do what he would, and would not do what he could. He did the next best thing, which was to lift up his voice and weep, and this he did manfully. This moment was a terrible one for all concerned, and especially for me, for now all eyes were directed to the primary cause of all this misery.

What was I to do? I was not prepared for such a turn of events. I could shoo an unwilling school to the playground, I could make unwilling feet kick, but how could I make an unholy face holy? Fortunately the idea of water came into my distracted mind, and I said: 'Take the fool down to the canal at once and wash him.' Immediately the thoughts and the eyes of the victim's sympathisers were diverted to the cleansing waters and their magical effect on the outraged features of the body. On their return I placed the ball again in the centre, blew my whistle and the ball was kicked off. All was excitement once more, and the game was played with enthusiasm until I called 'Time!'

Everyone left the field and scattered to various parts of the city, to tell their parents and neighbours of the great *tamasha* they had witnessed or in which they had taken part. The remarks made about me and the school in their homes over their curry and rice that night were, I expect, not all favourable.[40]

It is noteworthy that in this account the game is begun with the timely help of the teachers, positioned at each end of the field with sticks; most of these men were also Brahmin but, after one year of being with Biscoe they were evidently willing to obey him. One of these teachers, Tara Chand Kachroo, was the first to kick the football and, as already mentioned, he had joined the school in 1884 and was also among the first three to play cricket then.

By the spring of 1892 boating was well accepted by the teachers and boys and the first trip with four rowing boats and the Biscoe's new houseboat started for the Wular on 20 March, arriving at 4 pm where camp was set up. They stayed for a week, Biscoe likening it in his annual report, to the seaside camps in England. 'We get them by this means from their greater heathen festivals, with all their idolatry, etc., and show them the bright side of Christianity.'

Introducing Social Service to Kashmiri Boys

But rowing and football were less contentious than what he now determined to do: social service. Soon after Knowles had left in March, Biscoe began to make the pupils aware of the suffering going on around them every day: the ill treatment of animals, the indifference towards other people's troubles especially if those people were women, and the filth of the streets. To the sons of upper class Pandits, none of these were matters for their concern; they were at school to pass exams so as to obtain good employment. The first event, which occurred soon after the first football game and Wular trip, was a house fire in a street near the school at Fateh Kadal.

One morning while he was teaching the senior class, aged 17 to 22, he saw a man standing on the roof of a nearby house blowing a bugle. When he asked the boys what he was doing they said he is a policeman warning the citizens that a house has caught fire; and at that moment a column of smoke appeared, so he ordered the class to close their books and go with him to help at the fire. To his astonishment they refused, saying it was not their business and they were not coolies but gentlemen.

> So I ordered them to get a move on at once and was obliged to show them my big stick, and with that article drove them out of the school to the fire, a party from thirty to forty strong. I shall never forget what I then saw; it has been impressed deep on my brain, a woeful sight I never wish to see again. There stood, or rather danced an old woman mad with excitement, imploring the onlookers around to help her save her property. The crowd of men had taken up positions so that they might enjoy thoroughly the sight, squatting on the ground with their mouths open, and with hands shading their eyes from the heat. The woman implored them to help her, and to show her agony she took hold of the upper part of her garment at the neck in both hands and rent it right down the centre but they took not the least notice; they simply looked beyond her. She then put both hands to her head, and tore out two large tufts of hair, which she held out theatrically towards the men, again imploring their help; but it was of no use. However, when she offered them money for a pot of water, they went off to find pots with which to make some money. All this was enacted in shorter time far than it takes me to put it on paper.[41]

Then he saw that the police constables were busy with coolies collecting the woman's property that she had taken out of her house and were carrying it off to a boat for 'safe-keeping'. So he sent one boy back to the school to collect single sticks, which were handed to the teachers and large boys to guard the property from the police, while he sought for pots with which to carry water from the river. As chance would have it a large *kutchu* full of pots was coming slowly upstream, so he gave the boys money with which to buy the pots, but the owner would not sell them any, and had steered his boat out into the stream to show his mind on the subject, no doubt hoping thereby to send up the price of his goods. But they boarded the boat and took all the pots they needed and at once formed a line from the river to the house and passed up a stream of water. Out in the river the bargee shouted, 'You thieving *badmash*, I will report you to the Governor Sahib, the Resident Sahib and even to the Maharaja and you will be thrown out of the city to eat dirt.'

Having started the boys, Biscoe turned to the sightseers, 'Come on you there, take this pot and pass it along the line, *jheldi* (quickly).' The sightseers ignored the foreigner and his strange antics but turned to the boys, 'Stop it you stupid fellows, don't you realise how you are defiling your caste and your families?' The boys ignored the reproaches for some time, but a few slunk away and joined the crowd at a respectful distance. At this Biscoe put several jeerers in the line and made them hand along the earthen pots, using the coercive power of the single-sticks, which kept the pots moving. After a while the Governor of the city arrived with some officials and a small manual fire pump. They laughed heartily at seeing the Brahmin boys at work, but nevertheless supported them, which made the work easier for the boys.

Eventually the fire was put out, the owners settled down to mourn and weep over the ashes of their houses and the boys, pretty well tired out, soaking with water and covered with grime, went home to tell of their valour; and probably receive lectures from their parents for the dishonour they had brought upon all self-respecting Brahmins and their own families in particular.

To Biscoe this was a most important day in the school. Much later he wrote:

> However persuasive the preaching, or holy the book, duty to one's neighbours and duty towards God is most certainly not

learnt practically through mouth and ear only. Faith must be shown by works. Never was a day's schooling better lost; and many a school day has been lost since then, in so far as lectures and preaching are concerned, in our efforts to make boys into such men as we believe Almighty God wishes them to be.[42]

Making their sons row in European boats and play English football was bad enough but exposing them to public ridicule in the streets by forcing them to do the work of coolies was outrageous. There were missionaries in Kashmir who took a similar view of Biscoe's unorthodox activities and the person charged by the Bishop with investigating the matter was Rev. H.E. Perkins. In the 1870s he had been the Commissioner in Rawalpindi – a senior member of the Punjab Government – and a staunch supporter of the missionaries, especially Robert Clark. Subsequently he was ordained and joined the CMS and now held a senior position in the mission in Lahore. He and his wife arrived in Kashmir in April to replace the Knowles while they were on leave. Biscoe continued with the schools unaware of Perkins' charge to investigate him.

Two events occurred soon after the Perkins' arrival; a huge fire in the city which consumed 1,200 to 1,300 houses; and a day later the first case of cholera which rapidly developed into an epidemic.

The noise of the fire could be heard all over the city. Biscoe had been fighting the fires with the staff and boys all day. As he was returning up the river at the end of the day people cried out to him 'Biscoe Sahib, *shahbash*! The smell of your good deeds in our city has reached to Kabul and nearly to London.' As he got out of the *shikara* at Munshi Bagh, dirty and dishevelled, Perkins was on the steps,

'Biscoe, where have you been?'
  'That's fairly obvious isn't it?'
  'Is that the work of a missionary? Did you not remember that the weekly missionary prayer meeting is at 4.30 pm on Fridays?'
  'Yes! But the prayer meeting takes place every week but not a great fire like this!'[43]

As Perkins walked away having delivered his pious rebuke Biscoe thought, 'If his house was on fire and I happened to be passing and he called me to help him, should I have answered, I'm very sorry friend but I've got to be present at a Prayer Meeting!' On another occasion a lady missionary asked him if he thought it was the duty of a padre to go to a fire; after all, at the Great Fire of London the padres went into their churches and read the Litany.

But much worse than fires and missed prayer meetings was about to befall the country.

The Great Cholera Epidemic of 1892

The day after the fire, 9 May, the first cases of cholera occurred; on 12 May there were 38 cases; on 17 May, 150 cases; 23 May, 500 new cases, 250 deaths and 1,500 under treatment.[44] So began the worst cholera epidemic to afflict Kashmir. Cholera was endemic in the plains of India but had seldom affected Kashmir because the journey there took several weeks and any infective person would die before the end of the journey. However, after the cart road to Baramula was opened in 1890 the journey was reduced to a few days and the opportunity for cholera to reach Srinagar increased greatly; and once there the Jhelum River and the unhygienic conditions in the city favoured its rapid spread. And that is precisely what happened in May and June 1892. Although there had been ten epidemics in the nineteenth century, that of 1892 was the worst. In the city there were 500 deaths a day, the Mission Hospital staff was overwhelmed and the Indian Dr Thomas himself succumbed to the disease on the second day. According to Lawrence 5,781 persons died in Srinagar and more than 6,000 in the villages:

All business was stopped and the only shops which remained open were those of the sellers of white cloth for winding sheets. Men would not lend money and in the villages the people would sit all day long in the graveyards absolutely silent. In the city the people would go out at dawn to the gardens and parks in the suburbs returning at night to hear that more of their relatives and friends had perished. The long lines of coffins borne to the graveyards resembled an endless regiment on the march while on the river a sad procession of boats floated down to the burning ghats, and living passengers in other boats passed by with averted faces. Men telling me how they had lost all the members of their family would break into hysterical laughter and I have never seen such utter despair and helplessness as I saw in 1892.[45]

Biscoe tried to counter the terror and despair of the city folk by maintaining some school activities such as cricket but this soon had to stop. Not only did teachers from the Mission School show such courage, six boys came and offered their services to help look after the sick and one of them died of the disease. These were indeed brave people.

The epidemic abated by the middle of June and in July Biscoe organised a trip to Manasbal Lake in boats. While they were at the lake, Perkins arranged to visit the Central School and was taken round by Munshi Fazl-U-Din. He was a Catechist, that is to say someone learning about Christian beliefs but not yet baptised, so anxious to please a senior missionary. He took Perkins to the Persian class room where the Maulvi in charge of young Muslim boys was teaching them to read the Persian characters, using the Qur'an as his text book (probably because it was the only Persian text he had). 'Look how Mr Biscoe has the Qur'an taught in the Mission School,' said the Catechist.[46] Perkins did not raise this with Biscoe then but it appeared in his report to Lahore as an adverse comment on the school. Biscoe learnt of it the next year when his activities were reviewed.

The Maharaja's Visit to the Mission School

At some time after his arrival in Kashmir Perkins had invited the Maharaja to visit the Mission School at Fateh Kadal, possibly to ensure a continuation of the State grant or to smooth any difficulties that may have been provoked by Biscoe's recent activities.[47] With the waning of the cholera epidemic the invitation was taken up. Maharaja Pratap Singh arrived by boat with his brothers Ram

Singh and Amar Singh and attendant courtiers on 25 August 1892 and were received in the school hall, where all the boys were sitting on the floor. A small boy in coloured wedding clothes presented the Maharaja with a photo of the school 'fire brigade' set in a carved frame. Without a glance he immediately put it under his chair. Noticing the insult Raja Amar Singh picked it up and held it in his lap.

Munshi Hassan Ali was asked to translate the principal's message into Urdu for the Maharaja, who could not understand English very well; he wrote it in easy Urdu for the benefit of the missionaries, who were not fluent in the language. After many flowery phrases praising the Maharaja and his family, he related the good examination results of the senior pupils, there being 300 students in the school, and then mentioned that the school also provided physical exercises for the students, such as football, cricket, boxing and boating, which embolden the students and create in them the qualities so much admired in Englishmen. The administration of the school deserved credit for this and hoped that the fruits of the institution would spread through out the State, which is called Paradise. Finally he requested that the government continue to aid the institution as it had been to date. In reply the Maharaja said, 'Mr Perkins, the only reason for coming to this school is on account of your presence.'[48]

He was making it clear, by not replying to the principal, that he did not appreciate Biscoe's recent activities. As a devout Hindu himself he was concerned at him upsetting the Pandits by making their sons do menial work against their caste. Nevertheless, Perkins had been able to persuade him to continue financial help, for as the Maharaja's entourage departed his Private Secretary Pundit Vida Lall beckoned Biscoe with his finger and a wink to follow him to a side room where he held out a cloth bag containing 500 rupees in Chilkis (10 anna pieces) and ordered him to count the 800 coins. This was sufficient to meet the school budget for about two months and was most welcome. It would have been customary for Biscoe to share some of it privately with Vida Lall, who watched the counting as a hungry dog watches a stronger dog eating a juicy bone. But Biscoe took no notice of that look and the hungry Pandit left in anger.

Despite his differences with the Pandit parents, with Perkins and with the Maharaja, Biscoe at the close of 1892 was full of optimism. Blanche gave birth to a son on 21 October and two days later Biscoe wrote to tell his favourite brother Teddy in Africa the good news and ask him to be godfather to young Harold.

In his annual letter to the society he wrote:

> I love the work to which I have been appointed by the Parent Committee – it just suits me. I feel as if I were back at school again in my old age, and feeling anything but a pedagogue.[49]

He concluded the report with his aspiration for the school:

> We want to see manly Christians, men who can show their colours amongst their Muslim relations in their own villages; men who will make manly catechists, and who will love their work more than rupees, and who can stand up in the bazaars like men, not with shoulders up to their ears and with blinking eye and weak voice, but with a straight eye which can look their whole audience in the face and show by their whole gait what Christianity has done for them, and that they speak of those things which they believe and know from personal experience. Oh! For men with backbone, who can say 'no' and stick to it, and say 'yes' and mean it!

Little did he then know that his *beau ideal* of a 'man' had just transferred with two other 13-year-old boys from the State School to the Central School. When their first class was over they refused to join gymnastics saying that they had come to study not to play. They were ordered down to the parallel bars but Shenker Koul's arms were too weak to hold him, so two other boys supported him in his first gymnastic exercise. He accepted this with a good grace and later became an instructor himself and a leader among the boys at fires, at cholera epidemics and floods.[50] He never converted to Christianity but he became Biscoe's staunchest friend and colleague for the rest of his long life; they thought alike and all they achieved was done together.

First Differences Between Biscoe and the Church Missionary Society

Biscoe's ideas of manly Christians were not supported by the senior missionaries and, when Perkins left Kashmir in December, expecting to return in the spring, he took with him notes for a report to the Lahore Consultative Committee. Unaware of the impending report Biscoe wrote to the Secretary of the Society in London apologising for his lack of progress with language and appealing for financial support for the schools. On the first he wrote:

> I must confess that my jargon is only understood by those who are kind enough to give me a very patient hearing, and my sermons have to go through a terrible metamorphosis before they are fit to be preached. As to the hearing I won't offer an opinion. Of course this grieves me and I'm sure my patient Munshies suffer with me, but I have always been a fool at books and am not likely to change at this time of life. I have not turned lazy since becoming a missionary but book learning has never been my line.[51]

On school finances he wrote:

> When Mr Knowles returned to England I was left in charge of four schools, which are now reduced to three, Islamabad school having since been closed. The expenditure of the three schools is about Rs350 per month, of which Rs140 goes to salaries of two Christian masters. The total income is Rs160 a month, including Parent Committee's grant of Rs 80. Visitors to the school are as a rule not interested in education of natives, so I have no other course but to appeal to friends at home for funds to meet the remainder of the expenditure. Should Parent Committee, however, object I will have to close the schools.

The Parent Committee resolved that a report on the whole subject of these schools, especially as to the Christian teaching being given in them, be obtained from Lahore. Perkins' detailed report was received in January 1893; its conclusion was damning:

Owing to the absence of Kashmiri speaking missionaries and Christian masters, there is no possibility of Christian instruction for a large number of boys in the three schools in Srinagar. We therefore cannot support the application of further help for these schools.[52]

When Knowles in England saw the report on 1 March 1893 he vigorously defended Biscoe and the schools. He rejected the conclusion that there was inadequate scriptural instruction for, in each school every day there was a general assembly for Prayer and Reading with exposition of God's word, followed by Bible lessons for the senior classes. He continued:

I am at a loss to quite understand the minute which you kindly quoted from the Punjab and Sindh Missionary conference communications. These schools have always been most highly spoken of from a missionary's point of view by the Rev R Clark, other missionaries who have visited them and examined the boys from time to time, and I have said I cannot understand the minute – unless it is that Biscoe finds the language, or rather languages, a great hindrance to doing all that could otherwise be done. The burden of expense in connection with this work is a very heavy and wearing one, anywhere for the missionary-in-charge, but especially in Kashmir, where we cannot obtain any Government grant for the schools. It must be remembered too that school work in this country is comparatively new. There are, we think, rather exceptional circumstances, so some little stretch of charity, therefore, should be made towards us and we look for it.[53]

Biscoe wrote a detailed rebuttal as soon as he learnt of the adverse report from Robert Clark on 13 April:

Daily scripture instruction is given by Christian staff or visitors in the three schools; the absence of Kashmiri speaking missionaries is not an issue since it had never been the practice to teach the boys in Kashmiri; and Mr Knowles, who talks

Kashmiri like a native, never used Kashmiri in his teaching or addresses in the Central School because the boys object to be spoken to in Kashmiri and will answer in Urdu. And the reason there are so few Christian teachers is because a Hindu or Muslim teacher costs 6 to 10 rupees per month whilst a Christian master needs from 50 to 100 per month. Our two Christian masters' salaries with houses cost us Rs160 p.m., which is all the money received from the Mission, the balance of the schools cost has to be collected from private sources.

In the city are numbers of schools belonging to the Maharajah, who are able to offer inducement to the boys which we could not possibly do. The only reason the boys come to our school is because our English is known to be superior and now athletics are beginning to draw a few. The parents are told by the State Council not to send their sons to our school on the pain of dismissal from Government service. The Maulvis order their people to abstain from allowing their sons to attend our schools. Many of the boys came to our school in defiance of their parents' wishes. They dare not tell their parents that they learn scripture. Consequently we have boys coming late so as to miss the scripture lessons and it is not wise to press the boys too much on this point, unless you want vacant benches. When a boy has learnt to love us and become attached to the school then he will disregard the wishes of his parents in this respect and does as we tell him and gradually learns the manliness and beauty of the Christian religion.

It is not only from the Bible that he learns Christianity but often in the every day lessons a nail is driven home. And in the play field he learns many a Christian virtue which he would never have learnt any other way. I believe Christ Jesus our Lord is to be found anywhere and in everything if anyone has the desire to see Him – Christianity is a living religion and it is this life we try to put into the boys hearts and lives.[54]

Finally, he came to the delicate matter of his lack of progress on language. He had not attempted to learn Kashmiri, concentrating instead on Urdu; but this was proving difficult, especially having to read and write in the Persian script. He thought that if he were not required to know the Persian character he could take the exam soon.

> I know it is a great disgrace that I have not already passed both my language exams but I am rather inured to disgrace, as I have always been ploughed in exams; how I got my degree has always been a mystery and I passed my Bishop's exam on my conduct.
>
> If the Society has patience with me I shall no doubt scramble thro' the language exams and if they have not patience they had better dispense with my services and put in some one else who is more fitted for the work.[55]

His exasperation with what he thought peripheral to his main work was clear. Robert Clark had seen it all before and was sympathetic to young missionaries, 'for he knew not what distinguished man in embryo stood in their ranks'.[56] To those who would make a clean sweep of what they found, for whom the path to wisdom and victory was abundantly clear and only obstructed by older missionaries, he would quote Lord Napier's remark at a council of war, 'We are none of us infallible, even the youngest subaltern here'. He forwarded Biscoe's letter to Secretary Grey in London with the comment:

> I have told him that every missionary is required to write in the vernacular – as well as read and speak it. It may be well perhaps if you would write to him from home. He is an excellent missionary but has small gifts in acquiring a language or passing an exam; and his value to us as a missionary is probably far greater than that of some other missionaries who can learn a language and pass an exam easily.[57]

Biscoe asked Arthur Neve, who was fluent in Urdu and Kashmiri, to review the religious teaching in the schools and this he did in May. In his report he traversed the same ground as Biscoe had, with additional comments on the responses of students to his examination of their knowledge of scripture, and concluded that, 'In the present position of the mission in Kashmir and considering the probable future of the scholars, I consider that the religious teaching in the Mission School is of great value.'

Biscoe sent this report to Clark in early June:

> I am sending you Dr Neve's report of the scripture teaching in our school. If you think that Arthur Neve's report is a fair one, would you give the same publicity to it as the former ill report had. The former was a condemnation before trial and this is the report after the trial. As to the most fair I leave you to judge.[58]

And then to more congenial matters:

> We had a boat race this week in which our school four defeated easily the mission crew and a crew of officers, to the great disgust of the latter. All the world and his wife were present so the name of our school ascended somewhat. The name also ascended further by a crew of our school boys shooting through the Dal Gate, where every one else, boatmen and sahibs funked it. In haste, I remain yours very sincerely, not to say affectionately, CE Tyndale-Biscoe
>
> (The mission crew, comprised Cox Annie Corncale, stroke Biscoe, 2 Arthur Neve, 3 Ernest Neve, and bow Venables Green).

While his performance was being scrutinised adversely at the centre, boating and climbing flourished in 1893.[59] In the spring one party rowed to the Wular Lake in two four-oars and two pairs, covering the 40 miles in six hours with only one rest. Later in the year the fleet was enhanced by a fine 12-oared cutter built on the lines of a naval boat and carrying two sails as well. The funds for this had been given by Biscoe's sister and the boat was named for her the *Fanny*. In it a crew of 17 rowed to Manasbal Lake from sundown to midnight and the next day climbed a peak 5,300 feet above the lake. Since Hindus in Kashmir believed that the tops of

Figure 4 The 12-oar cutter Fanny *under sail on the Dal Lake*

mountains were the preserve of the gods this was an especial
achievement for city boys. At the end of the trip they rowed back
upstream from daybreak until late in the evening and

> although some told of their raw hands and blisters afterwards,
> none spoke of their troubles while there was work to be done.
> This first trip to the mountain top gave our party such an
> appetite for more mountain and other trips that the Brahmin
> priests never got the better of us again.[60]

The first real vindication of Biscoe's ideas and methods came at the
end of July 1893, a week after Blanche and Nora Neve, with baby
Harold had left the city for the cooler weather at Nil Nag, a lovely
little lake nestled in pine and fir forests 20 miles away and 1,000
feet above Srinagar.

The Great Flood of 1893 and Its Aftermath

Floods in Kashmir are caused by warm and continuous rain in the mountains which melts the snow and adds it to the flow of water and the consequent rise of the Jhelum River in the city. Early in July 1893 there was widespread warm, heavy rain which increased on 18 July and continued without a break for 52 hours, by which time the mountains were denuded of snow. A large flood was anticipated. The peak arrived on the morning of 21 July overwhelming the high banks protecting the city from flood. During the next few hours all the bridges except Amira Kadal were swept away. The first to go was Habba Kadal and when it collapsed the debris piled up against the next bridge and it collapsed and so forth. The low-lying cultivated land below the city as far as the Wular Lake was inundated. Buildings and crops were destroyed but because of the timely warnings of its coming there was little loss of life. The view from adjacent hills was of one vast lake across the Vale from Islamabad in the south to Baramula. It was thought that the flood would be absorbed in the Wular Lake but it continued roaring down the Jhelum gorge destroying the new suspension bridge across the river, so cutting the main road to Kashmir.[61]

On the morning of 21 July Geoffrey Millais, a close friend who lived near the church, and Biscoe had prepared for the coming flood by moving the American organ onto the roof of the church; Biscoe's pet monkey and young black bear were separately tied to chimneys on the roof of the adjacent kitchen. Then at 3 pm the bund broke at the Munshi Bagh and great waves came tumbling through, knocking down fences and then striking the front door of Knowles' house where the Biscoes were living. Arthur Neve arrived in a tin tub and Biscoe in his skiff and they rescued Knowles' precious papers and Bible translation from his library just before the bookcase fell into the water. The Neves expected their house to fall as well so all of them slept the night in Geoffrey Millais' houseboat moored nearby. They were jolted awake by the cries from the city as the houses fell and the bridges gave way.

Next morning they were out in boats with the Mission School boys, who had asked for the school boats so that they could pick up people stranded on rooftops or in trees; some poor people would not get into the boat for fear of being charged because the boatmen were reaping a rich harvest by charging exorbitant rates to rescue stranded people. For instance, Elizabeth Newman at the Women's Hospital had a difficult time rescuing her women patients because the boatmen wanted 100 rupees per ride. She was rescued by a British subaltern in a *shikara* who commandeered a boat for her patients. What was remarkable on this day was that the boys who joined in the rescue were the same boys who a year before were indifferent to the fate of a burning house near the school. Perkins had returned to Srinagar in June and it seems that the splendid performance of the school during the great flood changed his mind about Biscoe's approach to the work, for he gave a personal donation of 100 rupees to the school funds, the largest acknowledged in the report for 1893.

The next day as the flood abated they dug out their clothes and Blanche's jewellery from the mud in Knowles' house and moved everything they could rescue into their houseboat, *Shotover*, moored near Millais' houseboat.

Through August the Biscoes and Neves camped at Nil Nag. Here they built a cabin and Cecil's brother Julian, who was stationed in the Punjab, came up on leave from Sialkot via the Pir Panjal pass.[62] This became their summer holiday retreat every year thereafter.

In September they returned to Srinagar and lived in the houseboat, moored on the river. With no financial support from the society and a large shortfall in funding, Biscoe was once more facing the desperate task of raising funds from private donors. He decided to write a lively account of the current year's activities, print it locally and distribute it widely to potential supporters and British visitors to Kashmir. He adopted a breezy style, which would appeal to middle and upper class British people, who would not normally be interested in missionary activity. Because of his own interest in boating and his previous prowess in rowing for Cambridge and at Henley, he used boating analogies for his purposes and enlivened the text with his own sketches of Kashmir scenes and the photographs by Geoffrey Millais. The first report, or log, as he preferred to call it, was called *Tacking* and had a cover sketch of the *Fanny* under full sail on the Dal Lake. It began:

> Does anyone like sailing against the wind and tide? If not, then do not come aboard our ship; but if you do, then come along with us and help, and we will show you how we tack up against the never-changing wind and tide.
>
> To those who so kindly helped to keep our schools afloat last year, let me apologise for delaying so long in giving you an account of the last year's voyage. The cause of the delay has been my long illness from typhoid.[63]

The log begun in September was not distributed until April 1894 because Biscoe had contracted typhoid in October 1893. He and Blanche were living in their houseboat on the river and both became infected from the river water; fortunately she soon recovered. Typhoid was a common hazard of life in Kashmir and before the development of antibiotics was often fatal; recovery depended entirely on good nursing. Biscoe was therefore fortunate that he received excellent nursing from Elizabeth Newman, Nora Neve and Blanche and was attended by Ernest Neve. Both Neves wrote to Robert Clark to tell him that Biscoe had contracted typhoid and been comatose for two days in October with very high temperatures and in early November was showing signs of slow recovery. Arthur wrote, 'He will want a change when convalescent, in or out of Kashmir. But no (language) examination can be thought of.'[64] Biscoe's brother Julian was called from Sialkot, where he was stationed, to be with Blanche. And, erroneously hearing that Biscoe had died, Colonel Cockburn, a local businessman in Srinagar, wrote an ode for the departed soul.

Blanche wrote to the CMS Secretary in London, Wigram, on 5 November 1893, 'I think I ought to write and let you know how seriously ill my husband has been and still is although now without so much cause for anxiety. But my baby boy needs a male carer.'

There was no suitable house at Munshi Bagh as the Knowles' house was still damaged and they were to return in December, so they were moved to a large house at the Sheikh Bagh occupied by the first British Conservator of Forests, Dr McDonnell. This house had been built 50 years before by the last Governor of Kashmir under Sikh rule, Sheikh Imam-ud-Din, and subsequently was occupied by the British Officer on Special Duty during Gulab Singh's reign. By a coincidence Arthur Neve was at this very time negotiating with the State Government for a part of the Sheikh's garden to be the site of four permanent buildings for the missionaries and by the end of 1894 the Biscoes moved into their house on that site.

Recovery for Biscoe was very slow; the fever lasted three months and full recovery took 11 months. Elizabeth Newman used to come daily to nurse him, after her work in the hospital three miles away. One day a series of earthquake shocks occurred. Trees swayed, birds flew about scared and people ran out of their houses shouting. The old stone house rocked, the heavy roof beams shook and the occupants ran out of the house. She at once ran in and up the stairs to Biscoe's room where he was too ill to be moved. Seeing that he looked scared, she held him tight while the room swayed saying, 'Do not be afraid. God will take care of us', and did not leave him until the shaking ceased and all was normal once more.

By Christmas 1893 Blanche was able to write to Robert Clark, 'My husband is now at last slowly recovering and taking solid food.' But then there is a note of despair. 'The work seems unsuccessful but the All-wise knows why it should be so.' They had both been under much stress all year over the adverse report by Perkins and the constant worry of finances for the schools and they were also affected by the criticism from some of the local missionaries that instead of preaching in the bazaars Biscoe was spending his time on social service with the teachers and boys in the city. They were both convinced that this had weakened his resistance to the disease and greatly prolonged his recovery.

To add to their troubles their houseboat sank under a heavy load of new snow just when the Knowles returned to Srinagar. A Muslim eyeing the sunken wreckage said to Knowles, 'The padre sahib must be a very wicked man for God sends all these punishments upon him.'

Knowles wrote to London:

> The boys' school at rather a low ebb, owing to Biscoe's long-continued illness. The poor fellow has been as near as possible to death, and will take a long time to recover. It is the old tale Typhoid – our great enemy here. Until Biscoe is fit to resume his school labours I shall probably give a great deal of my time to this work but I am hoping by the middle of the spring to be free for evangelistic tours in the district.[65]

But that was not to be; he had to run the schools for most of the year.

Biscoe's recovery was protracted through January and February but he was well enough on 1 March to leave the old house at Sheikh Bagh and take the refloated houseboat to the Wular Lake for a five week convalescence with Blanche and Harold and their dog Taffy, and pet monkey, Sundri. While the houseboat floated gently round the lake he made delicate pen and wash sketches of the lake and the surrounding mountains, of fish being dried and village life. He tried to do a bit of sailing but was too weak, but he completed the log *Tacking* ending it with the words:

> Let me repeat that tacking against strong adverse winds and heavy tides is not the most cheering of all games, so that when one takes aboard a cheery companion, even if it be for a few hours, it is wonderful how it lightens the cargo and sends us on our way rejoicing.

In a covering letter to Secretary Gray at CMS Headquarters in London he wrote:

> I am writing from our houseboat in which we are returning to Srinagar after 5 weeks change at Wular Lake. I am nearly myself again but my legs are still very weak [...] I never expected to live, so that now I feel as though my life had been given back to me, and I hope to make better use of this spell of life than I did of the last [...] if it had not been for the great care expended on me I could not have lived through it.

Ernest Neve tended me most carefully for two months and then Arthur piloted me through the rest. We were very glad to have the Knowles back again in December. But it was a great grief to us to loose Miss Newman, who worked with such unselfish devotion and was beloved by the women in the city. We shall never see her like again I fear.[66] The work here is flourishing as far as institutions are concerned but as to spiritual results most disheartening. It is uphill all the way, real collar work; fortunately all hills have a down side so in God's own time we shall have more encouraging work.[67]

In another letter written at the same time he urges people to turn to God while they are healthy and not leave it until they are dying for then one is too sick to pray.

Back from the Wular trip he resumed school work but found his head wouldn't stand it, so Arthur Neve ordered the family off to Pahalgam. They went by houseboat to Islamabad and then by dandy and pony to Pahalgam. He tried to ride to the sacred Amarnath Cave but fainted and had to be carried back to Colonel Strahan's tent and dosed with brandy and a hot bath. He liked Strahan because he was the first European to cheer him in his work in the schools.[68]

In July he returned to the class room but again found the burden too great; he had no energy and his head seemed fuzzy most of the time so Arthur Neve sent them off to Nil Nag to stay in his hut in the forest. Meanwhile in Srinagar their house at Sheikh Bagh was nearing completion and in December they moved in. He named it Holton, after his home village in England; Blanche established the home that supported them for the next 53 years.

The new year began with snow about a foot deep. People tobogganed on the nearby hills and skated on the frozen Dal Lake.[69] Walter Lawrence had completed his settlement at the end of 1894 and left Kashmir and India to write his masterly book *The Valley of Kashmir* but would later return to serve with Curzon, Viceroy from 1898 to 1904. For Biscoe 1894 had been a lost year, and no log of school activities was written; but he now resumed full activity with renewed vigour.

2

Now Is the Day of Small Things, 1895–99

Now is the day of small things: it may not be ours to see great things, but others will.

> 1896 log, *Coxing in Kashmir*, p. 14

Family Support After Typhoid

The death of Biscoe's father in January 1895 was the catalyst for an increasing involvement of his immediate family in the Kashmir schools.[1] His mother had died four years before and so the family home of Holton Park in Oxfordshire passed to his eldest brother Stafford, and the other members of the family received their portions of the estate. Two of Biscoe's brothers were serving in India, Albert in the artillery and Julian in the cavalry, and Edward was in Africa. The three remaining members of the family in England were his sister Fanny and brothers George and Arthur. With their inheritance, George and Fanny decided to make an extended visit to Cecil and Blanche in Kashmir and they arrived in early April 1895. Albert took leave from his regiment in Lahore and accompanied them up the Jhelum Road and Julian joined them a month later, coming through the Pir Panjal Range by the old Mughal route from Sialkot.

Figure 5 Bible class in Sheikh Bagh, Biscoe speaking, Blanche at harmonium, 1895

Because the Maharaja was just about to come through from Jammu on his way to his summer capital of Srinagar, with a large following, they were unable to get tongas for the four day journey up the Jhelum Road, so Fanny travelled in an *ekka* – a comfortless conveyance – while Albert and George rode Albert's polo ponies, Josephus and 'the Wench', which he had brought with him. Five servants – bearer, *bihisti* [water-carrier], sweeper and two *syces* [grooms] with baggage came on four other ekkas. At Baramula they transferred to Biscoe's houseboat, *Shotover*, and arrived in Srinagar a day ahead of the Maharaja's party.

As they were approaching the city Arthur Neve came on board. He had been with the Chitral relief force, which had raised the siege of Chitral earlier that month,[2] and he had again hoped to get into Kafiristan, but had been thwarted in this and was now turning his thoughts to Hunza and Nagir. He and George walked through the city across the Amira Kadal bridge and so to the Sheikh Bagh – an orchard of about 10 acres with a bank or bund 12 feet high all round to protect from floods. In a corner of the Bagh was the new Holton cottage. They found Cecil taking a Sunday Bible class of

53

his school masters in the garden, singing hymns while Blanche played a baby organ. They were introduced to Harold, aged 3, and the spaniel Taffy. Geoffrey Millais came in to supper and Albert and George slept in tents in the garden.

George woke to a spring morning like home. *Chota hazari* at 7 am, breakfast at 10 am. Subhana the carpenter was working in the garden and a *durzi* (taylor) was working, sitting cross-legged, on the verandah. Silver and papier maché merchants and others came up to show them their wares. But when Biscoe thought his sister was about to be cheated he drove them off the verandah, much to the disgust of Fanny. Later, when he saw Punjabis making a short cut by walking through his garden, he chased them, caught one and annexed his turban. Fanny thought his behaviour shocking for a missionary; she was either unfamiliar with the way British people treated the local people in India, or she thought missionaries should behave better.

After tiffin at 2.30 pm, all of them, including Millais, went down the river in the school 12-oared cutter, rowed by teachers, to the Central School, just above the Third Bridge. All 500 boys had assembled to see the Maharaja come up the river to his palace below the First Bridge. The Maharaja's State Barge was paddled by 60 men in red and also towed by Queen Victoria's steam tug. A number of British officials were on board with His Highness, all looking rather bored. After the fleet had passed they went, some by boat up the Soonti Canal, or walking to the Dal Lake to tea with Millais on his houseboat.[3]

Two days later they attended the weekly school regatta staged on the Dal Lake, to which all the European community and visitors to Kashmir were invited, and given tea. Albert and George crewed one of the rowing boats with Geoffrey Millais and the Assistant Resident Chenevix Trench with Miss Losach as Cox, and were beaten by the 12-oared cutter rowed by masters and boys and coxed by Biscoe. There was also boxing on a floating island (of reeds), a tournament in *shikaras* and a water steeple chase. The next afternoon they went to the race course to see the school playing a cricket match against the Maharaja's team.

How things had changed in three years; now rowing in English boats was quite respectable and the Maharaja lent his name to a

Figure 6. Tyndale-Biscoe family in Sheikh Bagh, 1895. Standing L to R, brothers Albert, Julian, George; sitting: Harold, Blanche, Cecil, sister Frances

cricket match. And the new home in the Sheikh Bagh provided a comfortable sanctuary where the extended family could relax with their friends. A second house in the Sheikh Bagh was approved by the State Government in March for the women missionaries of the Church of England *Zenana* (Women's) Missionary Society under Elizabeth Hull's direction, and by June the concrete was in and the walls of the kitchen up and roof commenced, servants houses well on and the fencing to the river on both sides finished. 'Why they are so sharp I don't understand,' wrote Biscoe.

After the lost year of 1894 school activities had clearly resumed with full vigour. Biscoe went to the Central School at Fateh Kadal every week day from 11 am to 2.30 pm, either walking through the city or in one of the rowing boats with a crew of teachers.

Every Sunday he and Blanche held a Bible class for those teachers and old boys who wished to attend and they usually had an attendance of about 20, sitting in their garden.

But this was no ordinary Bible class: they were organising a special fund for waifs and strays in the city. As a result of the cholera epidemic of 1893 and the very severe winter of 1894–95, when the Dal Lake froze over, there were many homeless children in the streets, who walked barefoot in the snow, covered with a few scanty rags, some smoking *bang* (marijuana) in order to keep off hunger pains. Those in the Bible class suggested that they should help them, and so they started money-boxes in the three schools. In the first year the boys raised 11 rupees 12 annas, workmen in Public Works Department 20 rupees 8 annas, and Biscoe provided 29 rupees 9 annas, with which they supported eight boys until they were taken back by their families. The fund was named the 'Waifs and Strays Fund' with Hassan Ali as the treasurer and in later years the boys gave a much larger share of the funds needed. The account book for 1895–1902 remains today [2018] in the possession of his grandson, Munshi Ghulam Hassan in Srinagar.

Through the next three months, while Biscoe worked, Albert, George and Fanny enjoyed the Kashmiri countryside. They climbed the nearby peaks above the Dal Lake with Ernest Neve and they went trekking further afield to Pahalgam and the Hindu pilgrimage route to the Amarnath Cave beyond. Then through June and July the whole family, including by now Julian, moved up to the small lake Nil Nag, near the villages of Buzgu and Gogjipatra. Surrounded by a forest of pine and fir trees, and being 1,000 feet higher than the city, it had a cooler climate in the summer months. The lake had been formed about 50 years before by a large landslide that had impounded the stream and the drowned forest trees still survived as stumps above the surface. They bathed in the lake and walked in the forest and watched monkeys coming down to drink, and occasionally encountered a panther hunting for their dogs. This quiet retreat had been discovered by Arthur Neve some years before and he had built a holiday hut on its shore which they now shared with the Neves. With Ernest Neve they climbed Sunset Peak on the nearby Pir Panjal Range. Biscoe was with them during the week but had to return to Srinagar each weekend to take church services, riding in on his pony Snowball or on his bicycle, the first one in Kashmir. The bicycle caused much interest among the local people. While riding one night a man he passed fell down on the road convinced that he was dead because he had just seen a *djinn* go by on a very strange horse whose legs went round and round. For a few months after that people who saw him coming would shout out, 'Clear the way for the angel-horse is coming!'[4]

But Biscoe didn't relish these trips away from the family at Nil Nag, as a letter he wrote to Blanche shows:

Saturday 29 June 1895

My dearest B,

I hope you are as comfy as I am smoking the cig of peace after a wholesome dinner. Ramzana and Sadiq did me splendidly at dinner. I can't abide dining alone. It reminds me of my bachelor days in London. I was never meant to live alone I know. The first part of my ride was rather eventful. My poor Snowball took to rolling, I don't know why, and I certainly had no time to think. I fell away from him into the hedge so escaped splendidly. My pony went excellently and, without distressing himself, landed me opposite Ismailia's boat at 3.14 pm just 2 hrs 9 mins since I left you. The garden looked beautifully fresh and green after the rain and the house looked very cosy. It is quite cold here. I walked fairly hard to the Munshi Bagh and yet I shivered when walking through the Bagh.

Sunday 30 June, 3.30. Coolie just off so must close. I took service at 9 am, breakfast at Neves. We could not find the Church bell so service was late. Nearly 20 people in Church. Tiffin with Cockburns, who stuffed me. I shall dine with Hadows tonight. It's a lovely fresh day. I do hope Nora is mending. This fever is a great trial to her patience. I hope it is a fine day at Nil Nag so that you can get out for a decent walk.

I must now close with much love to you dear B and Bubbles and Fan and brothers.

I remain yours lovingly, C. E. Tyndale-Biscoe

While dining with the Hadows they shared a piece of gossip with him. Colonel Cockburn was apt to tire everyone by his incessant talking. One day after tiffin he called on Knowles. According to Knowles' orders the servants answered to the colonel's *koi hai* (Who's there?), '*Sahib baha gia*' (Sahib has gone out). The colonel said 'You liars', and walked straight into Knowles' study. Knowles had just time to disappear under the table but unfortunately showed a foot. The colonel seeing the foot said, 'A bad job Knowles being out, but I'll sit down and wait for him', and took up a newspaper, but watching Knowles' discomfort. Knowles having an engagement later had at long last to come out. Colonel Cockburn says, 'I had no idea you spent your afternoons under the table'.

Baltistan Expedition of Arthur Neve and George Tyndale-Biscoe, 1895

During this time George Tyndale-Biscoe became increasingly friendly with the Neve brothers and Arthur invited him to join him on his forthcoming journey to Hunza and Nagir. Having been unable to enter Kafiristan after the Chitral campaign, Arthur now wished to determine the possibility of extending missionary activity there. However, exploration had a higher priority since he eschewed the normal route there via Gilgit for another one. He was hoping that his party would cross by the Nushik La, a long disused pass through the mountains from Skardu in Baltistan to Nagir – and carry out medical work wherever they went. Arthur had already made two trips of exploration in the northern areas in 1882 and 1887 and, since George had no immediate job to call him back to England, he jumped at the chance to join the party. Meanwhile Julian and Albert returned to their regiments and Fanny remained at Sheikh Bagh with Blanche, who was expecting her second child in October. On the two month trip George wrote detailed letters to his family, copies of which are extant, and 18 years later Arthur wrote an account of the trip in his book *Thirty Years in Kashmir*.

They set off for Baltistan on 12 August by boat, first down the Jhelum River and then across the Wular Lake to Bandipur. Here they joined the recently constructed 200-mile mule track that

Figure 7 Arthur Neve, Mission Hospital, Srinagar

serviced the garrison at Gilgit. Through the summer months this track was heavily used by mule, pony and camel trains carrying supplies, as well as English travellers of several kinds – officers on duty travelling to or from Gilgit, others on leave hunting markhor, snow leopard or bear and intrepid ladies with very big caravans. George and his brothers and Fanny had covered the first part of the route a month before but this was a much more substantial affair, as reflected in their baggage, which was the equivalent of 12 coolie loads – one for the tents, one each for their personal stuff, two loads of medicines, one of books, three for food and three for camp beds, camera, oil, servant's bedding, ice axes and tent poles. With the baggage carried by five mules they set off to ascend the 8,000 feet Rhajdiangan Pass through forests of pine, fir, yew and walnut, eventually coming out onto meadows of lovely flowers – ragwort, potentillas, larkspur and columbine. Because the pass was overcast they missed a magnificent sight to the north. Godfrey Vigne, who had travelled the same route, more than 60 years before, described it:

> at the distance of a mile and a half rises a small eminence on the left towards which, on our approach, Nasim Khan suddenly started off in a gallop, calling on me to follow and loudly exclaiming, 'Sahib, sahib, ek tamasha, ek lakh' – literally he would show me a view worth ten thousand rupees. I quickly followed him and the stupendous peak of Diarmul, or Nanga Parbat, more than forty miles distant, in a straight line, but appearing to be much nearer, burst upon my sight, rising far above every other around it, and entirely cased in snow, except where its scarps were too precipitous for it to remain upon them. It was partially encircled by a broad belt of cloud and its finely-pointed summit glistening in the full blaze of the morning sun, relieved by the clear blue sky beyond it, presented, on account of its isolated situation, an appearance of extreme altitude.[5]

Arthur had seen the sight in 1887 when he was moved to write in verse:

> King amidst kingly mountains, monarch o'er snowy height,
> Girdled with glacial fountains, fenced by avalanche might,
> Battlements towering skywards, pinnacles glistening bright,
> Who shall dispute Diyamir, the crown that's thine by right?[6]

As George and Arthur crossed the pass in cloud, the first serious expedition to climb Nanga Parbat had preceded them by a month. Led by A.F. Mummery, it was the most experienced team of climbers of the day, and they were on that day exploring two possible routes on the western side of the great mountain; but ten days later Mummery and his two Gurkha companions disappeared, presumably swept away by an avalanche, while attempting to cross a col of 20,400 feet now called Mummery's Col.[7]

From the Rhajdiangan Pass they descended to the Kishenganga river and stayed overnight at Gurais. Here the Englishman in charge of the Gilgit road lived with his family in English comfort and they enjoyed a game of badminton and ate raspberries and cream. They set off next day up the Kishenganga to its headwaters and the 14,000 feet Burzil Pass, the most dangerous place on the route to Gilgit, especially in winter when snow lies many feet deep and the cold is intense; every year many porters and animals would die attempting to cross the pass and the thought of it brought dread to the men who had been forced to carry loads to Gilgit before the mule track was completed in 1890. Neve had seen the anguish of villagers in Kashmir being forcibly taken for the Gilgit transport, and their suffering when he had continued over the pass in 1882 and 1887. But now 800 camels and 3,000 mules and ponies replaced forced labour or *begar*. On this trip they left the Gilgit route here and instead went east across the barren Deosai high plains, heading for Skardu, four day's march away. The Deosai was treeless and uninhabited and at over 12,000 feet was cold and windswept. They had to carry firewood and at night the men sheltered behind low stone walls that had been built many years before; George and Arthur also preferred these to their tent. They descended 6,000 feet to the Indus River with views across it of the high peaks of the Karakorum, again described by Vigne:

> I, the first European who had ever beheld them (so I believe) gazed downwards from a height of six or seven thousand feet upon the sandy plains and green orchards of the valley of the Indus at Skardu […] whilst on the north, and wherever the eye could rove, arose with surpassing grandeur, a vast assemblage of the enormous summits that compose the Tibetan Himalaya.[8]

Like Vigne before them, Arthur and George entered the town of Skardu where they were entertained by the Wazir or Governor,

Ram Ju Durr, who was known to Neve from Srinagar, and the Raja of Baltistan. Neither of them was happy about Neve's proposal to try to cross to Hunza by the Nushik La as they said it had not been used for many years because it was dangerous. However, when he assured them that he would not endanger the men they agreed to supply him with 25 coolies and more if needed.

Arthur's reputation for surgery had preceded them and from early morning the Dak Bungalow where they were staying was besieged by the sick. When he gave someone medicine and instructions all the people gathered round shouted out the instructions after him and explained them at more length to the patient. Most of his treatments were for people's eyes caused by the very smoky conditions in their houses and at each town or village where they stopped he would carry out many operations for cataract and trichiasis, or in-turned eyelids,[9] the results of which gave immense joy to the sufferers.

On August 24 they left Skardu early and walked down to the swift flowing Indus River, here about 500 feet wide, and crossed it on a large raft made of inflated animal hides, which carried their whole party of 34 men and four ponies rapidly downstream, diagonally to the far side near the junction with the Shigar River. They walked all morning up the wide, formerly glaciated Shigar valley through cultivated fields and ripening fruit. An avenue of poplars led them to the oasis of Shigar where they were met by the local band, comprising three flutes, four drums and two great brass trumpets, which struck up and marched in front of them. Soon several local officials fell in behind them and the whole procession crossed the polo ground and arrived at the Dak Bungalow where they met a solitary Swedish missionary, Gustafson, of singular appearance. His face was untouched by sun or wind; he had a long red beard, blue serge trousers, black tail coat and brown hat. He occupied two rooms of the four in the bungalow where he had lived for the past two years helping the poorer people with amateur doctoring and other matters but largely ignored by the Raja and hindered by the Kashmiri officials. Arthur and George occupied the remaining rooms and for the rest of the day were fed on delicious fruit and entertained by the Raja of Shigar, the Wazir and other people; it included a lively game of polo 'on the finest polo ground in the Himalayas', which had been announced by the beating of the drums.

The band sat at the end of the ground and played a sort of running accompaniment to the game, playing a loud triumphal air when a goal was hit or when the Raja had run down the field with the ball. At the end of the game the winning side stood in front of the band and cheered holding their sticks aloft, and then came a little way down the ground and sat in a row. The other side retired to the further end of the ground and walked slowly up towards the winners salaaming very low and throwing a little earth over their shoulders. Then the winners went forward to meet them. Then all salaamed down to the ground and embraced. The ground was then invaded by little boys with hockey sticks.

Early the next morning many people had gathered around the bungalow waiting to see the Doctor Sahib. He began with a short address in Hindustani, which was translated into Balti by a very smart lad who declaimed with great spirit. Gustafson then preached to them and sang a Balti hymn after which Neve began examining the patients, giving each a note for medicines. Most of these were chronic cases of rheumatism, dyspepsia, asthmatic bronchitis and opthalmia for which he could do little. When all had been seen the pills and medicine bottles were put out on a table by the window, and Neve gave them out as fast as the people presented their notes. Gustafson stood by and poured out the mixture of Epsom salts-Senna, which was the favourite concoction, and the lad held a sensor of lotion wherewith he rubbed the legs, arms and backs of those who required to be so rubbed. Minor ailments having been attended to, Neve began to operate on the more serious cases, having converted the little wooden pavilion where the Raja watched polo into an operating theatre. Each day he did 15 or 20 operations, comprising cataracts, trichiasis, tumours and tooth extractions, all the while being watched by a large crowd of interested onlookers. On several occasions through the day Gustafson would sing one of the Balti hymns he had composed and speak a few words of some simple Christian truths. The next two days more people came and Neve did several cataract operations before breakfast and continued until 6 pm each day.

Figure 8 Skin raft on Shigar River, Baltistan, 1895

This left little time to organise the next phase of the journey to the Nushik La but Wazir Haider agreed to accompany them and make the forward arrangements for food and porters, and on their fourth morning they began the journey up the fertile Shigar valley. Harvesting was in full swing accompanied by the singing of the women as they cut and carried the buckwheat and millet to the threshing floors where cattle trod it out and men winnowed it. The flat tops of the houses shone gold with apricots laid out to dry in the sun. The kernels were extracted and pressed to provide oil for lighting and cooking and much of the dried fruit not kept for the coming winter was carried down to Srinagar by the men.

For four days they travelled up the valley, camping each night near a village where Neve would attend to the sick and Gustafson would preach to them, something that they seemed willing to listen to.

At one point they had to cross the Braldo river, a large tributary of the Shigar, on a raft of 20 inflated skins, six men at a time. So it took their large party two hours to accomplish. The final village, Arandu, was at 9,700 feet where no trees grew and the people lived for nine months of the year in underground cellars; they were not Baltis but people who had crossed the Nushik La from Nagir three generations before and settled in this inhospitable place.[10] They were very reluctant to carry for Neve's party but the men from Shigar were now anxious to get back to their harvest and few of them stayed on. Before they left Gustafson told Neve that Wazir Haider had impressed the villagers – *begar* – and had not paid them. Yet none had complained to Neve, which amazed him, and he sought to remedy the matter – not a big one for him as a day's pay was 5 annas per man.[11]

All was now ready for the attempt to cross the Nushik La. As well as Arthur and George the party consisted of their cook and 13 coolies for their kit; then there was Wazir Haider and his gun carrier, a guide who had been across the pass 30 years before, five *shikaris* (hunters) who carried native ice axes, 16 coolies for the Wazir and for carrying extra blankets and food, a goat herd and 17 sheep and goats for milk and meat. On 2 September the whole party of men and beasts started across the snout of the great Chogo Lungma Glacier towards the narrow entrance to its tributary, the Kero Lungma nullah on the further side. They travelled for nine miles, which took eight hours, and camped at Domok where there were some circular sleeping shelters and birch trees. Before nightfall 14 more coolies came in from villages below Arandu to replace some Arandu men so they were a party of 56 in camp that night at an altitude of 11,000 feet. As George wrote, 'It was rather a weird sight, the groups of long haired wild looking Baltis sitting round their various camp-fires amongst the birch trees'. All the next day they climbed up the Kero valley, either on the glacier itself or scrambling across the lateral moraine on one side or the other until they reached the upper basin fed by seven glaciers and here they made their final camp at 16,000 feet where they found a piece of level ground and some old stone shelters from which they disturbed a brown bear. After a very cold night they made an early start and tramped across the firm snowfield to the col that formed the Nushik La. However, it was a large cornice that required Neve to cut through it and then cut steps down the slope on the further side for the porters and George to follow. While Neve had crampons the rest of the party slipped a lot in their grass shoes and became much distressed, all except the *shikaris* who were accustomed to these conditions. While they could now see clearly all the way down to the surface of the Hispar Glacier and the route to Nagir, their way was totally blocked by a large bergschrund, about 30 feet wide and 60 feet deep. At no point was there a bridge of avalanche snow that they could have used to cross it so they reluctantly – and the porters thankfully – climbed back to the pass and made a bivouac among the rocks. The most recent previous crossing had been made three years before but much earlier in the season when there was a bridge across the bergschrund. This was by members of Martin Conway's expedition, which was exploring the northern glaciers from Nagir and crossed the Nushik La in early July as far as Arandu and then returned to Nagir.[12]

With their goal now thwarted they decided to return to Shigar and then follow the Indus River upstream to Ladakh and return to Srinagar via the Zoji La. Once decided they rapidly descended to Arandu, where the villagers were much relieved to welcome their men back from the unpromising venture. Then it was a rapid nine hour trip down the turbulent Shigar River on the goat skin raft to Shigar, where more patients were treated by Neve and Gustafson provided his Balti homilies and hymns. But according to Neve they were more attentive when he spoke to them, even though it had to be translated from Hindustani.

From Shigar they travelled the high route north of the Indus River, crossing two snow-covered passes before dropping down to the river itself, where they found it confined to an extremely narrow gorge less than 20 feet wide but presumably immensely deep and swift. They crossed it on a cantilevered log bridge, leaving behind the Muslim Baltis and entering Buddhist Ladakh, and joined the main road from Leh to Kashmir. And here also Gustafson left them to return to his solitary life in Shigar. Eight more days travel through Kargil, across the Zoji La and down the Sind valley brought them to the shores of the Dal Lake, where Ernest Neve met them with breakfast and they were paddled across the lake to their respective homes in Srinagar.

For Arthur Neve this was his least successful summer trip into the high mountains but for George it was high adventure, which he recorded in great detail for his family. At Sheikh Bagh he was welcomed back by Cecil, Blanche and Fanny and young Harold. A week later Blanche gave birth to the new baby, Julian; Fanny and George departed soon after for England but George had already decided to return the next year to help Cecil in an unpaid capacity – and maybe make another trip with Arthur Neve sometime. Soon after they left Cecil and Blanche took off for a quiet time in their houseboat on the Wular Lake, so that she could recuperate and he could begin to write up the year's activities.

Coaching in Kashmir

This had been the best year since he came to Kashmir and the 1895 log would continue the boating theme and be called *Coaching in Kashmir*. The schools were flourishing with increased numbers, now over 500 and, more significantly, the sons of the wealthy families in the city were now attending. He was not certain that this was a good thing and wrote:

> For some reason unknown to me the sons of the big men here are leaving the State school and coming to the Mission school. One has to be very careful in one's treatment of them, as they imagine they are dukes, and if one is too severe upon their cheek they leave.[13]

Govind Ram was one student who experienced the careful treatment when he claimed that he, as a Brahmin, knew everything and could do anything. Can you box? Yes. Defend your nose! After three strikes that he could not defend it from, he agrees that he doesn't know everything.

The unknown reason for the change in attitude by the wealthy families – even if their sons came home with sore noses – was probably due to the endorsement of the Mission Schools by the British Resident, Sir Hugh Barnes, who with his wife and many Europeans attended the end of year Prize Day. Afterwards the Resident's party was rowed home in the 12-oared cutter manned by school boys, which so impressed him that he advised the Maharaja to send the eldest son of the Raja of Nagir to the Mission

School instead of the State School, which he did. The Mission School now included boys from Afghanistan, Bengal, Dras, Nagir, Nepal, Punjab, Poonch and Ladakh. As Biscoe wrote in the log:

> Boys of rich parents, boys related to the Maharaja, boys of saintly Brahmin and Devotees, sons of the despised boatmen, shopkeepers class, waifs off the street, all are shoved together in the Mission boat, both literal and metaphorical – all have to be licked into shape no matter birth, race, colour, the same regime for all, prince and pauper.[14]

And while he was pleased to report that two boys passed the Entrance exam into the Punjab University, he reiterated the point that passing exams was not the whole purpose of the school.

> We do not believe in educating the boys simply to pass examinations; we try to educate the whole man, so that when the boy leaves the school he may be a good citizen. If you simply train the mind, so that the boys can pass an examination, you make a conceited discontented monkey, who, if he does not get employment, curses those who gave him the education and all in authority, and uses his monkey brain to write spiteful letters to the papers against the British Government, etc, etc, and imagines he is fit to hold a responsible position simply because he is a BA or FA or MA, when his right title should be ASS. No, we try to give the boys the best education in our power, but let them clearly understand that a degree is not the end or aim of all things, it is simply a dead skeleton which has to be filled with a real man, i.e. one who has a humble and brave spirit, one who is ready to take a back seat, and, at the same time, one who would die rather than be a coward.[15]

This was written ten years after the founding of the Indian National Congress and the beginning of the movement for Indian independence from British rule. It encapsulates Biscoe's attitude to the movement that would grow in importance throughout his career. Fifty years later in a letter to his son Julian he wrote,

'Education in India has much to answer for, for it has made a God of examinations and forgotten that character is the one thing needful. Oh for men instead of biped BAs.'[16]

At the end of 1895 a fresh young missionary woman joined Miss Hull in the Church of England *Zenana* Mission Society (CEZMS) but, since the house she was to share with Miss Hull was not ready and Miss Hull was away, she moved into Holton Cottage with the Biscoes. Irene Petrie was well prepared for her vocation, having already learnt Urdu and soon began to learn Kashmiri as well. While Blanche liked her, she was soon under Biscoe's spell and began teaching 80 boys in Habba Kadal School, near the Sheikh Bagh and taking a Bible class in the garden. She wrote in March:

> What an immense silent work the Mission Schools are doing. One would like to hear all Christians with tongues and pens and purses to see and hear what I have seen and heard. Then Mr Tyndale-Biscoe would no longer wish in vain for some University men as assistants and for sufficient funds.[17]

In the spring she joined the annual ten day trip to the Wular Lake and wrote a full description of it.[18] A party of 50 left Sheikh Bagh on 8 April in a flotilla of boats that included the Biscoe's houseboat and the two rowing boats, *Blanche* and *Fanny*. As well as the Biscoe family and Irene there was another missionary woman, several servants, nine masters and the wife of one of them, 20 boys, a Pundit cook for the Hindus who had to eat separately, and Ishmailia the boatman.

Biscoe took the boys on two trips across the lake and, while returning from the second a storm came up – the much feared Nag Korn – and the boats had to stand to until the storm eased. Kashmiri boats would swamp in such circumstances but the rowing boats were safe. Nevertheless, some of the boys were nervous and one 12-year-old, Rago, began to cry. On asking him what was the matter, between his sobs he said, 'I don't mind dying myself but my mother will be very sad'. One of the teachers, Poonoo, who had been one of the first crew to row a boat, cheered him by saying, 'These clouds are nothing. They are like Mr Hadow for he makes a great noise but doesn't do you any harm'. However, news of the storm got back to Srinagar and the rumour started that the boys had been drowned. The Governor telegraphed the parents' concern, and was reassured that all was well. At the end of the camp as the boats rowed back through the city the bridges were lined with people and the rowers responded by raising their oars and giving three ringing cheers, which were warmly echoed from the crowd.

Ladakh Expedition by Ernest Neve and Cecil Tyndale-Biscoe, 1896

A few days after their return, George arrived back from England to begin his voluntary offer of assistance to the schools, which he continued for the next six years. Leaving George to stay with Blanche and the children, Biscoe left at the end of May for the only trip he ever made to Ladakh.[19]

Biscoe was to have gone with Ernest Neve but could not get away in time and instead was invited to join Captain Chenevix Trench, the Assistant Resident, who was making an official visit to Leh with a large party. As Biscoe could not leave with the main party he made several double marches and caught up with them at Kargil. Leaving Sheikh Bagh at 10:30 pm on 29 May he was paddled across the lake by Ishmailia and at Ganderbal mounted his pony at 3 am, changed ponies at 7 am and reached Gund at 10:30 am. After a quick breakfast with Captain Godfrey[20] and the Governor, he was off again on a fresh pony and reached the beautiful upland of Sonamarg at 7 pm where he camped for the night. The next day, being a Sunday he couldn't travel until midnight and so he spent the day with the Postmaster and bathed in the icy cold river.

Unbeknownst to Biscoe, Aurel Stein was camped not far away at Mohand Marg. Aurel Stein was Principal of the Lahore College of Punjab University and in his own time was earning a great reputation as an archaeological explorer of Central Asia and northern India. He had discovered this place a few years before and every summer he would return to it to work on ancient Kashmiri Sanskrit texts and to enjoy its beauty and solitude.

Figure 9 Ernest Neve, Mission Hospital, Srinagar

Currently he was completing his English translation of Kalhana's *Rajah Tiringini* or the *Chronicle of the Kings of Kashmir*, which was written in Sanskrit in 1150. On his first visit to Kashmir six years before he had learnt of the existence of the oldest complete copy of the work, which was jealously guarded by a Pandit family in Srinagar. At the same time he met Pandit Govind Kaul who was as keen as he to save the manuscript and see it translated. By the next year the family had agreed to let Stein translate it and he arranged for Govind Kaul to join him in Lahore to carry out the task together. Each summer he spent weeks at a time in Kashmir, verifying Kalhana's descriptions of buildings and geographical features, extracting useful information as he went from conversations with

71

local people well-versed in the traditional lore of Kashmir, and amassing encyclopaedic knowledge of the valley. The result was a translation of the text into English complete with commentary, notes, geographical memoir and maps, which finally appeared in two volumes in 1900.[21] A few days after Biscoe passed through Stein wrote to his sister-in-law in Hungary:

> I enjoy the freedom and work eleven hours a day. After dinner I take down Kashmiri tales from the mouth of a peasant bard and am thus collecting valuable material which I will put to good use in Europe. Hatim the story teller is known throughout the Sind Valley and to my great pleasure was brought up here by the authorities.[22]

Had Biscoe called on Stein that Sunday it is not clear how much they would have had in common? Certainly they knew each other because Stein was the chief examiner for the Punjab University Entrance that Biscoe's senior students sat for and in later years they knew each other well. But Stein's closest friends among the missionaries were the Neves with whom he stayed when he was in Srinagar. His attitude towards the scholarly Kashmiri Pandits was very different to Biscoe's; he respected their knowledge of the ancient texts and they respected Stein's fluency in Sanskrit.

As soon as Sunday ended, Biscoe set off for the Zoji La with five ponies and his servant Ramzana, who whiled away the night march with stories of the ancient kings of Kashmir, like Hatim was doing with Stein. They crossed the snow-covered pass at dawn, the ponies slipping on the track, and began the steep descent to Matayan for the second night. Having crossed the divide, which holds back the moisture from the plains, the land had changed dramatically being arid except where people had carried snow-fed mountain streams in irrigation channels to water the alluvial flats. Over the next two days they travelled along the hot dry valley leading down to the Suru River, which they crossed by a new suspension bridge to reach Kargil and the official party. Here Biscoe watched Trench expose the chicanery of the Kashmiri Governor of the province before the whole community. The Governor, a member of the powerful Dhar family of Srinagar, had been charged with storing a large quantity of grain in the old fort at Kargil against the coming winter. He produced the books which showed that the grain had been collected but Trench asked to see the store for himself. This the Governor tried in vain to obstruct but eventually the doors of the store rooms were opened and were all empty. He had sold the lot and pocketed the proceeds. The next day the community assembled in Durbar to hear the words of the Commissioner, for all had heard that the Governor had been caught out in his defrauding that none dared mention because he was a powerful man with the ear of the Maharaja. Now his time had come to be humbled. 'There we all were, in a circle, sitting in an orchard near a rushing river, and surrounded by the great mountains as silent witness at the great Court of Justice.' Many years later Biscoe met his son, an old boy of the school, working as an honest official and recalled this encounter with the father.

Four more marches took them to Leh and on the way they visited two Buddhist monasteries and marvelled at the massive, 30 feet high, rock carving of the Buddha at Mulbe and were entertained by the monks at Lamayuru to music, songs and intricate dances. Biscoe was fascinated by the small clay medallions of the Buddha that he saw in crevices in the Mana walls that devout Buddhist must always pass on the left side. He was told that the medallions are made of the ashes of deceased lamas, mixed with clay and pressed into moulds and sun dried or baked and painted. They were irreverently referred to as potted lamas[23] and he brought two back with him.

Many years later – about 1944 – I found them while rummaging in his study, and he gave them to me, along with a Ladakhi flint and steel that people then carried on their belt for lighting fires (see p. 82), and a Thanka from Hemis monastery.

In Leh Biscoe finally caught up with Ernest Neve, who was already busy attending to patients at the small hospital of the resident Moravian missionaries. These people had been working in Ladakh since 1875 with the permission of the former Maharaja, Ranbir Singh. They were Lutheran by religion and Scandinavian by birth – Gustafson in Shigar was one of them – and had provided medical services to the Ladakhis as well as a small school in Leh. They admitted that mission work among Buddhists and Lamaists was not easy and they had made few converts to Christianity, although one was at that time a student in the Mission School in Srinagar. As one of them later wrote:

A Buddhist Lama who has understood the doctrines of his system to a certain degree looks down with contempt on every other wisdom, and is quite capable of enveloping himself in as much conceit as the ordinary Mussulman does. The laity, who have to be satisfied with the grossest idolatry, are kept in strict dependence on the ecclesiastical institutions; for the monasteries have developed into a sort of banking establishments, and there is hardly a peasant who is not in debt to one or the other monastery [...] Hard to conquer though both are, Mohammedism as well as Buddhism, they were both weakened by being brought in contact with each other. This can plainly be seen in Leh. The adherents of both religions are most bigoted in those territories where they never get to see adherents of other creeds. In a religiously mixed population the belief in the infallibility of any particular religion is often shaken, and in consequence of this the religious convictions of any one creed become weaker.[24]

But somehow Christianity was thought to be immune to this hazard and these good people laboured on for many years, suffering death from typhus and typhoid. Indeed, Neve and Biscoe visited the small cemetery at Leh to honour the graves of two Lutheran missionaries who had died of typhus five years before – Rev. Redslob, the founder of the mission, and Dr Marx, a scholar of Tibetan, who had translated the most important historical work of the country, the *Book of the Kings of Ladakh*, but did not live to see it published.

While Neve was busy each day at the hospital, Biscoe took himself off to explore the nearby Khardong Pass of 17,400 feet over which caravans go on their way to and from Central Asia. Because it was so hot in the daytime he left on a pony in the evening but lost his way in the dark. When the moon rose Biscoe found himself under the snout of a glacier near the top of the pass but he was feeling the effects of the altitude so badly that he descended as fast as he could, reaching Leh at 8 am and retired to bed for the rest of the day. This was his first and last venture into higher altitudes.

A few days later he and Neve visited the famous monastery of Hemis 20 miles from Leh. It was then the wealthiest monastery in Ladakh with 500 monks and each year a special religious play was enacted, lasting two days. Many people from all over Ladakh gathered for the performance. Neve thought its object was to illustrate the struggle of demons for the soul of man and the value of priestly intercession, while Biscoe thought it was to show all the known and unknown horrors of hell and the power of the monks in a future life. Monks dressed in hideous masks representing various animals danced round a fire into which a clay figure of a man was thrown, all accompanied by an orchestra of shawms (copper trumpets 15 feet long), cymbals, clarinets and drums. Two clowns appeared who stealthily biffed the devils and then 13 richly dressed figures with black hats and benign faces, representing the priests came dancing down the steps and slowly drove off the devils and sprinkled water to douse the fire. The audience thoroughly enjoyed the show and Biscoe thought they were too jolly and cheery a lot to believe much in devils and saw the humour of it all.

From Leh they retraced the journey out as far as Mulbe but then followed the Suru River to the village of that name, which is under the massif of Nun Kun (23,500 feet or 7,634 metres), then crossed a pass into the Wardwan valley and thence to the main Vale of Kashmir. At the end of each day's march Neve would treat patients, some of whom would follow them from camp to camp for later treatment. He performed 42 operations for cataract on the trip and after each operation he would hold up his fingers and ask the patient to count them. Biscoe described the joy that spread across the man's face as he realised he could really see and it was no dream or sorcery but naked fact that his sight was restored.

Soon they reached the Jhelum River and were thankful to rest their feet and lazily glide downstream to Srinagar and home.

The relationship of the two men on this trip is curious. Both published accounts of the trip some years later but, while Biscoe describes being in Neve's company from Leh back to Srinagar, Neve nowhere mentions Biscoe at all. Neve's account is the more scholarly one with descriptions of the geographic formations passed through and the historical and religious associations of places seen; Biscoe's is a more light-hearted account. It seems likely that they had much less pleasure in each other's company than their respective brothers had enjoyed the previous year in Baltistan. And, while Ernest Neve made many more excursions into the mountains around Kashmir, Biscoe never again travelled far from the immediate environs of Srinagar while in Kashmir. His experience of high altitude in Leh may have convinced him that his chronic ill health was not up to such exertions. Indeed, he was again ill in October and November of 1896.

Soon after his return, George presented the school with a 15-seat *shikara* to be propelled with Kashmiri paddles rather than English oars and early in August the first crew of Brahmin boys were on the water – although with their heads covered to avoid shaming their families by being seen to do the work of low caste *hangis* (boatmen). This crew came from the Rainawari Branch School, under the plucky leadership of Pandit Amar Chand, and they paddled all the way down the Jhelum River and under the bridges crowded with jeering townsfolk. In later years it was remembered with pride by boys from that school.[25]

However, that event changed the attitude of the others and by the next year the number of racing *shikaras* had increased to seven that could each seat 15 and one really long one that could seat 35 paddlers. The latter was built in the Central School with funds provided by Irene Petrie from the sale of her pictures. So, as had happened five years before when English rowing boats were introduced, initial resistance soon gave way to enthusiastic acceptance by the boys and teachers despite opposition from the general public in the city. The low repute of Kashmiris for what the British termed 'manly pursuits' was being rapidly dispelled when they were given leadership.

Financial Concerns Again

And while these achievements pleased Biscoe they still did not do him much good in missionary circles, where his lack of converts and inability to master the languages of the country, resulted in less financial support than other schools received.

This is clearly seen in the accounts published at the end of the log for 1896, *Coxing in Kashmir*. These show that the grant from the parent body, the Church Missionary Society (CMS), amounted to one-fifth of the total expenses of the schools; there was no grant from the State and the main sources of funds were contributed by members of the Tyndale-Biscoe family and other private donations (30 per cent each) and the balance from fees and fines.

He poured out his troubles in a letter to Robert Clark, who was his immediate superior as Secretary of the Punjab and Sindh Corresponding Committee of the CMS in Amritsar. He began by explaining George's background, and his reasons for joining him but not wishing to be a missionary:

> He has private means and so he gives his services free [...]
> We were brought up in a God-fearing home with its never dying
> influences but it was not until George was 18 when at Bradfield
> College that he really learnt his need of a personal Saviour and
> accepted Christ as such. The instrument of this spiritual light
> was the memoirs of Captain Hedley Vicars, which I had sent to
> him when at school and delightful letters I received from him
> at this time. My being able to help him a bit has naturally drawn
> us together and he has always backed up my work out here
> when many of my relations and friends took the opposite line.
> After school he went to Kings College [sic] London where he
> did well and from there launched out into his engineering
> profession in 1891 and served for his first 2.5 years in Sir
> Douglas Fox's office. Last year he came out on a visit and was
> so impressed with the usefulness of the work that on his return
> he decided to throw in his lot with us [...] While I was in
> Ladakh this year he took over my duties which he fulfilled
> most satisfactorily. He is a man of deeds and not words and will
> be a blessing here where words are cheap and action scarce.

You are aware that the work here has grown very much of late so that my brother's help has only just come in time [...] We have five schools, one of which my wife generally looks after. We have over 700 boys with 26 masters to pay and our numbers increase. I continually receive petitions from unworked parts of the town and from villages to open schools amongst them. We have been very successful this year passing 2/2 for the FA Punjab University and 8/10 for the middle exam. And 5 members of my Bible class (100) went for the General Lake Scripture Prize and they were only beaten by 2 [hot] men from Delhi. I entered them for the senior when they could have entered for the juniors. This month too I have completed my fight to make these conceited pandits to do despised and low caste work of boatmen. Five years ago I could not get them to row an English boat with me like sahibs; now you would see me being paddled to school in a native boat by 15 holy Brahmins doing the real menial work of a *Hangi* and this not by compulsion but because they like it and have learnt that real gentlemen may do hard work after all.[26]

He goes on to raise his problems of funding the work:

I have never said anything about this before as I didn't know until the other day that other school masters' lot was any better than my own. I find this wear and tear does not fall to the lot of all scholastic missionaries. Some of the supporters are opposed to educational work thinking that we spend our time over secular subjects and cramp out the scriptural but this is not the case. I know of no school in England which has so much scripture taught as in our main school. Nearly all my time is spent in addresses and scripture classes in the school or at my home. Of late we have had so many boys coming to read scripture out of school at my house that we have had to deter them from coming from lack of teachers. I am a great believer in out of school work and look upon it as if not a more important time than in school. It is the time when you get to know your boys personally and they to know you.

Then there are the old boys who are out at work who have to be kept hold of through night school etc. The work is endless and still it grows and opportunities are lost for lack of workers and the needful.

I could of course get more help from the CMS public if I wrote more, telling of the religious conversations I have with the boys and of the persecution that some undergo because they have had the courage to confess their belief in Christ openly. But I won't do that as you know a native's words are not the same as a European's and what would be perfectly true as a fact would give quite a wrong impression to those at home who do not know the native's character. I have seen some pamphlets written about certain Kashmiri Pandits and their wonderful Christian lives, which is utterly false. So I refrain from falling in the same error but when by God's grace we shall have steered some of these young fellows into port then will be the time to show our supporters that their money has not been spent in vain. It is the age of advertising one's work but I would rather not, so it is my own fault and no one else's that I have hitherto been left to fight the money question more or less alone. Please forgive this jaw but I know I have your sympathy otherwise I would not write thus.

Yours very gratefully, CE Tyndale-Biscoe

Robert Clark (then aged 72) was sympathetic and at the next meeting of his committee got the CMS grant to the Kashmir schools raised from 1,800 rupees to 3,000 rupees; and accepted George Biscoe as an honorary agent in local connexion. He also wrote to the CMS Secretary in London in May 1897:

I have received your letter of 30 April regarding the Rev C.E. Tyndale-Biscoe's application for furlough. This will come before CC [Corresponding Committee (in Lahore)]; but as Mr Biscoe asks for a reply from PC [Parent Committee (in London)] I have brought it before members who are now here [...] You will doubtless remember that CC have already corresponded with Mr Biscoe before, on the subject of his exam. He expressed his inability to pass the exam and thought himself unworthy to be a missionary and thought it would be better for him to go home; and for the Society to send someone who would do the work better than he. Mr Perkins when in Kashmir, doubted his being ever able to pass the exam. He works in English all day long, and knows enough Kashmiri to carry on his school work and to converse with the people; and he did not feel able to do much more than this [...] He is looked on here as one of the best and most useful missionaries. It will be remembered that some of the best missionaries who have been in India were not conversant with the vernacular.

He has 900 boys with 35 masters, hardly any fees and no Government Grant (in Kashmir). His expenses are some Rs 700 per month of which he receives some Rs 250 from PC and he raises the rest. CC recommended that when he goes on furlough the school be made over to Mr Knowles, who can then depute the management to his brother, Mr George Biscoe (an Honorary worker who declines to be officially connected with the Society but works most heartily with his brother for us).[27]

Despite his problems with finance, the 1896 log, *Coxing in Kashmir*, gives an optimistic account of the year's activities, including a lively account of the camping trip to the Wular Lake and the beginning of paddling in *shikaras*.

If anyone had prophesised of this unheard of action six year's ago they would have turned up the whites of their eyes and said, 'O, Ram, Ram, preserve us, may Saraswati [the Goddess of learning] cease to ride on a goose',[28] but that will never be.

Reflecting the concerns expressed in his letter to Clark he concludes the log by assuring his readers:

Let me say that, although this educational work has small results to show so far, we are forging ahead, and that we are working not merely for the present, but for generations to come […] Think of our crew of over 700 twenty year's hence, all of them *pater familias* with many a young hopeful around them following in the wake of their dads. Therefore I ask you to come and look at our crew sometimes, and help us to turn our very difficulties into energy and power for driving ahead. Now is the day of small things: it may not be ours to see great things, but others will. Let us hasten on that time, knowing that we are on the winning side.[29]

So ended 1896 for Biscoe, with optimism for the coming year, encouraged by the increased support of the CMS. George was well established in the schools as Jog Sahib, and Blanche and Irene were involved in the nearby junior school at Habba Kadal.

Ladakh Expedition by Arthur Neve, Geoffrey Millais and George Tyndale-Biscoe, 1897

George, as he had hoped, was invited by Arthur Neve to join him and Geoffrey Millais on his summer expedition, this time to explore the then unknown region north of the Nubra River – the Sasser Peaks and the Panamik Glacier – north of Leh.[30] They left Srinagar in July 1897 and crossed into Ladakh by the Zoji La, following the same route as Ernest Neve and Biscoe had traversed the year before to Leh. On the way they caught up with a party of lady missionaries, including Irene Petrie, also travelling to Leh. They travelled together for two days during which time Irene was feverish so her party decided to rest up for a day or two. She had been unwell before leaving Srinagar and Blanche, who well knew the early signs of typhoid, had tried to dissuade her from going but she was determined to get into the cooler hills. Arthur Neve thought it was not serious and dosed her with quinine and his party of three men then continued on to Leh. The women's party continued slowly but after two days Irene became weaker and eventually had to be carried the last march into Leh on a bed, and was there cared for by the Moravian missionaries. Neve saw her again and now suspected that she had typhoid and if so the crisis would be expected in about ten days. Since the only treatment at that time was careful nursing to allow the body to cure itself, there was nothing more he could do for her so he decided to pursue his plans on the understanding that he would return if she got worse.

Mounted on yaks the three men ascended the Khardong La, from which Biscoe had turned back the previous year, and like him they experienced mountain sickness until they had descended on the northern side to the Shyok River. They crossed it on a ferry and continued up the tributary Nubra River to the village of Tirit, where Neve treated the people and arranged for porters for their forward trip up the Panamik Glacier. One man in a very loud voice from a housetop successfully called the men by name from halfway up the opposite mountainside. As Neve wrote, 'a Ladakhi might well replace a foghorn'. At Panamik the next evening they sought information about the high pastures in the Panamik valley from the village grey-beards and from this judged how they could climb to the top of the glacier. They carried a camp up the valley to 17,000 feet where they found small shepherds shelters. This became their base camp and from there they were able to climb to the head of the glacier and reach the dividing range at 22,000 feet. This gave them a magnificent view of Sasser Kangri (25,170 feet) and the Popache Glacier that flowed southwest from it, as well as several other high peaks on the eastern end of the Karakoram Himalaya. Geoffrey Millais photographed the peaks while George measured out a base line for their sketch map of the area. The map that Neve subsequently published was the first description of this area.[31] They were unequipped to do more and so returned the way they had come, stopping in the villages for Neve to treat people, particularly for cataract which he performed under the most extraordinary conditions. At the Shyok River were three blind women who implored him to treat them. At first he demurred but then decided to try. In his words:

> I had my box of instruments, but how should I sterilize them, and how should I light a fire? I told the Ladakhis and they tried to strike sparks with flint and steel, but the tinder seemed moist. One of them then produced a little gunpowder and placed it on a stone, tore off a rag from his shirt and fraying it

out laid it by the powder, then with flint and steel ignited it. Then a cooking pot was produced and soon water was boiling. What an anachronism between the aseptic surgery aimed at and the primeval method of fire production! While the instruments were being boiled I cleaned the eyes and instilled cocaine; then kneeling in the sand, removed the three cataracts, completing the operations just before a gust of wind came, laden with dust and grit, which would have put a stop to the work. The gratitude of the people knew no bounds.[32]

When they returned to Leh the next day they learnt that Irene Petrie had died some days before and was already buried alongside the graves of the Moravian missionaries Redslob and Marx. The speed with which she had succumbed to the typhoid was unusual and may have been due to the unaccustomed altitude. At any rate, there was now nothing to keep them longer and they made a rapid return journey, doing double marches. In Srinagar a memorial service was held for Irene at which both Knowles and Biscoe spoke. While Knowles dwelt on the hereafter, Biscoe emphasised the present, 'Therefore my beloved brethren, be ye steadfast, unmoveable, always abounding in the work of the Lord, forasmuch as ye know that your labour in not in vain in the Lord.'[33] Both Blanche and Cecil were much affected by Irene's untimely death as they had become very fond of her during the two years she had stayed and worked with them. Ten years later, when their only daughter was born they named her Frances Irene.

Despite the loss of Irene, 1897 was a successful year for the schools, as the log *Paddling in Kashmir*, published in December, attested. In the five schools, staffed by 41 teachers, there were now between 850 and 1,000 boys, who put on a massed drill for Prize Day. As the title proclaimed, this was the first year that boating in Kashmiri *shikaras* using Kashmiri paddles took off with five crews each of 15 paddles and one of 31 paddles. And Biscoe used the theme to describe the various strokes that Kashmiri boatmen used: the ordinary leisurely stroke used when the boat is empty or is only carrying *nikka pice* (poor) passengers; through the *sahib ko* stroke, which is long and strong beginning slowly and gradually quickening for a few minutes, then back to slow, this is the stroke that can be maintained for hours; to the showy stroke for weddings and festivities – two ordinary strokes and then a loud smack as the flat of the paddle hits the water. The school crews aimed for the middle stroke – strong and not showy, except for the Prize Day when the smacking stroke was used. And he gave some lively examples of what he meant.

First Home Furlough, 1898

At the end of the year Cecil and Blanche and their two boys left for a year's furlough in Britain. They visited Julian and Albert at their postings near Peshawar and then sailed for England, which they reached in time for Christmas at Holton with most of the extended family. Stafford was established now as the squire of Holton with his wife and family of seven children. Fanny was there, as well as all his brothers, except George in Kashmir, Cecil and Albert with their wives and young families. A group photo of the family was taken in the garden and another of the ten children indoors.

For the next ten months Cecil travelled around Britain speaking to schools and churches about the work in Kashmir. In all he spoke to 95 meetings that year. It was a condition of missionaries taking a year's leave that they speak to supporters in order to raise funds for the society but they were nevertheless expected to rely on friends and relations to provide them with accommodation. It was not an easy vacation and quite a few of the places they visited were not particularly welcoming. At one school the headmaster introduced Biscoe to the assembled boys with the words, 'Here's a missionary to speak to you', and promptly left the room. However, at many other places he was welcomed and enjoyed meeting old friends, including several he had got to know in Kashmir, such as Walter Lawrence, soon to return to India as Private Secretary to the Viceroy Lord Curzon, and the current Resident, Sir Adelbert Talbot, also on leave.

Biscoe also had discussions at CMS headquarters about the ongoing financial support for the Kashmir work, a constant worry to him. He compared the resources available in Kashmir, where the

State gave no support, with the much more favourable resources from the Punjab Government to the Mission School in Amritsar.[34] His arguments were clearly persuasive because head office sanctioned additional funds for the Kashmir schools and also made a request through the British Resident to the State Government which was eventually successful.

In the new year of 1899 they began the journey back to Kashmir. Blanche and the children travelled by steamer with a governess and two relatives who were coming out to help in the school, Augustus Tyndale an engineer who would start a Technical School, and Blanche's brother, L'Estrange Burges a mathematician; meanwhile Julian and Cecil travelled overland through France, Greece and Turkey to the Levant and Palestine, taking in the main sites of the Holy Land, which Cecil sketched. They joined the family at Port Said and all travelled on together to India.

When they reached Baramula they were met by George and some of the teachers in the cutter *Fanny* and escorted to the city, where they were met by hundreds of boys and old boys who unharnessed the ponies and dragged their tongas to the Sheikh Bagh, like pious Hindus drag the carriage of Jagar Nath on holy days. Thus began a happy and successful year for Biscoe. He much appreciated the support and friendship he had received in London and wrote to the Secretary in May:

> Let me say this which has been in my heart and mind many times since I left England and that it is the kindness and consideration that I met with at all times at Salisbury Square. It seems extraordinary to me that the Secretaries, who have so many cares and such a quantity of men and matters on their minds could take so much personal interest in insignificant individuals. It is evidently this Power which the Secretaries possess and use, which goes so far to make the Society not a Society but a family. I can only say again I thank the Committee most warmly for all their kindness to me when I was in England, and so I return to my work a stronger man than when I was here before, for I know that we are being backed up by personal friends.[35]

In the log for 1899 *Towing in Kashmir* Biscoe especially mentioned the supporters and helpers which he called towers. By the end of the year the total enrolments topped 1,100 in six schools; the Governor of the Punjab attended the annual regatta as the Chief Guest and visited the Central School. They were also much helped by the strong support of Walter Lawrence, now back in Delhi, who strongly advised Robert Clark that the CMS 'should always send very special men to Kashmir, because the eyes of India are on them there.'[36]

Maharaja Pratap Singh

More significant than the approbation of the British authorities though, was the friendliness shown to Biscoe by Maharaja Pratap Singh this year, in contrast to his earlier coolness. Pratap Singh was a lonely man since he had been deposed from the affairs of State by the British ten years before. He did not trust his younger brother Raja Amar Singh, who now ran the State, and instead devoted himself to religious matters. As a pious Hindu he was interested in Christianity and he had several private meetings with Biscoe, when they discussed religion and other matters. He had a distinctive way of speaking and some of his remarks were recalled by Biscoe.

The Maharaja was especially interested in the Prayer Book, which he studied carefully.

Mr. Biscoe, he said. You of course, know the part of your prayer book called Litany?

Indeed, I do Maharaja Sahib. Why? What about it?

Oh there is one part of Litany that I love very much. I read it often and often. Can you guess what it is?

No, Maharaja Sahib, I'm afraid I can't.

It is the part which says 'from battle and murder, and from sudden death, good Lord deliver us.' That is what I like best in all of Prayer Book.[37]

Poor Pratap Singh, he always lived in fear of assassination or poisoning or witchcraft. Every night when he went to bed, a

Figure 10 Pratap Singh, Maharaja of Jammu and Kashmir, 1885-1925

Brahmin priest would walk round the bed repeating powerful mantras, (holy verses or incantations), and a chalk mark would be made on the floor round the bed. His Highness was then safe from sorcery during the hours of darkness, so long as he remained within the circle.

On another occasion the Maharaja questioned Biscoe about the Holy Communion Service.

This Holy Communion, in your religion. Is it compulsory for all persons to attend?

No, Maharaja Sahib. It is for each person to decide for himself.

I see. So anyone may go or not, just as he chooses?

Yes, that is so.

Does the Resident Sahib attend the Holy Communion?

I'm sorry Maharaja Sahib, but that is a question that I cannot discuss with you. It is an entirely personal matter for each person to decide for himself.

There was a pause, and then the Maharaja asked, does the Assistant Resident attend Holy Communion?

Maharaja Sahib, I have told you this is a matter I cannot discuss with you.

Acha. Another pause, and then. Does Colonel Cockburn attend the Holy Communion?

Really, Maharaja Sahib, I must ask you to stop asking me such questions. Because they are personal and private concerns about which I cannot speak to you.

Oh, indeed! *Ap ka nak kiun aisa tera hai?* (Why have you got such a crooked nose?)

My nose Maharaja Sahib? Why my nose was knocked crooked as a boy when I went in for boxing.

Boxing? Boxing? What is boxing?

Don't you know about boxing? The noble art of self defence? Now supposing I tried to hit you on the nose with my fist, could you defend yourself? And Biscoe put up his fists and made a feint as if to hit the Maharaja on the nose.[38]

The Maharaja immediately put his hands up to cover his face and let out a loud chuckle of laughter. Immediately the door was thrown open and a couple of guards came rushing in with swords half drawn, thinking that the Maharaja was calling for help. He looked up and shouted to them.

Jao! Jao! (Get out! Get out!) Can't you see I am having a private talk with the padre Sahib? Tell me more about this boxing.

And so Biscoe explained why he wanted the boys to learn to box, not to win competitions but so that they could learn to stand up for themselves and help to defend the weak and the helpless, and grow up to be brave and true, instead of cringing.

Mr. Biscoe, said the Maharaja, like his grandfather Maharaja Gulab Singh before him. You are wasting your time. You will never make the boys brave, for all my Kashmiri people are cowards.

But many times in the past nine years Biscoe had seen that that was not true.

Conclusions on the First Decade

Two themes stand out in Biscoe's first decade in Kashmir: his unresolved conflict with the CMS over the lack of converts; and the remarkable speed with which the young Hindu and Muslim men, who formed the staff of the schools, embraced his ideas for social reform even against their parents and religious leaders and the contempt of the Maharaja.

On the first matter his troubles began in 1892–93. Rumours had got back to London that Biscoe was encouraging prize fighting among the boys and that he was offending the Kashmir authorities and the Hindu community by making the boys do sweepers' work. Then the adverse report to the Punjab Committee by H.E. Perkins, who considered that the Mission School under Biscoe was not performing as a missionary endeavour because it was not making converts or employing Christian teachers, whereas the schools in the Punjab were doing both. Perkins chided Biscoe for busying himself with fighting fires in the city instead of attending prayer meetings.

This attitude completely baffled Biscoe but probably should not have done so; it reflected the thinking of the evangelical movement in the Anglican Church that had prevailed for the best part of a century and certainly in India since 1833. For the evangelical movement, the primary purpose of missionary endeavour was the urgent need to bring all people to Christ – to preach the message that all people are sinners and their only way to salvation in the life hereafter was through the blood sacrifice of Jesus. During the first 30 years of the nineteenth century the church authorities endeavoured to persuade the East India Company that governed British India to actively encourage the conversion of Indians to Christianity and, by progressive regulation, to discourage Hindu religious practices that were contrary to this.[39] Doing good works or trying to change the social customs of the society in which one lived was not only irrelevant but actually sinful because it implied that a person could help themselves to salvation – pride in self, called supererogation, 'which hath the nature of sin'. Furthermore, by busying oneself with such matters one was neglecting the primary purpose of the missionary call to preach the good news and make as many converts as possible. The mystical/magical effect of baptism was the necessary and sufficient purpose for the follower of Christ.

This was not Biscoe's idea of the Christian life at all. He had little time for theology and the more esoteric aspects of the Christian faith. In his own words, written to me 50 years later:

We learnt that Christianity was a practical life, that is, following our Master who came to the Earth to teach us how to live and treat our fellows, viz to live the unselfish life [...] I was never troubled over beliefs as I was never clever enough to go into the matter. It all seemed plain to me; that those who tried to follow the Master had to do some fighting. It was quite easy to follow the devil – any fool could do that. To be a Christian you must be ready to fight the evils in yourself and to protect the weaker brothers. That was one reason, or *the* reason why I was so keen on boxing. Not prize fighting; I have no use for it; but to be able to protect the weak. Perhaps the reason I had no religious doubts, because I realized what following Jesus Christ's life meant for the World [...] No, I believe we are put in the World, as at school, preparing for the Greater Life ahead. There is no death but life abundant. I feel to be still at school, preparing for the greater life, hoping that I with others may be thought fit for some kind of usefulness somewhere.[40]

Confident in his beliefs, Biscoe pursued his own form of missionary endeavour despite the discouragement from some members of the CMS and the opposition of the Kashmir State Government. However, he did have the support and even admiration of the British ruling class in India, who appreciated what he was achieving with Kashmiri boys, and who supported him with donations. While the financial support was in fact quite meagre, the moral support of his peers in India and in Britain sustained him and he pitched his story to them.

This evident support from the British establishment posed an awkward problem for the CMS. While many in the society disapproved of his approach to mission work, they could not gainsay the credit it brought to the society, especially when he toured Britain in 1897–98, speaking in schools and churches on behalf of the CMS. This complicated relationship between the society and Biscoe continued to the end of his career.

On the second matter, the speed with which his ideas were embraced by the Kashmiri teachers and students was remarkable. From the time of the first Maharaja, Gulab Singh, in 1854 and even before, the Kashmiri had a reputation for being cowardly, cringing and contemptible; willing to lie and cheat if he could get away with it and entirely without self-respect. Early visitors to Kashmir, such as William Moorcroft[41] and Victor Jacquemont[42] described the appalling conditions that the Kashmiris suffered under the tyrannies of the Afghans and later the Sikhs; and these did not improve under the Dogra rule that followed, so that survival depended on being subservient and evasive. What Biscoe offered the Kashmiri was self-respect and pride in their own worth, something they had not experienced before. And many of them, such as Amar Chand, Hassan Ali and Shenker Koul seized the challenge and became fiercely loyal to this cocksparrow of an Englishman, who couldn't speak their language but believed in them and loved them. And because he did not require them to abandon their own religion in order to follow him, he didn't make them dependant on him like the so-called 'rice Christians' of other missionaries. In this regard his relationship to them was more like that of a British officer towards his Indian sepoys in the army.

So the century ended. But as the new century began Biscoe and his Kashmiri colleagues were to be challenged from another and quite different quarter, and one that nearly finished him off: Annie Besant.

3

The Challenge, 1900–05

We know now who are our friends and who are our
enemies, who to trust and who not to trust, we have
unmasked our enemies' guns.

1901 log, *Punting in Kashmir*, p. 21

The new century began in Kashmir as a year of plenty and in
the opening months the Mission Schools enjoyed their
traditional activities of camping at the Wular Lake and
climbing in the Pir Panjal mountains. A technical department had
been started in the Central School under the guidance of Biscoe's
cousin Augustus Tyndale in order to encourage Hindu boys to
develop skills in metal work and carpentry and so improve the
quality of local handcrafts. Two rowing boats were made during
the year.

The ever present worry of finance was aggravated early in the
year by the decision of the Church Missionary Society (CMS) to
cut the grant by 500 rupees per month, just two years after they had
agreed to raise it substantially. Biscoe wrote cheerfully enough in
reply, 'We every now and then raise the fees and lose from 100 to
150 boys in consequence, but in a few months we gain that number
and then are in position to raise them again.'[1] However, after Raja
Amar Singh visited the school the Kashmir State Council looked on
them more favourably by providing a grant of 200 rupees per month.

Cholera Again

Then in August 1900 cholera came to Srinagar again as bad as in 1892. The Mission Hospital reported 7,600 cases of which 4,256 died, and 35,000 visits were registered at the dispensary:

> They came from the picturesque balconied houses by the riverside where the merchants and trades people dwell; from the secluded courtyards adjoining mosque or shrine, the home of mullahs and religious teachers; but chiefly from the narrow, crowded alleys where the sun scarcely penetrates, and courts where the air is poisoned by the festering heaps of filth, where disease is ever rampant and epidemics are bred.[2]

Cholera had always been a frightening disease because its origin was not known and its effects could be so swift and terrible. Two views prevailed at the end of the nineteenth century about its cause although both recognised its association with filthy streets and housing. The older medical view was that cholera was caused by miasmas from stinking cess pools, as this quote from the Annual Report of the Mission Hospital implies, but by 1900 it was becoming known that it is caused by a bacterium and is carried in infected water.[3]

Biscoe noted in his diary in early September, 'City frightened, 50 deaths in a day, chiefly at Chatterbal where there is no tap water.'[4] But unlike in 1892 when most deaths were in the city, Neve noted that most of those in 1900 were in remoter villages, reflecting the sanitary improvements in the city, including piped water, which had come by 1900.[5]

All six schools stayed open during the cholera epidemic, the boys kept busy at school and games, and boat races went up and down the river to raise the morale of the city. Whenever any member of the crews died their place was quickly filled. The masters behaved splendidly all through a really trying time and put their backs into the work of saving life, not merely giving medicine and then departing but sitting up with the sick and nursing those attacked. Out of the thousand masters and boys in the six schools 20 contracted the disease and five died.

Figure 11 The school fleet of seven racing shikaras, *cutter* Fanny *and two rowing boats upstream of 3rd Bridge. Shahi Hamdan Mosque and Hari Parbat Fort behind the bridge*

One who died was Tara Chand Padi, who had been on the staff since Biscoe's first year, and it struck him down swiftly. In the morning of 9 September 1900 he was supervising the games and late that same evening Biscoe was told he was dying. He rushed to his home in the city but Tara Chand was already unconscious and was being massaged by two other teachers, Bala Koul the Dispenser and Gana Koul. Biscoe gave him brandy and as he did so Tara Chand breathed his last. Biscoe was asked to leave but the teachers continued to massage his body through the night to spare the women and to protect Biscoe from being accused by them of causing his death. This made a huge impression on Biscoe, both the loss of a loyal teacher and also the nobility of his colleagues who stayed with him despite the fear that cholera engendered in everyone then.

In the next school log Biscoe wrote:

His loss to us has been great, for he possessed the power of decisiveness, most rare in a Kashmiri. He could not only make his boys do what they said they would not do, but made them like it. On account of this gift he taught scores of timid boys to swim, and lazy conceited fellows to paddle in the school boats, which some continue to call low-caste work.[6]

His tragic loss was a powerful incentive for the action that would come to dominate the New Year – an Engineer Corps in the schools to clean the city. However, before that began they were confronted with another challenge to clean up in the city.

When the boys went out on to the open spaces to play football they were frequently troubled by hooligans and the masters were accordingly involved in protecting them. But there was a more troubling threat from men attempting to cajole the younger boys away with offers of sweets in order to abduct them for sex. On one occasion when a band of these men were driven off one dropped a notebook, which was the record of the Srinagar Sodomy Society with the names of its members and the names of the boys they were interested in abducting. With this evidence Biscoe and his masters attempted to bring the perpetrators to justice. As he wrote in his annual report 26 October 1901:

> The police at first would not help us, so for three months or so our masters had to use their fists and otherwise defend their charges. At last we succeeded in getting the authorities to move and seven were convicted.[7]

While this was a signal achievement, those exposed were senior and influential men in Srinagar with powerful friends in the Hindu establishment and resentment simmered in the city. To add to his troubles he discovered that some foreigners were also engaged in paedophilia and during the next three years he attempted, through the British Resident, to have such men expelled from Kashmir.

The School Engineering Corps

After the 1892 cholera epidemic, Walter Lawrence and Biscoe had agreed that cleaning up the streets of the city was the most important action needed to save the city from another such visitation. Dr Mitra, the Chief Medical Officer of the city had greatly improved the main streets by paving them and bringing piped water to the main centres, but in the smaller alleyways conditions remained as before. No houses had sanitation so that the sewage generated in every house ended up in the gutters outside. In 1894 after he recovered from typhoid Biscoe had tried to keep the street near the Central School clean as an example to the neighbourhood. Dr Mitra had then lent the school a manual fire engine and twice a week the boys hosed the street, until the Mullah of the nearby mosque arrived and asked who had given leave to clean the street? He said the street was his property and he did not want it cleaned. To which Biscoe replied that he intended to wash the street and if he did not move he would be hosed down the street himself; which he was. But he never interfered again and even sent his boys to the school.[8]

At the beginning of 1901 the Mission School created an Engineering Corps of volunteer boys and teachers before the cholera returned in the warmer months. They offered their services to any city household that asked for help. Dr Mitra again lent a fire pump as well as baskets, spades and shovels, and the school boats were used to bring sand. Seventy households initially asked for help in January and work began on them, despite jeering from bystanders who said they were doing unclean work. When the news got back to the Hindu Dharam Sabha they were ordered not to persist with this sanitation work, and many were very frightened; so were the householders who all withdrew their requests for help with sanitation. However, several brave members of the Corps, including Darim Chand and Balk Koul, turned their energies to cleaning up around the Mission Dispensary at the Seventh Bridge (Zaina Kadal) and finished the job in face of a large crowd of jeerers; they were encouraged by several European visitors joining them and by one important Brahmin ally, Pandit Mahdu, the *Tehsildar* or Chief Executive Officer of Srinagar, who publicly supported the school and insisted that his son should participate.

Opposition from the Dharam Sabha, however, increased and on 25 February 1901 a telegram was sent to the Maharaja in Jammu

Figure 12 The Tehsildar of Srinagar, Pandit Mahdu and sons, 1901

complaining of the latest outrage by the missionaries. Three days later Arthur Neve gave a public lecture at the Central School on the importance of sanitation to prevent cholera and the President of the Dharam Sabha came to protest but after the talk he praised the staff and Biscoe for their noble efforts for the good of the city and wished them all success.[9] The depth of the opposition was fuelled in Biscoe's view by the pent up fury of the parents and friends of the paedophiles that he had succeeded in getting convicted a month before. Articles appeared in Hindu newspapers in Lahore

Figure 13 Rago Nath Temple, the seat of the Dharam Sabha, and Biscoe on houseboat Shotover

and Benares, embellished with stories that Biscoe was paying his staff and students 5 rupees for each dead dog they would drag through the streets in order to defile their caste and force them to become Christians.

On 1 March the Hindu members of the school staff were called before the Dharam Sabha to answer charges against them. Back on his own ground the president, who a day or so before had praised them, reverted to his prior opinion; they were cursed and ill treated, and ordered to desist or face excommunication, with the result that most began to waver. A week later one of them, Balak Ram, who had been on the staff for six years, argued in the assembly against continuing, whereupon Biscoe thrashed him in front of all the staff. Balak Ram left the school determined to run Biscoe into the courts but the lawyers said they couldn't take his case because Biscoe had more money and could settle the judge. Nevertheless, Biscoe had made an enemy who was now a willing recruit for an opposition Hindu school. This intemperate action by Biscoe indicated the stress that he was under and at the end of March he became ill – he thought from the stink of the cess pools they had been cleaning – but possibly from the stress itself. While he lay ill, in early April, Blanche gave birth to their third son, Eric, who much later would become his father's successor in the work.

Annie Besant and Sri Pratap School

The report in the Benares newspapers of the Srinagar events was read by a singular English woman, Annie Besant, who three years before in 1898 had founded the Central Hindu College in Benares in order to educate Hindu Brahmin boys in their ancestral religion, while inculcating what she saw as the central lesson of the *Bhagavadgita* 'that union with the divine life may be achieved and maintained in the midst of worldly affairs'. She was deeply opposed to the policy of the British administration in India of encouraging the use of English as the medium of education and discouraging the study of Indian culture and history. Her action in starting the college was declared by the Lieutenant-Governor of the United Provinces, Sir Bampfylde Fuller, to be a disloyal act, using education to cloak her political purposes. This so outraged the Maharaja of Jammu and Kashmir that he provided a large sum of money to the college which transformed its fortunes.[10] He was now to do the same in Kashmir.

What she read of Biscoe's actions in Srinagar epitomised all that she deplored and she quickly contacted the Maharaja in Jammu and was invited by him to visit Kashmir as his guest. She arrived with the court entourage in April and one British official with His Highness's party asked Biscoe what mischief he had been up to because she had come to investigate the evil doings of the missionary, making Brahmin staff do sweepers work in the city.[11]

Their first encounter was unfortunately ill timed and did nothing to bring about an understanding between them. And this was a pity because in very many ways they thought alike – in fact too much alike perhaps. In the *Central Hindu College Magazine* for 1901[12] she wrote that her aim was to develop a sense of social duty in the boys, alongside the ancient virtues of reverence, self-reliance, freedom, moderation, calmness, gentleness, justice and courtesy, so that they might become pious Aryan gentlemen able to hold their own with Western citizens – aims that, although couched in different language, were remarkably similar to Biscoe's.

Annie Besant was 16 years older than Biscoe and until 1889 had been a vigorous and effective campaigner for women's suffrage in England and stirred up much controversy by her public advocacy for contraception to help working class women prevent unwanted pregnancies; she was also an ardent atheist and spoke in public places in London on the topic. Indeed, in about 1888 when Biscoe was a curate in Whitechapel he heard her speaking there and encouraged a large dray to be driven past her several times until she cried out, 'Men of England, can none of you stop that dray?' A year later she astonished her numerous supporters by renouncing atheism in favour of the occult as promulgated by Madame Helena Blavatsky. Ten years before Blavatsky had founded the international headquarters of the Theosophical Society at Adyar, near Madras.[13] Besant went to live in India in 1893 where she learnt Sanskrit, studied Hindu mythology and history, and made an excellent translation of the *Bhagavadgita,* which was later to be read by Gandhi and influenced his thinking. She assumed Indian dress and involved herself in championing Indian culture against the encroachments of British influence and power over Indians. Her earlier views on women's rights changed; she strongly opposed the 1891 Age of Consent Bill introduced in British India to prevent the consummation of marriage of girls under 12 by defining it as rape, and she revised her views on the education of girls for a life independent of marriage. Some years after her visit to Kashmir, when she had succeeded Blavatsky as President of the Theosophical Society, she did found a school for girls in Benares in association with the College for boys, at about the same time as Biscoe began a school for girls in Srinagar (see Chapter 4).

Although he did not know any of this when she arrived in Kashmir, Biscoe was confident that when he met her he could convince her of his real purposes in trying to clean the city. Their first meeting came sooner than expected[14] when on 6 June 1901 Biscoe saw a European woman in Indian dress speaking to old Colonel Cockburn, a great admirer of his, outside the British Resident's garden. Says Cockburn to the lady, 'I wish to introduce to you the man who turns Hindu monkeys into men and makes their tails fall off'. 'Don't insult Hindus before me,' said she angrily and walked off. This was a very bad start and, in order to try to make amends Biscoe called upon her later at the palace that the Maharaja had provided for her and their meeting was polite but cool. Later, when the Headmaster of the Central School, Lachman Singh, called on her to invite her to see for herself what they were doing she declined.

This was not surprising as plans were already underweigh for her to start a rival school directly across the Jhelum River from the Central Mission School, the express purpose being to crush the Mission School by providing for Hindu boys an alternative like the Central Hindu College she had founded in Benares. In this she had the strong support of the Maharaja's Private Secretary, Dya Kishen Koul, and many influential people in Srinagar, including the Governor and the Head of the Dharam Sabha, who became members of the management committee. It was named Sri Pratap College in honour of the Maharaja, and an Australian couple, Mr and Mrs Wilson, also Theosophists, were put in charge. Three teachers from the Mission School, Balak Ram, Ram Chand and Shiv Koul, defected to the new school and took 300 pupils with them.[15] Meanwhile Annie Besant gave lectures in Srinagar to the English community[16] on arousing in Indians a sense of self-respect and pride in the greatness of Indian religious and cultural traditions, especially the Hindu wisdom that she so much admired.[17]

This was a very serious crisis for the Mission Schools, now reduced to a rump. Many other teachers, with the strong disapproval of the Dharam Sabha still fresh in their minds, were also wavering. Biscoe called the staff together and told them that they were free to go but for old times' sake he would like to box with each of them before they left. He then waited outside the building, but no one emerged. When he went in again they all said they wished to stay: he had given them an excuse they could use outside, that he would beat them if they left the school. As he later wrote in his annual letter, 'the opposition has put my men on their metal'.

The Maharaja's attitude to the situation that had now developed in the city was ambivalent. He clearly admired Besant and must have approved the new school but when she asked him to turn Biscoe out of Kashmir for breaking the caste of Brahmins he replied that he had known Mr Biscoe for 11 years and he had done nothing but good.

And one month after the new school began Biscoe was called to the palace where they had a congenial meeting and the Maharaja asked that the boys should swim past his palace and down the river. On 13 July 1901, 147 masters and boys did just that, watched by the Maharaja and his court.[18] They were accompanied by a visiting medical missionary, Dr Theodore Pennell from Bannu, who swam with a blue puggaree on his head. A few days later Pennell was travelling in the hills near Pahalgam when he met Annie Besant and another English woman making the Hindu pilgrimage, barefoot, to the sacred Amarnath Cave on the slopes of Mount Kolahoi.[19] Deep inside the glacier an icy stalactite meets an icy stalagmite in a representation of the sacred union of Shiva and Saraswati and each year thousands of Hindu pilgrims trek up the mountain to view it and receive *darshan*. So also, presumably, did the two English women.

Despite the challenge of the school across the river, the Mission Schools continued with their normal activities during the second half of 1901. These included an unusual geography lesson to challenge the prevailing belief of devout Kashmiris that the Earth is flat and the sea is composed of melted butter and sugar. Three of the most senior masters – Shenker Koul, Mahanand Razdan and Din Mohammad – were sent at the end of July to visit Karachi, Bombay and then to visit the fabled island of Sri Lanka to see what the sea is made of and what beings inhabited the sacred Isle. They were unable to get a ship to Ceylon but returned in September full of the wonders of their travels; but when they said the sea is salt the priests declared that they obviously had not reached the sea. While they now taught that the sea is salty, some of their pupils were more cautious in their written exams, writing, 'the sea is salty, or so says Mr Biscoe'.

Another initiative in this troubled year was the founding of a special fund to help teachers who fell sick or their families if they died like Tara Chand Padi had. There was no insurance of any sort in Kashmir so this was a novel idea. It was started with a large donation by a supporter of the schools and was to be augmented by regular contributions from each member of staff and was managed and audited by the staff themselves.

In October ten boats each with a crew of 15 engaged in a marathon race from the city up river 15 miles and back, which took all day. And slowly the number of students increased as some came back and others joined. At the end of the year Biscoe could write in the school log:

> The masters have had to put up with a great deal of bullying in the city, and persecution from their relatives, and in some cases the relatives have had to suffer with them. Nevertheless, some of them have behaved right nobly and pluckily, and have proved again, for the hundredth time, that the Kashmiri has got some 'bottom', if you can only find it and puddle it well. We look to men like these to raise the men of this country – aye and the poor women too, held down by cruel, unjust and senseless so-called religious laws. It even has been the case that all kinds of evil are perpetrated in the name of religion, and the priests have always been at the bottom of it.
>
> Well, we are coming out of the year's wars all the stronger, as one does from all trials or persecution. We know where we are, which we really did not properly know before.
>
> We know now who are our friends and who are our enemies, who to trust and who not to trust, we have unmasked our enemies guns. We lived before in a fool's paradise, not knowing the waters in which we were punting.[20]

He goes on to defend his approach to education, stung by the remark put to him in the past year, 'Your business is to teach and not to meddle with matters outside your school'.

> Well, what is meant by teaching and the matters outside the school? If by teaching and inside school is meant only teaching boys to pass examinations and to behave themselves in school, then we have exceeded our rights. But my idea of teaching and

educating boys is rather different to this, and I think all honest men will agree with me.

If I see boys coming to school continually dirty in body, diseased in skin and with pale and unhealthy-looking faces and slack demeanour, I consider it my duty to go into the matter. Of course, we can clean their skins of dirt in school and give them sulphur ointment and other medicines for their diseases, but this is repeated over and over again because we have not got to the root of the disease, which is in their unhealthy and unsanitary conditions of life. They themselves continually express the desire for healthier surroundings. Are we to say, 'This is nothing to do with us? We can only look after your brains and care nothing for your bodies! You can do what you like and live as you please in your homes, so long as you behave yourself during school hours?'

Surely no self-respecting man would say this, if he had the least heart in his work or cared the least bit for his fellow-creatures, though they be of a different nation and religion. If education means anything, it includes all his being, his body as well as brain and soul. Education that falls short of this is no education.

Breakdown

Despite the optimistic end to the year in the school log the toll on Biscoe had been great. Hardly had the new year begun than he was again unwell and Ernest Neve ordered him to get away for a change of air and rest. So in February 1902 he took a houseboat to the Wular Lake with Blanche, Harold and Julian. But on their return he was ill in bed for all of March and was still sick in April. Fortunately the Knowles by then had returned from furlough and Knowles was available to take over the schools as he had done in 1894.

The strain was not confined to Biscoe and the Mission Schools; at Sri Pratap College the Wilsons were not happy either, and when she called on the Biscoes she could not look at them straight, and in the middle of the year he apologised to Biscoe for having taken on the job as he had been told untruths about him and about the work being done in the Mission Schools.[21] Also Balak Ram, the teacher who defected to the new school, became very ill in July, with a swollen tongue filling the whole of his mouth and was given less than two weeks to live; some unkind people told him that *djinns* had done this because of his treatment of Biscoe. He asked to see Biscoe to seek his forgiveness so, with Amar Chand Biscoe visited him and he let them carry him to a boat and thence to hospital where Arthur Neve soon cured him.[22] Less than a month after this the idea of using the school boats to take sick people from the hospital for outings was first raised at a staff meeting; in later years this became a strong tradition in all the schools.

The summer holidays of July and August were spent at Nil Nag and included other family members – Albert and his wife and baby, George and his new wife Isobel, and Nora Neve. They tried to make a long trip to a mountain lake called Konsanag but Biscoe was once again laid low, this time with shingles, and the trip was abandoned.

At the end of the summer George and Isobel left Kashmir to return to Oxford so that he could study theology and become ordained in preparation for joining the CMS. George had worked with Cecil for seven years in Kashmir, unpaid and not a member of the CMS, and his going now was an added stress to Biscoe's health. George was a much more gentle man than his brother and his reason for leaving during these tumultuous times is not clear. Unless it was that he could no longer support Biscoe's forthright way of meeting crises; certainly he never again worked with him in Kashmir. Soon after they left Biscoe suffered what Arthur Neve described as neurasthenia or a nervous breakdown, which would now be described as post-traumatic stress disorder and in November he ordered Biscoe to leave Kashmir for three months of complete rest.[23] Blanche and the three boys stayed in Kashmir while Knowles took charge of the schools and was helped in this by other local missionaries. Neve accompanied Biscoe to Delhi, where they both visited the Viceroy, Lord Curzon (known as King George). He then went to Dehra Dun where he began his recuperation at the home of Colonel and Mrs Strahan, who had been his strong supporters in his first two years in Kashmir, and he was happy to go to them now. He stayed with them for six weeks and wrote almost daily to Blanche:

30 November. Dearest B, […] and then go on to Dehra Dun and I trust have some rest and peace. Please forgive a short scrawl but I've been rushed today. My heart is much with you though the body is not. Your ever loving Cecil.

4 December. I have not much to say, you see I write every day, I have not missed one yet. I can more than sympathise with Mrs La Touche, if I feel bad over a few weeks what must a year be. Ever so much love, your very loving Cecil.

17 December. I think what a slackster I have become that I play patience most evenings and am becoming quite adept at killing time.

26 December. We are in a very nice bungalow, the best dak bungalow I've seen in way of finish inside. The Strahans make it all so nice for me and treat me as a son. They don't wish me to leave them at all. Their son at Mandalay has wired to say that he will be delighted to look after me. I wish you were here dearest to enjoy the Strahans and this quiet change. Much love sweetest.

15 January 1903. Benares. I soon got sick of the Hindu sights, *puja* galore but woke up to interest when I saw a youth in one of the many box caves doing what I thought was Sandow's exercises and felt quite cheered up, in that I had at last found a man, but alas he was only doing an excessive sort of puja to Shiva. I felt more sick and soon turned homewards. The Hindus here have no respect for the Sahib as they are soaked with idolatry and all that that means. I shall not go to the river again. [In his diary for this date he writes, 'The view of the temples was fine but I loathed the whole show as it smelt of Annie Besant and Hindu filth'.]24

He left Calcutta on 25 January on the SS Kasara for Chittagong and Burma. The officers on the ship were strong in their dislike of missionaries and he had a difficult time defending his calling. But while at Chittagong he went ashore with the Captain and on his return he skilfully rowed a sampan from the jetty to the ship anchored mid stream and earned the admiration of the officers and the epithet 'a boy parson and a mad one'.

At Akyab on the Arakan Coast he was entertained by a young and rather lonely Englishman who he befriended, and in a letter to Blanche on 30 January wrote:

> He talked freely to me of his private affairs and seemed so glad to have someone to talk to. It has not been a one sided business only, for it is generally the case that one is helped by those one wishes to help [...] I shall feel much lighter when my face is turned homewards and my dear ones get nearer and nearer.[25]

When the ship reached Rangoon he took the train to Mandalay to stay with the Strahan's son and marvelled at the ornate palaces of the former ruler, Theebaw, deposed by the British 17 years before. He wrote down some of Theebaw's titles, which included Lord of Many White Elephants, Lord of Gold, Silver, Rubies, Amber and Jade, Descendant of the Sun, Arbiter of Life, Possessor of Boundless Dominion and Supreme Wisdom.

One of the Buddhist temples built of teak and lavishly decorated with gold leaf had been appropriated by the invaders for the garrison's church services, and Biscoe wrote that it was

> the most uncomfortable service I have ever been to and quite in keeping with the heathen building in which it took place. The service was a perfect farce. If this is a specimen of a garrison compulsory service the sooner they are discontinued the better. I do not at all wonder at the officers going away for shooting on Sundays.[26]

In Mandalay he wrote to Blanche on his fortieth birthday, 8 February 1903, thanking her for her loving birthday wishes.

> I am looking forward to another year of happiness with my loved ones and I trust to make it a happier one for my sweetest of wives and do my level best to keep her young by giving her

a mind at rest. Tell the boys to give you the tightest of hugs from me. Dear little men, how I long to see them.[27]

He returned to Rangoon by paddle steamer down the Irrawaddy river, sketching the sites and strange boats he passed. At Rangoon he caught another steamer for the four days trip to Colombo, where he was entertained by many missionary colleagues and other old friends. He visited Trinity College, Kandy, a famous Mission School, which he sketched. But when he inspected the dormitories he found evidence of the boys smoking and how they left their dormitories at night, both of which activities they admitted to but the principal was unaware of.

At the beginning of March 1903 he spent three days in Bombay where he sketched the Girgaum Church where he and Blanche had been married 12 years before, and then sailed on to Karachi where he stayed with other missionaries before taking the train to Multan. Here he met Pandit Shenker Koul, who he had sent to help the incumbent principal of the local CMS School get it in order after the Indian Christian headmaster 'like Sircar of old had fought Johnson-Smyth and made his life unbearable, hence his illness. Shenker got the school in order quickly'. This is a reference to Biscoe's former headmaster in Srinagar whom he had replaced with Lachman Singh in 1896. After a few days in Lahore with missionary colleagues it was on by train to Pindi travelling with Mrs Wilson and her boy. What did they talk about? Theosophy? The Sri Pratap School? Or his breakdown? Nothing is revealed except the bare diary entry for 10 March. At Rawalpindi he stayed with his brother Albert and joined his troops in gunnery practice before setting off on the long trip back to Srinagar, which he reached on the evening of 17 March where 'all looked so sweet and clean'.

The next morning he and Blanche were welcomed at the Central School and at Habba Kadal primary school, which was decorated in his honour, followed by several days visiting and receiving friends and supporters glad to see him back. He was feeling fit and ready to tackle his work but within the week he was embroiled in two unsavoury matters, which must have undone much of the benefit of the time away.

The first was to bring the evidence before the British Resident of the behaviour of a Belgian living in a houseboat in Srinagar. This was because foreigners in Kashmir were not subject to State law but were under the jurisdiction of the British Resident. Count Borgrave, who being wealthy, attempted to abduct Kashmiri girls for his pleasure. On one occasion a year before he had seen a girl on the way to her wedding and ordered his servants to abduct her. Unfortunately for him her family gathered other men from the village and came back to rescue the bride and carried off the Count himself and strung him up to a beam. He was rescued by his servants before he strangled but the villagers ran him into the courts. The judge, not having authority to try a foreigner dismissed the charges and instead imprisoned the villagers. Now a year had passed and the Count was at his mischief again and this time Biscoe organised a trial in his house, chaired by the Assistant Resident, and the 14 witnesses were emboldened to speak the truth and the Count was ordered to leave Kashmir forthwith. The Count was incensed at the decision and threatened to burn down the Mission School, so a guard had to be maintained for the week until he left.

While all this was going on Biscoe discovered at dinner in his own home that one of his guests, a fellow missionary from another society, was a paedophile, who made a set for the good looking boys in the school. Biscoe called on the man in his houseboat to warn him not to 'hunt with the hares and the hounds'. Bruce responded by threatening to take Biscoe to court for defamation of character. He also complained to the CMS in Lahore demanding that Biscoe desist or he would seek legal action. A year later Biscoe learnt that he was threatening to sue the CMS in London unless they expelled Biscoe from the society. They did not do so and Bruce did not press his charge. Perhaps he was mindful of the harsh fate of Oscar Wilde just ten years before, who sued his accuser and ended up being convicted himself.[28] At all events, Biscoe succeeded in having him ordered to leave Kashmir in 1905. Biscoe's actions in getting both men removed from Kashmir was primarily to protect the boys in the schools from predatory foreigners, who were immune from Kashmir law, but his fierce response was surely coloured by the memories of his own school days when he was the prey of older boys and had to learn to box in order to defend himself. It also added to his difficulty in fighting against local paedophiles that foreigners were engaged in the same practice.

A month later he faced another challenge when he discovered boys in the school reading an illustrated pornographic book. His punishment was unusual; he asked Arthur Neve how much paper a person could safely eat and when the answer came back, three ounces, he assembled the school and ordered the boy who had brought the book to school to eat several pages with the help of a glass of water. When the boy protested that to eat the paper would defile his body it was pointed out to him that he had already taken it into his mind and heart and that it was unfair that his stomach should not also share in the feast. When he had swallowed the paper, Biscoe told the rest of the school that they might all bring such books to school tomorrow and eat them in public. However, it was not sufficient to punish the boys for reading such books, it was more important in his view to seek out the vendors and makers of the books and punish them, and this they did. Biscoe took the offending book to the Chief Judge of the Kashmir Court and after telling Biscoe that Hindu law permits a certain amount of impurity he agreed that this book exceeded it and such perpetrators could get two years imprisonment if convicted. Next Biscoe cleared it with the British Resident who agreed that he could take it up with the police, provided that there was no row. Armed with these two sanctions he organised his staff and the police to raid the shops and the houses where Brahmin priests were making the books. But when he asked the Superintendent of Police to make a public example by arresting them, the Superintendent said that could not be done because one of the priests was His Highness's chaplain who leads his worship every morning and night. Undeterred Biscoe persuaded the Superintendent to take the matter to the State Durbar and the Maharaja agreed that the makers of such a book should be brought before the court. Although the Judge let them off with a small fine, Biscoe concluded 'from the punishment of a boy eating filthy paper came the result that certain holy men had to "eat fear", *kauf khun* as the Kashmiris say'.[29] As he wrote to London later:

> So we got ourselves a bit disliked over the business in certain quarters. It is splendid training for my men, making them identify themselves on the side of purity. It is excellent for them when the scoundrels of the town are their enemies, as a native as a rule makes friends with all sorts.[30]

Having made enemies of important people in June, the school staff became heroes in July when the city was again inundated by a massive flood like that of 1893, which destroyed over a thousand houses and left those that survived immersed in mud. Food shortages began soon after and the State authorities called on the missionaries to help in assessing damage and distributing food. The Mission School was given half the city and the job of distributing compensation to householders for damage, a task that took a month to accomplish.

Funding Troubles

While Biscoe had been away in the first months of 1903, his friends in Kashmir got up an appeal for funds for the schools. They were fully aware of the great stress he was constantly exposed to in trying to meet the monthly expenses with insufficient resources. The school log for 1901, *Punting in Kashmir*, contained a full analysis of the finances of the Kashmir schools compared to a similar school in the Punjab, concluding with an earnest appeal for supporters to give generously. He relied on the regular funds from the CMS, a lesser amount from the Kashmir Government and fees but there was always a large shortfall, which could only be met by donations from supporters and members of his own family. In 1901 the shortfall was 27 per cent of the budget, compared to 42 per cent from CMS.[31]

The appeal referred to the funding problems and criticised the CMS for not doing more to support the schools. When the appeal was seen by the Parent Committee of the CMS in London, Biscoe received a stern rebuke from Lahore for the irregularity and the apparent slur on the society. This letter was waiting for him on his return to Kashmir and he tried without success to explain that he had not been involved in the matter at all:

> I fear I know little about this appeal for the schools and it was only a day or two ago that I heard of it. It was got up when I was away on sick leave. I believe the appeal was printed by Mrs George Moule in England, and I have never heard of any copies being in this country. The Europeans here know that it is no easy matter for me to run my schools here and that I have to collect about Rs300 per mensem, to keep them going, and some of them were anxious that this financial burden might be lightened a bit. The Europeans here as you know give very liberally towards the CMS work here.[32]

And the reply:

> As you cannot furnish me with a copy of the appeal regarding which I enquired I would mention the point that Parent Committee adverted to. It states that the school work is 'deserving of more aid and recognition [...] specially from the Parent Society' and suggests that your recent breakdown was brought about by the financial responsibilities of the school. One can understand the enthusiastic friends, whose sympathy and help is so welcome and so valuable, putting the things in this way from their point of view. At the same time you will understand that PC feel they have done not a little for the Srinagar School, considering their financial position and the needs of other schools. In 1898 they added Rs300 per month to the Rs100 they were already giving and thus showed their great appreciation of your earnest and effective work; and they would not wish it to be supposed that they had shown themselves unmindful of this. No doubt a word from you to the friends who have acted without showing you the appeal before issuing it would set matters right, by modifying the way in which the matter is put.[33]

This correspondence got overtaken by the great flood and what followed so his response was curt and to the point:

> I am sending you a copy of the school accounts for the last year, as I believe the PC wishes to see them. I am not writing a Report this year, as I hardly think it is worth the expense and trouble. You will have heard of the great flood. Many thousands of houses destroyed. None of the mission houses fell. Hoping to see you before long and find you in better health than I am.[34]

Second Home Leave

In November 1903 the Biscoe family left Kashmir for a year's furlough, reaching Holton for Christmas. Before they had left Kashmir his close friends had urged him to see a neurologist in London and they collected £20 to cover the fee. So after Christmas, Biscoe saw Sir Victor Horsley in Harley Street, who told him that he was in a critical condition and could have heart failure at any moment. What he needed was complete rest for six weeks with absolutely no stress whatsoever – no books, no writing, no visitors, not even Blanche – but daily massage and plenty of food. He signed into the Reste in Bournemouth where all his clothes and books were taken from him and he could only read what the Matron allowed him to. He lasted a month under this regimen and then demanded to be allowed to leave but couldn't do so because he had no clothes. He agreed to stay longer if his wife approved, which she did, so he stayed for another two weeks by which time he had put on much weight. Whether he was improved in his mind and heart was another matter for even as late as August 1904, there was doubt at CMS London that the Medical Board would allow him to return to Kashmir.

After he left the sanatorium his view of the future must have improved for he changed his mind and wrote a report of the activities of 1903, which was published in London in August 1904 with the title *Plugging in Kashmir*. As he explains at the beginning, plugging is putting that last ounce of effort into grabbing victory from the jaws of defeat and he illustrated his point with a vivid description of the great rowing race of 1885 at Henley when he coxed Cambridge to victory. He likened the past three years in Kashmir to such a race and implied that the Kashmir schools had triumphed over the forces of Annie Besant. Certainly the number of students had now risen to 1,100, the highest ever, and there he had a greater sense of camaraderie with his staff. Unlike the former logs this one explicitly lists the senior Kashmiri teachers and their individual responsibilities:

Leaders in Social Reform

Pandit Mahanand Razdan	Waifs and Stray Society
Pandit Suraj Raina	Dixon Benevolent Fund
Pandit Bagwan Das	Sanitation Committee
Din Mohammad	Vigilance Committee
Pandit Shenker Koul	Knights Errant [help to women and girls]
Munshi Hassan Ali	Sandeman Loan Fund
Pandit Vishn Koul	Ambulance Volunteers
Pandit Nath Ram	Anti-Billingsgate [bad language]
Mr Lachman Singh	Anti-Ignorant Club
Pandit Kanta Warikoo	Social Club
Pandits M.R., S.K. and D.M.	Court Martial
Headmasters	Manual Labour Effort

In the acknowledgements to supporters no donations are listed, presumably because in England he had no access to the accounts, but telling comments are made about the help of three, who 'gave a leg up' and for Mr C.M. Hadow, Manager of the Kashmir Carpet factory, whose 'active sympathy and advice has often quieted my troubled spirit and helped us over many a difficulty'.

He clearly recognised the need for an additional missionary to help him with the five schools and he pressed this point with the Secretary of the CMS in London, Durrant, when he visited him in December.[35] He said that if a colleague is not sent it will mean that the schools will have to be closed and if they are the scholars will almost certainly go over to Annie Besant's school. This was quite a new piece of information for Durrant and most serious if the work was handed over to an anti-Christian society.

The problem for the CMS was that the Kashmir schools did not make converts to Christianity and for the most part did not employ Christians on the staff, whereas in the Punjab the Christian community was growing rapidly and the Mission Schools were largely staffed by Indian Christians. For a society dedicated to the propagation of the Christian faith but with limited resources this posed an acute dilemma. In his response Durrant wrote:

> If the branch schools are really efficient from a missionary point of view (and this is of course the main consideration) no effort should be spared to keep them open and under the control of the Mission. For these reasons the Committee realizes your need and will do their best to send you out a competent educational missionary as soon as ever such a one can be found [...] They pray that you may have during this fresh term of missionary service a full measure of physical health.[36]

The need for another missionary for Biscoe was strongly supported from Kashmir. Wade wrote to Durrant, 'we are greatly in need of extra help for Kashmir where the Rev C.E. Tyndale-Biscoe should certainly not be left alone, or he is likely to breakdown'.[37] And Arthur Neve wrote:

> May I put plainly on record my opinion that it is essential that Mr Tyndale-Biscoe should have a co-worker in the school. Failing that I am sure that in three years he would again become neurasthenic and would return to England and *remain*.[38]

The advocacy worked for within a year F.E. Lucey was recruited to Kashmir and proved to be a most congenial helper for Biscoe, working with him for the next 16 years.

Similar Educational Developments in America and Britain

The year 1904 was important in another way for it was the year when two other men were independently developing ideas for outdoor activities for boys with the purpose of improving their fitness and social awareness, Robert Baden-Powell in England and Ernest Thompson Seton in America.[39] Seton had for many years been developing woodcraft for boys in America based on the old skills of the Indians, his main purpose being 'to make a man'. His ideal of a man was Chief Tecumseh:

> a great hunter, a great leader, clean, manly, strong, courteous, fearless, gentle with his strength, dignified, silent and friendly, equipped for emergencies and filled with a religion that consisted not of books and creeds or occasional observances, but of a desire to help those that had need of help.[40]

In 1904 Seton published *The Red Book or How to Play Indian*[41] and during October to early December 1904 he visited Britain to spread his ideas by lecturing in schools across the country. The virtue of Seton's plan was that it gave young people 'something to do, something to think about and something to enjoy in the woods with a view always to character building'.[42]

In this same year after his discharge from the nursing home, Biscoe also toured Britain, lecturing on the Kashmir schools to some of the same schools that Seton visited although not on the same dates. There is no record that they met but their ideas – and even phrases – are extraordinarily similar. Seton, who was a distinguished artist/naturalist, invoked Tecumseh as his ideal man while Biscoe invoked Jesus as his. Just four years before during the great cholera epidemic when the masters and boys were called on to perform many deeds of courage Biscoe had coined the school motto, *In All Things Be Men*, and the badge of crossed Kashmiri paddles to represent humility and service.

Well behind Seton and Biscoe was Baden-Powell, who wrote his first essay on the topic in the *Eton College Chronicle* in December 1904. He was, of course, by then the hero of Mafeking and the youngest General in the British Army so anything he wrote, and he wrote much, would be eagerly read. Nine-year-old Julian Tyndale-Biscoe read an article he wrote in January 1905 entitled 'The World's workers and the World's shirkers',[43] in which he included missionaries among the shirkers, so Julian wrote to tell him, 'You don't know my Daddy'. It is highly unlikely that the two men met in the early months of 1905 before the Biscoes returned to Kashmir but they may have begun a correspondence because B.P. discussed his ideas with anyone who was interested, including boys' organisations such as the Boys' Brigade. He was appalled at what he saw as moral and physical slackness and his purpose was to inculcate into British youth the virtues of manliness, obedience to leaders, country and God, and help to people in need; precisely the things that Biscoe had been doing for more than a decade in Kashmir – as he often wrote, making men from jellyfish. Their family backgrounds were also similar; B.P. had served in the 13th Hussars in India for 11 years, like Biscoe's brother Julian in the 11th Hussars, and in Africa he was in the 1896 Matabele campaign that Biscoe's other brother Edward took part in,[44] and they both had a profound belief in the excellence of British imperial purpose. While Biscoe certainly knew who B.P. was, B.P. would not have known of Biscoe but may have known his brothers.

When Seton returned to Britain in 1906 for a second promotional tour of his book and ideas he sent a copy to Baden-Powell who enthused about it and they developed a close collaboration in the next two years leading up to the publication of *Scouting for Boys* and the inauguration of the Boy Scout movement in 1908. It was an instant success across Britain and Seton was made the official representative in North America. However, he was much aggrieved to discover that B.P. had used large parts of his earlier book without acknowledgement and their relationship soured and ended in litigation for breach of copyright. Seton always claimed that he, not B.P., was the real founder of scouting but it was B.P.'s flair for publicity and his formidable reputation as a war hero that promoted scouting as a world-wide phenomenon. Two years later (1910) Biscoe adopted scouting in his schools and in 1920 Baden-Powell wrote the foreword to Biscoe's first small book, *Character Building in Kashmir*,[45] and they maintained a personal correspondence thereafter.

Cecil and Blanche, with their youngest son, Eric returned to Kashmir in March 1905, refreshed by their year in England and confident that Cecil had recovered from his neurasthenia and having been assured by CMS that he would have an assistant to help him with the work. The two older boys were left at boarding school in England and lived with relatives in the holidays, not seeing their father for six years and their mother for the next two years. So strong was this cruel custom of the British of not educating their sons in India that even for the Biscoes, deeply involved in education, they could not contemplate their own sons attending their father's school. Of the three boys only Julian seemed to be unaffected by the experience; for Harold and later Eric the years in England at school were miserable. Young Rudyard Kipling had the same experience and wrote bitterly of the cruelty imposed on him during his exile.[46]

Back in Kashmir the schools were flourishing with a record enrolment of 1,500 boys, so clearly the Sri Pratap Hindu School had not had a lasting effect on the fortunes of the five Mission Schools and, indeed healthy rivalry between the schools was beginning to occur. Crews of boys took more than 150 convalescent patients from the Mission Hospital for rides on the Dal Lake and they saved more than a dozen from drowning; and 400 new boys were taught to swim. When the city was again flooded the school crews rescued those in distress much to the chagrin of the boatmen who were unable to charge exorbitant prices. 'You can imagine how the boatmen love them and what sweet words they give them. It is of course just lovely being cursed on these occasions.'

These words were in a pamphlet Biscoe published in September 1905 for his supporters, which he called *Plugging again in Kashmir* as a stop gap for a school log on his return to Kashmir. In it he asks rhetorically:

> Why do the boys crowd into the Mission Schools where they will have to learn a religion contrary to their own, where the fees are more, where they will be obliged to go against their inclinations to take part in all sorts of bodily exercise and where the rod is by no means an unknown quantity. The answer is *Rupees*. They believe that they will get on better in the money market and this is no doubt true.

Having got this multitude of young lives in our hands we try to keep our eyes on the end, which is NOT rupees, nor University exams, which is the key to the said rupees but to the CHARACTER of each individual boy.[47]

And then he introduces his new system for assessing the character of every boy and rewarding not memory or genius or sporting prowess but those who try to fulfil the whole duty of man. Each teacher is responsible for his class of 25 boys and once each term each boy is assessed and has the opportunity for instant redress if he thinks he has been unfairly judged. Out of a total of 4,000 marks, 900 are awarded for 'mind', that is to say 100 for each subject taught; 1,000 for 'body', 200 for each sport but not for winning but for achieving an appropriate standard for age; and for 'soul' 2,100 divided between scripture 200, conduct towards teachers 400, conduct towards other boys 300, conduct towards the school 200, conduct towards the city 200, manners 400, cleanliness 200 and regular attendance 200.

Here was the actual outcome of the ideas just beginning to circulate in Britain and yet in later years Biscoe was described as a 'Baden-Powell disciple!'[48] But as he was wont to say, 'You can achieve a lot in this world if you don't mind who gets the credit.'

4

Exceedingly a Bad Man,
1905–10

He is exceedingly a bad man, illiterate, deceitful, ill-mannered, uncultured, cunning, and man too much fond of cricket.

1908 log, More Odds and Ends of School Life in
Kashmir, p. 14

Political Scene and British Attitudes to Educated and Free-Thinking Indians

Throughout 1904, while the Biscoes were in England, the British Government in India had been engaged in an extraordinary and inept invasion of Tibet. It was conceived by the Viceroy, George Curzon and was led by Colonel Francis Younghusband, who had gained renown for his journey from China to Kashmir across the Karakoram Mountains in 1887 and his subsequent explorations in Hunza and Kashgar.[1] While Younghusband was the political leader of the expedition the forces that accompanied him were led by General MacDonald, who resented his subordinate role and maintained frosty relations with the leader. In consequence, when the invaders met the Tibetan forces and were politely told to leave, a misunderstanding arose and the Tibetan forces were massacred by the superior weapons of the British. Lhasa was occupied and the Tibetan Government obliged to sign a treaty with the Indian Government of open access for 75 years. This treaty, drawn up by Younghusband, considerably exceeded his commission and was subsequently abrogated by the Government in Britain which was appalled by the outcome of what had been intended to be a peaceful trade mission. Curzon avoided the opprobrium that should have been his, and Younghusband became the scapegoat. Curzon became embroiled in a bitter conflict with the Commander in Chief of Indian forces, Lord Kitchener, and when Curzon offered to resign in August 1905 it was accepted with alacrity by the British Government; he was replaced as Viceroy by Lord Minto, who had just finished a term as Governor General of Canada. However, before he left India, Curzon rewarded Younghusband with a Knighthood (but of the lowest rank, Knight Commander of the Indian Empire) and appointed him over the heads of more senior civil servants to the plum position of Resident in Kashmir, which he took up in June 1906.

In retrospect the Tibetan invasion marked the high tide of British Imperialism and the long ebb now began, although not discerned by most of the British in India, including Younghusband and Biscoe. To all of these people the aspirations of educated Indians for a greater share in the administration of the country and eventual independence, like Australia, Canada and New Zealand had already achieved, was unimaginable and wholly unacceptable. They were also fearful that the fiftieth anniversary of the 1857 Mutiny might provoke another uprising.[2]

Minto was a very different person from Curzon. Curzon thought any reforms 'would run a very fair chance of spoiling the natives', whereas Minto wanted to engage with leading Indians who aspired to independence and he immediately opened conversations with them. In this he was supported by the Secretary for India in the newly elected Liberal Government in Britain, Lord Morley, who believed that the British should not be in India at all and favoured the aspirations of Indian independence. When they introduced reforms that brought Indians into the councils of government they were strongly opposed by the civil service but they persisted and thus began the slow reform that in 40 years would bring independence to the country. One of their strongest opponents was the Lieutenant-Governor of East Bengal, Sir Bampfylde Fuller, who threatened to deprive schools of their government grants if their students were involved in political agitation and sedition. When he was not allowed to do this he offered to resign and Minto and Morley promptly accepted it.[3] This provoked uproar among the British civil service but this and their other initiatives were welcomed by leading Indians and by a small number of English people working in India. Notable among these was Charles Andrews who joined the Cambridge Brotherhood in Delhi in March 1904.[4] Like Biscoe he had been at Cambridge and was a keen oarsman, and had graduated in classics and theology in 1895; he was subsequently ordained into the Church of England and offered himself as a missionary to India. Soon after his arrival in India he was captivated by Indian culture and made close friends with several Indian colleagues in the brotherhood, especially the Vice Principal, Sushil Kumar Rudra who 'made India from the first not a strange land but a familiar country'.[5] He deplored the attitude prevalent among the British that it was a dangerous policy to educate Indians. When in September 1906 a letter appeared in the Lahore newspaper, *The Civil and Military Gazette*, that referred contemptuously to Indian nationalists as a handful of mis-educated malcontents who could and should be dealt with like ill-disciplined schoolboys, Andrews replied, 'It is not less education but more, a thousand times more, that is needed [...] by a reactionary policy we may more easily alienate them by social ostracism and the closing of doors.'[6] His view was ridiculed as someone new to India and out of touch with reality, but he was defended in the same paper in October by Dr Theodore Pennell of Bannu – already met in Kashmir swimming down the Jhelum River with the Mission School boys in 1901 – who wrote:

> The arrogant spirit of *vae victus* [woe to the vanquished] will do more to undermine the loyalty of Indians than all the high schools and colleges that were ever founded in this land. The time has gone by when natives can be hectored into submission.[7]

Andrews' letter brought him national recognition as a supporter and friend of Indians. He was sought out by some of the leaders, such as Lala Lajpat Rai of Lahore and Ramanda Chatterjee of Bengal. The latter invited him to contribute articles to his newly launched political journal, *The Modern Review*, which greatly increased the impact of his thinking. He was also invited to attend the Indian National Congress in December 1906 where he met other leaders in the movement for Indian independence such as G.K. Gokhale, the President of the Indian Congress, with whom he established a close friendship.[8]

In Kashmir matters were different. Younghusband arrived in Srinagar in June 1906 as the new Resident and soon established good relations with Maharaja Pratap Singh and with his brother Raja Amar Singh, much helped by them all holding similar views on Indian agitators. As the fiftieth anniversary of the start of the 1857 Mutiny approached, Pratap Singh told Younghusband that the courts in Calcutta were too lenient towards sedition and that hanging was the proper punishment for Bengali agitators.[9] And Amar Singh wrote, 'A movement like this which has the effect of inoculating the students' mind with germs of mischievous political ideas should be immediately nipped in the bud.'[10] He gave instructions to keep close watch over all agitations and their promoters and authorised them to adopt measures consistent with the situation to prevent and put a stop to seditious and politically dangerous movements.

When informed of these opinions by Younghusband, Lord Minto said, 'I cannot say I value highly the opinions of his Maharaja and quite between ourselves Younghusband with his curiously reserved manner is underneath it all nervous and inclined to exaggeration.'

However, Younghusband and Biscoe established very cordial relations from the first and. soon after their arrival Sir Francis and Lady Younghusband attended the Mission School's annual Prize Day as the guests of honour, along with Raja Amar Singh and Bishop Lefroy of Lahore.[11] At a palace banquet in 1908 Younghusband gave what Biscoe considered a memorable speech against sedition.

Preparing for the worst, 70 British residents in Kashmir, including Cecil Hadow and Biscoe, joined the First Punjab Rifles and had regular rifle practice. Biscoe wrote:

> Riots in Pindi led by Lajpat Rai. Hindus trying to emulate mutiny of 1857 (fiftieth anniversary). Col. Delanie with his cavalry 11th Bengal Lancers seize Lajpat Rai at Pindi station, tie him to a sowar's saddle and bring him to the cantonments. The rioters burn down Porter's chapel, try to kill Porter.[12]

The rioters were actually Sikh farmers protesting at a new regulation – the Canal Colonisation Bill – to control the subdivision of irrigated land being pressed through in the face of popular protests. Lala Lajpat Rai believed that the riots were organised by the police with a view to arresting the popular leaders, which they did, and he was deported to Mandalay by the Viceroy's order. However, Minto was far from happy with this outcome and the following month he repealed the bill and soon after he released Lajpat Rai.[13] Minto was sensible to the distinction between lawful protest and sedition.

Biscoe and Andrews met for the first time in November that year at a meeting of missionaries in Lahore and Biscoe recorded their first encounter in his diary.

> In Lahore with A. Neve for Missionary meeting. Andrews lectured in chapel on 2 St Johns [the miracle at Canaan]. Later I met Andrews at Wigram's and twitted him on seeing two Saint Johns. Although it was before dinner he was nettled and tried to kick me but I caught his heel and made him hop round the room on one leg.[14]

Not a happy introduction, nor one likely to open understanding between them. In the following days Andrews gave a lecture in Lahore on Indian Nationalism, reported in the *Indian Review* of January 1907, and Biscoe read a paper on 'Why men do not go to church'. In the subsequent discussion the Indian Christians said bitter things of the missionaries but no one answered them. One Indian padre said 'we need Mr Biscoe to teach our children discipline and gave an instance of the need'.[15]

While they did meet occasionally in the next few years it is unlikely that they ever read each other's writings. At this time

Andrews was touring northern India collecting material for a book on the state of the Church in India, based on the lives of Indian and English men and women and it was published in 1908. He was profoundly shocked by some of the missionary literature he read.

> I remember being given at Delhi a whole series of pamphlets published by a missionary who had been employed at a station not far distant. These contained nothing but a number of bitter attacks upon what was considered to be the vulnerable points in the armour of Hinduism. Such a form of controversy led on to counter attacks. Abuse was poured upon the Christian religion in turn.[16]

It is not certain that this passage refers to Biscoe but the 1908 book is explicit in the danger of the missionary being seen as a 'Sahib' – a member of the foreign ruling class living apart from the people and imposing on them the mores of England, so Biscoe's attitude to educated Indians and his emphasis on British values were at odds with Andrews' emphasis on embracing Hindu thinking and culture. In Andrews' 1912 book, *The Renaissance in India*, he does not refer to Biscoe but does refer to Irene Petrie in Kashmir, who had died in Leh 16 years before (see Chapter 2).

Andrews became increasingly involved in the movement for Indian independence as well as for the condition of Indian indentured labour in South Africa, where he got to know the young Mohandas Gandhi and was highly influential in abolition of the pernicious practice, and he severed his ties with the Cambridge Brotherhood and with conventional Christianity. Biscoe continued to follow his lights for the advancement of Kashmiris through practical Christianity and social service. And continued to distrust the motives of educated Indians who he felt were ungrateful for the benefits of British rule. Andrews was ahead of his time, Biscoe was of his time.

Development of the Mission School Team

When the Biscoes returned to Kashmir in March 1905 they received a grand welcome from the school staff but soon thereafter two events occurred which tested the relationship greatly, although the eventual outcome led to a far stronger team that went on to achieve important reforms in Kashmir society.

One event was the reinstatement of Pandit Amar Chand as headmaster of the Rainawari Branch School in September 1905. Amar Chand first met Biscoe at Baramula in December 1890 but later had been appointed by Biscoe to the headship of this branch school and had distinguished his leadership by his school being the first to crew a boat with Kashmiri paddles rather than English oars. While Biscoe was in England in 1904 his deputy, J.H. Knowles, dismissed Amar Chand for paedophilia, a serious matter if true, so on his return Biscoe held a court martial with five senior teachers to investigate the charge against Amar Chand. As Biscoe described in the 1906 log:

> I as a foreigner and no lawyer am not up to all their peculiar manners, customs and devices and am likely to fail in getting at the truth. But the court martial is composed of Kashmiris who know their own race and in every case so far have settled the matter smartly and sharply.[17]

In this case the evidence was that on successive days two boys had each appeared before Knowles' house crying and when asked the reason told him that Amar Chand their headmaster had tried to do bad work with them, so Knowles dismissed Amar Chand and appointed as headmaster, Ganga Dhar. The court martial found that Ganga Dhar had instigated the boys and that it was false, so Biscoe dismissed Ganga Dhar from service and ordered Amar Chand reinstated as headmaster. The other staff of the school brought Amar Chand on their shoulders to Rainawari School, placing him on his headmaster's chair with great rejoicing!

The other event that Biscoe learnt of in August 1905 was that three Brahmins – one a teacher in the Mission School, one a 20-year-old student in the school and the third an old boy of the school – had inveigled a young panditani to accompany them on a *doonga* for three days where they seduced her. Being thus dishonoured her husband drove her from his house. For a Mission

School that had put in the forefront of its activities the uplift of women this was a grievous blow. Biscoe assembled the staff and boys and asked Dr Henry Holland, who was working at the Mission Hospital while Arthur Neve was on leave, to deliver a pep talk on sexual matters. After Holland left, Biscoe ordered the three men, all orthodox Hindus, to each be given 20 strokes of the cane by a strong municipal sweeper and pay him for his service. His choice of an outcaste sweeper was to bring home to them and everyone else the enormity of what they had done to the woman, making her an outcaste for life.[18]

He then took the teacher aside and said that he must suffer more than the other two on account of his position in the school; he must carry a heavy load the 220 miles to Gilgit and on his return bring back an equivalent load of dried apricots in order that he might think over his behaviour and repent. His photograph would be sent to the British officials along the road to ensure that he carried the loads himself. For two years he would not comply with the punishment and so lost his job as a teacher in the Mission School. Then in 1907 he sent Biscoe a message to say that if he would take him back he was willing to carry out the punishment.[19] Biscoe agreed and he returned from the 440-mile journey fitter than he had ever been and apparently grateful for the experience. He was taken back on the staff and remained for the rest of his career. A year earlier one of the senior teachers, Tara Chand Kachroo, reported that the husband of the woman had taken her back, so the episode ended better than at first thought possible.[20]

What these two incidents did in their quite different ways were greatly to strengthen the relationship between Biscoe and the Kashmiri staff for they showed that he was just, even though at times he could be very severe. In 1906 he also discovered that half the staff were in debt to money lenders who charged up to 40 per cent and did not want to be paid off, so he began a Loan Fund, initially with a donation of 300 rupees from his brother Albert,[21] to take over these debts in return for a charge of only ten per cent, half to go to the lender and half to build up the Loan Fund itself. In this way the teachers were relieved of their debts and the fund was soon able to help others in financial difficulties. This was quite distinct from the Dixon Benevolent Fund, begun in 1901 and to which all staff had to contribute each month, to help the widows of staff that died, like Tara Chand Padi, and also to provide pensions to retired staff. While both schemes are the norm a century later, in 1906 they were unknown in Kashmir and provided the teachers with independence. As Biscoe wrote, 'The men therefore stand on their own legs and I can say I'm no longer your father and mother! You are fledged! Look after yourselves! Fly in the air of freedom!'[22]

The school log for the year 1906 also spells out in some detail Biscoe's philosophy and vividly evokes the relationship that had by then developed between him and the masters in the five schools. Almost all of them were men who had grown up in the schools as boys and had been imbued with his ideas of social service. As he wrote:

In the East the teacher is in the place of honour next to the parent. Hence it comes to pass if you take on your old students, you have men tied to you by a bond at once ancient and strong, for both religion and custom demand this reverence of pupil for teacher. Where custom and religion are joined together, woe betides the man who has the temerity to break the bond.[23]

But not all were so bonded. His headmaster, Lachman Singh, was a Christian from Calcutta who had been appointed in 1897 but because he was not a Kashmiri he had not enjoyed as good a relationship with Biscoe as some of the local men who had come up through the school and its traditions. So when in February 1906 he asked for a year's leave to go to England to further his studies Biscoe was happy to let him go with the thought that he probably would not return. As he wrote two years later:

We have not been fortunate in our school with regard to native Christians. The headmaster who was here when I arrived 18 years ago left my first term to join the Arya Samaj.[24] The second man nearly worried me to death with his insulting behaviour as I tried to act towards him as a Christian brother and be principal of the school as well; he was a Bengali babu.

The third fought with the then principal (GWTB), the fifth I turned out for immorality, he was a Pathan Christian and this last man was my sixth. So it comes to pass that my Hindu teachers do the living and the Christians the talking. When I say living I mean the acts of kindness, visiting the sick, helping the distressed etc. I suppose the reason is that the Native Christians here are foreigners and cannot mix with the Kashmiris.[25]

With these thoughts in his mind Biscoe put an advertisement in the *Civil and Military Gazette*, 'Wanted a headmaster for CMS School, Srinagar. No one with a proud look or high stomach need apply to the Rev. C.E. Tyndale-Biscoe.'[26] Within a few days he received a post card from Canon Allnut, Head of the Cambridge Brotherhood in Delhi, very grieved, and saying that the advertisement had upset the whole of Delhi. It is most likely that C.F. Andrews with his great sympathy for Indians and Hindu culture instigated the response. There is irony in the fact that Andrews was at this time pressing for his close friend, Sushil Rudra, an Indian to be appointed Principal of St Stephens College against opposition of the English brothers, so might have had sympathy with Biscoe's wish to appoint a Kashmiri Hindu rather than an Indian Christian.

There were 70 applicants for the position but Biscoe accepted none of them; he said he could see by their letters that they had high stomachs and probably proud looks above them. Instead he appointed Pandit Shenker Koul as headmaster, who had joined the school as a boy of 13 in 1892, and he remained in the post for 35 years.

The first challenge came a few months later with the news of much loss of life in a storm on the Wular Lake. As previously mentioned it was a dangerous place because of the sudden storms that could drive down from the surrounding mountains and overturn the flat-bottomed boats, and because no boatman could swim. Biscoe put it to his staff that they should swim across the lake to show the community that knowing how to swim could reduce the danger of the lake. On 17 July 1906 the first ever crossing of the Wular Lake was attempted by four swimmers – Darim

Figure 14 Biscoe and Darim Chand, the first to swim across the Wular Lake,
17 July 1906

Chand, Asad Joo, Gana Koul and Nedou – and Biscoe, with
Dr Sam Barton in a boat as a precaution.[27] Three swimmers gave
up but Darim Chand and Biscoe completed the swim to Baba
Shukr-u-Din. After the swim their boat was chased by police
attempting to catch boatmen to tow an official's boat up river to
Srinagar. The two Englishmen lay down in the boat out of sight

and, as they closed in the police shouted to the crew to halt or else. Then the two Englishmen stood up and the police completely changed their tune and said they had come to offer any assistance they required. When this was declined they raced off to find another boat to press gang for the unpaid towing.

One year later, Biscoe took his 6-year-old son Eric with him to watch the Wular swim when 11 swimmers began, and seven crossed the Lake in 3–4 hours.[28] From then on it became an annual event. On one occasion some of the local villagers asked to swim with the party and when asked how it was that they could swim they said that since the first crossing they had lost their fear of the lake and had all learnt to swim.

Development of the Character Form and the School Crest and Motto

By the end of 1906 there is a new optimism in his writing; the tribulations of the past 15 years had been overcome and he now had a staunch headmaster who thought like he did and was courageous as well, and a loyal team devoted to him and willing to tackle with him whatever might befall. Another important factor was that he now had two English assistants – F.E. Lucey and C.F. Hall – which relieved him of much of the load of running the five schools, 56 teachers and 1,040 boys. Frank Lucey, who arrived in 1905, proved to be a great support; he was especially sent in response to Biscoe's nervous breakdown and as he later wrote, 'I am not prepared to lose Lucey. Since my breakdown I have been obliged to run half steam so don't count me as a whole worker. I can't run at 120 lbs pressure.'[29]

The school log for 1906, *Training in Kashmir*, introduced the final version of the Character Form, which followed the preliminary ideas presented the previous year on his return from England, and described the system of marking and its purposes. The key elements of the scheme were: the personal relationship in and out of school of each student with his form master; the meeting of each student with Biscoe and the form master three times a year for assessment and completion of the Character form; and the emphasis in the distribution of marks of the boy's personal achievements in esprit de corps and social service to others. While marks could be earned for scholastic or sporting success these were tempered by the background of each boy. So a boy from a well to do family who did well at games or swimming might get no more marks than an undernourished boy from a poor family who tried harder but achieved less.

> If we always reward the strong, as is the custom of the world, we discourage the weak and often they give up trying. The strong will do well without more aid. Therefore let us go for the weak ones and give them encouragement.[30]

It seems that it worked and that the boys took up the challenge of helping anyone or any animal they saw in trouble. They wore on their shirts a metal replica of the school badge and motto and when asked why they did this or that kind action would reply, 'It is the School Motto, In All Things Be Men'. The badge comprised two Kashmiri heart-shaped paddles crossed over each other. Paddles represented hard work or strength, the heart shape represented kindness and being crossed represented self sacrifice. The badge and motto first appeared in the 1899 log but only in 1906 was its significance described in detail. Nevertheless, it is remarkable that the concept of wearing a badge to declare that one is ready to help was established by Biscoe and enthusiastically adopted by the boys in Kashmir several years before Baden-Powell instituted a similar concept with Scout badges. The good deeds that the boys accomplished were noted on their character forms and Biscoe also kept a notebook in which he recorded particularly noteworthy actions. Any boy whose action saved a person's life was inscribed on an honours board in the school hall; but there were no boards for academic or sporting prowess.

In 1909 he brought his ideas together in a booklet titled *Character Building in Kashmir* which replaced in that year the annual school log recording the year's activities and a list of those who had supported the schools. This pamphlet compared the state of affairs when he had arrived in Kashmir in 1890 with the changes that had been achieved in 18 years and it concluded with a quotation from John Stuart Mill:

> The prosperity of a country after all depends not on the abundance of its revenues, nor on the strength of its fortifications, nor in the beauty of its public buildings, but it consists in the number of its citizens who are men of character. Here are to be found its true interests, its chief strength, its real power; that which raises, strengthens, dignifies a country, that which spreads her power, creates her influence, makes her respected and submitted to, bends the hearts of millions, and bows down the pride of nations to her. In a word, her true throne, crown, and sceptre are to be found in an aristocracy not of money, but an aristocracy of character.[31]

Bakkal's Response and Challenge

Mama Bakkal was one boy who responded to the challenges of the school. He came from a devout Muslim family and had been warned by his father not to listen to the religious teachings of the missionaries, but he threw himself into the school activities: sporting, academic and the social work for the betterment of the city folk. He had been a small boy during the great cholera epidemic of 1900 and saw what the teachers and older boys did then and during the subsequent street clean up by the engineers' corps. So when a heavy snowfall in January 1907 caused Lucey's houseboat to capsize he was among the senior boys who came to help rescue his belongings. Among the things Bakkal rescued was a picture of Jesus with the words 'This have I done for you; what have you done for me?' The question seemed to be for him and soon after he went to Biscoe seeking to become a Christian. While many people came to Biscoe with protestations of wanting to 'go Christian' these were easily seen off. Indeed, he had often been criticised for not having made any converts to Christianity in his 17 years in Kashmir. Now he was faced with the first serious inquirer, one of the senior boys in the school. Biscoe warned Bakkal of the persecution he would have to endure and possible death, to which he replied; with the help of God he would be ready for both. 'I told him I could not move in this matter until he had told his father for he was only 16 years of age. He left with my blessing.'

As expected his father was very upset and kept him at home for several days in an attempt to get him to change his mind, and was aided in this by the local Mullah, who became angry at the intransigence of this young boy who refused to listen to reason. When beatings did not change him he was taken to the top of the house and tied to diagonally crossed beams, like the school badge, and left without food or water; but still he would not change. For many weeks he had a very severe time of persecution which he bore bravely and cheerfully, for he possessed a very cheerful disposition. Biscoe visited his father and said to him:

> I am a father of boys and therefore I sympathise with you for I would be very upset if one of my sons gave up Christianity; but I would not be angry with my boy but with the man who was the cause of my son's change of faith if it was a matter of proselytising. If this change in your son's faith were caused by me or any other man's words then he need not distress himself for it would all come to naught, but if God Almighty had spoken to the boy's soul then what could he or any one else do to prevent it?[32]

He quite accepted this view and was comforted and gave his son leave to return to school, but this happy state of things did not last for long and he was not seen at school for several months.

On returning from his summer holiday at Nil Nag, Biscoe met Mama Bakkal on the Bund and hardly recognised him; he was so changed from the terrible time he had been through.[33] So he could not allow him to return home and arranged for him to be accommodated at the Mission Hospital from whence he could travel to school each day. But this was not to be, as a party of zealots were lying in wait to capture him on his road to or from school, so they put on an escort of the school's three best boxers to guard him.

All went well until 11 September when the guard were ambushed outside the school and a scuffle ensued as the guards held on to his arms and the enemy on to his legs. When Lucey appeared the battle went in the school's favour and the prize was safely landed in the school. The school was besieged for three hours by an angry, howling mob and when Lucey tried to arrange Bakkal's escape by the river they were followed in other boats. However, with their superior skills in boating, the school crew were able to sink the pursuing boats and, as the occupants could not swim they gave up the chase.

The next day Biscoe and Henry Holland drove him in disguise to Baramula from where he was escorted by other missionaries to Baring High School, Batala, where Biscoe's brother George was principal. Having completed his studies in England and been accepted by the CMS, George had arrived in November 1906 with his wife Isobel and their son Francis.[34] A month later Biscoe was with George and Isobel awaiting Blanche's return from 6 months in Britain where she had been caring for the two elder boys.[35]

Bakkal was baptised at the end of 1907 and took the name Samuel. A year later Biscoe wrote:

> The boy who became a Christian last year is doing very well at Batala. May he not fall victim to the disease which is more prevalent than any other in this country to so-called educated young men, viz the swelled head. I try to combat it by putting my fellows to all sorts of manual labour.[36]

It seems that he did not succumb to the disease; he matriculated from that school and then studied for his BA at Allahabad University and then his Bachelor of Teaching at Lahore, where he introduced his fellow students to the joys of social service by leading them in putting out a fire and saving a neighbouring house. He returned briefly to Kashmir in 1912, when he was again subjected to the anger of some Muslims in the city before continuing his studies towards a BA. He passes out of this story until after World War I, in which he served with Indian troops in France and Palestine, when he returns to Kashmir as the Executive Officer of the State Granaries.[37] But his tumultuous conversion continued to reverberate in Srinagar for another year or more.

Conflict with Dya Kishen Koul and Lachman Singh

Lachman Singh did not go to England in 1906 but returned to Kashmir a year later bent on revenge against Biscoe, and the conversion of Bakkal provided him with a cause.

He arrived in February 1907, soon after the incident with Lucey's houseboat, and started the National School above Habba Kadal Bridge with the help of the Maharaja's Private Secretary, Dya Kishen Koul, who had also helped Annie Besant five years before. Like her, he tried to get Biscoe evicted from Kashmir. Dya Kishen Koul was a very powerful man in Kashmir because he had direct access to the Maharaja and knew how to control him. For instance, when Biscoe took Lucey to meet the Maharaja in June 1906 he was drowsy with opium, given to him by Dya Kishen Koul, who would arrange for the opium to be given when he did not wish the visit to be a success.[38] Not only did Lachman Singh have this important backing but the Prime Minister, Pandit Amar Nath Koul, was able to get the new school recognised by the Punjab University. However, when the Punjab University asked Dr Ewing to inspect the school he found it empty of boys; when he asked for the school registers he was told they are locked in a box and the man with the key is not available. So he recommended withdrawal of recognition. However, a year later it was operating along with five other schools besides the Mission School, as Biscoe's letter to London in June 1908 indicates:

The School work year by year increases, as it is not simply a teaching in school machine, it works various other businesses outside the power station.[39] It is supplying electricity more and more in this city of 130,000 people outside. Also the other companies are increasing and running strong: 1. The State High School with six branches. 2. The Sri Pratap Hindu College and four branches. 3. The Islamia High School and branches. 4. The State model and normal schools. 5. Arya Samaj schools. 6. National High School (Lachman Singh) and various private schools, so Srinagar is becoming quite a seat of learning and we must hold our own.[40]

One way the school was 'supplying electricity' was through the beginning of inter-school sports tournaments but the State school team were most unsporting. They blocked the goal with boys, called the umpire a liar and sat on the ground for 25 minutes refusing to play. Biscoe and Moore, the Principal of Sri Pratap School visited the Resident to report the rotten behaviour.[41]

But rotten behaviour of a different kind was brewing: Younghusband said that he had received three letters threatening that Biscoe would be killed if he was not expelled from Kashmir, and that he must be careful as the police had failed so far to find the authors. Younghusband, unknown to Biscoe, had visited Raja Amar Singh and told him that he was responsible for Biscoe's life, so Biscoe was given a police guard for six weeks. Biscoe kept a bright look out going to and from school different ways each day, kept a loaded revolver under his pillow and each night set up an elaborate booby trap on the staircase, which he removed early in the morning so that no servant would know of it. When after a month the police had still failed to find the author of the letters Younghusband told Raja Amar Singh that he would send to Simla for an English CID man to do the trick. Thereupon the Raja called a Cabinet meeting and it transpired that Dya Kishen Koul was the author of the letters, Lachman Singh being his accomplice. The hapless accomplice was ordered to leave Kashmir the next day, never to return but Dya Kishen Koul was untouched – too big a person.

Raja Amar Singh himself fared much worse from the same enemy at Court; his sudden death in Jammu at the age of 42 on 25 March 1909 occurred after he had attended a nautch party at the home of Dya Kishen Koul. It was supposed that he was given powdered glass in his food. The college students were so furious that they lay in wait for Dya Kishen Koul and as he left the party drunk they dragged him from his carriage and beat him with their shoes and left him in the gutter. The police then took charge of the 'drunk' and put him in the lock-up. When next morning they visited the drunk, lo it was none other than the great Dya Kishen Koul. Dya Kishen Koul left Jammu at once, never to return.[42]

Maharaja Pratap Singh had no male heir until the time when Annie Besant visited Kashmir in 1901; when the long-awaited event occurred that year her spiritual interventions were initially credited with it, but when the hapless boy died in 1905 she fell out of favour with the Maharaja. Without an heir of his own, the 10-year-old son of Raja Amar Singh would inherit the Gadi instead and the Maharaja was warned by the British Government that if the boy, Raja Hari Singh, were poisoned the State would be incorporated into British India. Three months after the death of Raja Amar Singh Younghusband, proposed that Biscoe should become the official tutor of the Heir to the Gadi. In this he was supported by the Prime Minister, Diwan Amar Nath, whose own son, Badri Nath, had been tutored by Biscoe. When Biscoe asked the Prime Minister why he wanted him as tutor for the boy he replied, 'He needs discipline. I cannot give it for he always kicks my shins.' Biscoe accepted on condition that the prince should never enter the palace.[43] The Maharaja would not agree to this so Hari Singh was sent to Mayo College, Ajmer, for his education, and survived to become the fourth and last Maharaja of Jammu and Kashmir in 1925. Dya Kishen Koul was banished from Kashmir by Younghusband and took up a similar post with the Maharaja of Ulwur. However, he was back in Kashmir in the first years of Hari Singh's reign and was eventually made to leave the State in 1931 because 'his presence was definitely against His Highness' interests.[44]

At the end of 1908 Biscoe wrote:

> You will remember an account of the Muslim boy who became a Christian last year, and had to go through some severe persecution and how our school was besieged for some hours, and how the boy finally escaped to the Punjab, etc. Well, the Muslims quieted down and the father of the boy and we were good friends and all went well until this summer when a Christian master whom I had dismissed turned up in Kashmir and started a rival school with the hope of damaging the Mission School, and amongst the many tricks that he tried was to stir up the Muslims against me on account of this Christian boy and so get me into trouble with the authorities, and he hoped that I should be sent out of the country. The authorities were obliged to take the matter up and in the investigation the

police managed to secure some of the letters that this boy had written to his father and which showed plainly that the boy had become a Christian of his own free will and that he was a very true Christian. On account of this fact the plot came to naught and the plotter was expelled out of the country as he was foolish enough to threaten my life. The manner of my death as described in the various letters differed somewhat for I was to be murdered in the bazaar, shot and strangled. I will only quote from one:

To the Members of the Mission Society,

Srinagar, Kashmir, April 1 1908

Protector of the Poor

We, the inhabitants – Hindus and Muslims – of Kashmir respectively beg to state that there is at the present moment a mission high school in Kashmir. Our boys attend the said school. But as long as there was Mr. Knowles there was everything in perfect order, and our boys gained much learning and ability under him. But since the arrival of Mr. Biscoe he has done nothing to improve the teaching of the boys, but has devoted himself soul and heart to all sorts of athletic entertainments and, above all, is attracting the boys towards his Christian religion, and notwithstanding the repeated warnings from the Maharaja Sahib, he has always given a deaf ear to all such, and it so happened once that he had forced some Moslem boys to dine with him, quite against their wishes or religion, and made a compromise with the parents of the boys by bribing them, and now he is stretching forth his hands on Hindu boys, and the result is this, that 500 boys have been kept back from attending the school, and when asked to give them the discharge certificates, he did not give these and made a great fuss, and now all the students are wandering here and there. All these events are indeed earning a very bad reputation for the school and the Society, and a complaint has been made to the Maharaja, and a full and stern explanation has been asked, and we hope a copy of the same complaint has been forwarded to you. Now we want this, that if Mr. Biscoe is allowed to remain in

*Kashmir as a Principal of the school, not a single boy will
attend it, and the Society will have to close it for good, but
if a man like [Mr Knowles/Lucey?] and an M.A., is put in
his place the school will flourish a good deal and we all will
do our utmost to help it in every way. Therefore, please,
Sir, transfer Mr. Biscoe, for he is exceedingly a bad man,
illiterate, deceitful, ill-mannered, uncultured, cunning, and
man too much fond of cricket.*

He ends, 'It is well sometimes to hear the unvarnished
truth!'[45]

And another of the same tenor from Sri Pratap College:

We, the students of S.P. College Srinagar, send the copy of a
resolution passed at a meeting today:-
    We strongly condemn the action of Mr. C.E. Tyndale-
Biscoe in turning out a few of his students simply for putting
on khadi[46] and invite the attention of H.H.'s Government
Jammu and Kashmir to make an enquiry into the matter.
Further, a copy of the above resolution be sent to Mr Biscoe.
    Students, S.P. College Srinagar

However his own staff took a different view and within days of the
departure of Lachman Singh they presented Biscoe with a white
cane to mark the fact that he had not beaten anyone during the
last term![47]

Diwan Badri Nath

Dya Kishen Koul's successor as Private Secretary to the Maharaja
was none other than Badri Nath, the 36-year-old son of the Prime
Minister and a good friend of Biscoe. As a young man of 19, Badri
Nath's father had asked Biscoe to prepare Badri Nath for Oxford
University.[48] This was in 1892 when Biscoe was beginning to
introduce his ideas on boating and swimming to Kashmir. Biscoe
agreed to prepare him on three conditions: the fee would be paid in
advance, he would be allowed to teach the youth manners, and he

must have lessons in swimming. They agreed to all three conditions but when Badri Nath arrived for his first lesson he had not brought the fee – he promised it the next time. No, said Biscoe, no fee no lesson, so he went home and brought the fee. 'Now come with me to the lake for your first swimming lesson.' 'No,' said Badri Nath, 'I cannot learn to swim because I am a gentleman.' 'That is decidedly interesting. If your mother fell in the river what would you do?' 'Call a coolie and send him after her.' 'And if there was no coolie at hand, what would you do?' He scratched his head but made no reply so they set off on bicycles for the lake. On the way his bicycle got a puncture, but to no avail, they continued on foot and he had his first swimming lesson. A few years later Biscoe met him again at Cambridge – not Oxford – where he was Cox of the Trinity College rowing crew and glad that he could swim. He graduated with an MA from Cambridge and LL.B from Dublin and then returned to Kashmir where he entered the Maharaja's service, and in 1909 became his Private Secretary and a firm friend and helper of Biscoe.

Soon after he took up this post he called on Biscoe and asked him if there was anything he could do for him. As it happened, two Hindu boys at the school had recently stood up in the school assembly and publicly declared their intention to become Christians. This had led to strong pressure from their families and priests but they persisted in their intentions. Late at night Biscoe received a caller who told him that he had overheard several senior men at Court agreeing that the only course was to poison the two boys. While he was pondering what to do Badri Nath called on him and asked Biscoe if there was any way he could be of help. He mentioned the plot to kill the boys. Badri Nath told Biscoe he was just off to Gulmarg to see the Maharaja and that he should meet him in two days time at a particular discrete place at noon. Each day a gun was fired from the Hari Parbat Fort at noon which could be heard at Gulmarg. At the appointed hour and place Biscoe saw a villager walking along the track; as they neared each other Biscoe heard the voice of Badri Nath tell him the matter had been settled and the boys were safe. However, they also changed their minds about converting to Christianity!

Dr Kate Knowles and Recognition of Women's Needs

On their journey to India in March 1905 the Biscoes were accompanied by a new recruit for Kashmir, Dr Kate Knowles (no relation of Hinton Knowles). She was to join the medical staff of the Mission Hospital at Islamabad that had been started in 1900 by Dr Minnie Gomery and Miss Kate Newnham, presently on furlough. When asked about her reactions to the appointment of Dr Kate Knowles to Islamabad Dr Gomery was enthusiastic and said she liked Knowles when they met in Peshawar and it would be good to share the medical responsibilities.[49]

Kate Knowles was an unusual recruit, being an older woman with a wider experience than most of the new recruits. At 39 she was three years younger than Cecil and a year older than Blanche. She had been a school teacher for several years before undertaking medical studies at the London School of Medicine from which she had graduated the previous year. She had long harboured an ambition to be a medical missionary and now at last her ambition was to be fulfilled. She was eager to begin work immediately by re-opening the hospital but was unaware of the subtle difficulties that awaited her in Kashmir.

The first difficulty was the prejudice of the senior men of the mission against a forceful and able woman. The local secretary in Lahore, Ireland Jones wrote to the London secretary in May:

Miss Knowles is proving very importunate about Islamabad and her letters come in 2 or 3 a week. Dr E. Neve advised me that she should stay in Srinagar this summer; he still adheres to that opinion. She urges that she be allowed to go to Islamabad in August. My fear is that if she once gets established at Islamabad there will be little prospect of Miss Gomery ever going there again. I fear we shall not find Miss K. a person easy to provide for and she does not seem to know very clearly the principle of being one in an organised body. Her doctrinal history and natural character of which you have told me when I met her at your house may account for a good deal.[50]

Despite their concerns she did re-open the hospital at Islamabad in September with two nurses, Miss Foy and Miss Coverdale, and her friend Dr Janet Vaughan, who

> came for three months and but for her help I should have had to close the hospital, as it would have entailed more work on Miss Coverdale than she has force for and I should have been unable to do any of the major operations which bring us the bulk of our in patients and draw most attention to the hospital.[51]

Knowles had the hospital going well when Gomery and Newnham returned in April 1906. Ireland Jones wrote to her before they arrived:

> Dr Gomery will once more take up responsible charge with you as her colleague in all the work. You recognise as we all do that mutual relations will need very wise action on all sides. May God enable you all so to work together and to live together in all the manifold relations of home life, hospital work and itineration that there may be real happiness in the ministry for Christ at Islamabad, and much blessing to all who come within the influence of the hospital and its missionary workers.[52]

But trouble soon began because Knowles, newly graduated from London, had introduced new standards that showed up the work of the others. Added to this was the fact, unknown to Knowles that Gomery and Newnham were in a much closer relationship than anyone knew. By the end of June the situation was so bad that Ireland Jones came up to Kashmir and, with Arthur Neve and Biscoe made a special visit to Islamabad to try to resolve the issue. When it became apparent to all that Gomery and Newnham were inseparable, Knowles had to go and was understandably aggrieved. Both doctors wrote to Jones after the meeting. Gomery wrote:

> There is peace after the storm, thank God, real peace but still a very great soreness and pain [...] Your reference to my

friendship with Miss Newnham brings up an old grief which we had both hoped was a thing of the past. Words seem useless in this connection but I must just tell you once again simply and earnestly that we both recognise this friendship as a gift from God to be used for his glory and by his grace never to be a hindrance to anyone else. If it seemed worth while to go into this matter as it probably is not, you could I believe prove that this has not been a real difficulty to others (Miss Churchill Taylor for instance). Miss Robinson is the only one who could really have felt such difficulty and in that case it was due partly to over sensitiveness and no doubt partly to the fault of Miss N and myself, as in those early days we had not learned the necessity of being especially watchful. That experience taught us a lesson we have never forgotten. I am very sorry for Dr Knowles for I fear she feels very much injured just because she never perceived the difficulty and I fear does not even now and I am deeply sorry to be the means of bringing it to her knowledge in such a painful way.[53]

And Knowles wrote:

Very many thanks for your sympathy. I think you three men need it too, for it must have been very trying for you all [...] What I think, judging from her very few remarks, has been the source of the unhappiness is that she, and I think the others, although saying 'I'll try' started out with the conviction of failure (while I acted as though I were in my future home, they regarded and regard me as a visitor) and I think she still has it, though she will not say yes, when I ask her if she and the others feel strongly that they will be happier and the work go more smoothly if I go, because it seems a pity to waste time if they do [...] The reforms carried out have been such as to make life possible for a third or fourth without those who preceded me found it impossible. I think the lack of outside interests makes the two regard molehills as mountains, perspective is upset. I know for myself that since I have had the school and the boys to think about, many things which especially when I was tired seemed overwhelmingly important are now quite easily bearable.[54]

Ireland Jones seemed to conclude that Knowles was the problem even though conceding that she was good at her work:

She lacks perception and fails to see that her 'bossing' methods are hard to bear. She also deprecates very openly Miss G's professional methods, which she considers old fashioned and defective. Naturally this tries Miss G. much [...] They [Neves] do not want her in Srinagar and we could only suggest that she should open work in a hired house on a small scale, in Baramula, which is much larger than Islamabad and growing [...] Work is sure to grow under Miss K's hand and her high aims at a big affair. I write at once to hear what you and the Medical Committee feels.[55]

The Neve brothers who ran the hospital in Srinagar were not in the least interested in having a woman doctor in their hospital where they had for long been the sole doctors with women nurses; they did not want a forceful woman doctor in their hospital and had no intention of opening a gynaecological ward to accommodate such a person. So for the rest of 1906, and the first half of 1907, Knowles did not practice as a medical missionary, but spent her time becoming proficient in Kashmiri, which she did.

London did not approve of the Baramula option and said that two doctors were needed at Islamabad and she should be reinstated and, if necessary, Miss Newnham be transferred.[56] This did not accord with the views of the Neves or Ireland Jones:

I am sending you A. Neve's and H.U. Weitbrecht's opinions on the suggestion of the Medical Committee about turning out Miss Newnham and re-instating Dr Knowles at Islamabad. It is a mistake to think that Miss N is the sole cause of friction. It is as acute professionally between Dr Gomery and Dr K.K. I am sure Dr K.K. would never consent to be re-instated on the terms suggested by the Medical Committee. Dr K.K.'S character, her energy tenacity of purpose (verging on wilfulness) undoubted professional zeal and capacity point to an independent sphere. If she came to the Mission Hospital it would require opening an entirely separate gynaecological wing, which they do not want to do.

[A. Neve's comments] We should regret any unsettlement of the admirable self-sacrificing work carried on by the 3 ladies at Islamabad. The work has been founded by Dr G. and Miss N. with whom Miss Coverdale works happily and loyally [...] Dr Gomery is retiring and perhaps cautious but she holds her own views with perspicuity and tenacity [...] she regards Dr K.K. as in some ways her antithesis, more surgical than evangelical, ambitious of big things, pushing her own views and unsympathetic. I write from her point of view with no wish to depreciate Miss Knowles' many pleasant and admirable qualities, but I fear she has not the tact to work as Dr G's colleague [...] after the failure to work harmoniously in 1906 it would indeed be hopeless to expect that after removing Miss N. the sorely wounded spirit of Dr Gomery could find happiness in uncongenial companionship. Weitbrecht concurs.[57]

However, when Weitbrecht went to Kashmir in July, Knowles was working in the Srinagar Hospital because the Neves' niece was called back to England suddenly.[58] But this was only a temporary arrangement.

The one male missionary who was sympathetic to Knowles was Biscoe who had watched from the sidelines as she was thwarted in her desire to work hard as a doctor for Kashmiris. Like him she was less interested in preaching – itineration – than in doing, and towards the end of 1907 he offered her a room in the branch school at Habba Kadal for a small dispensary for women in Srinagar city.[59] It was very popular with the city women and soon outgrew the one room, especially when Knowles started to do surgery as well. So she spread into another classroom, and then another, until a day came when the whole building was occupied by her dispensary. The headmaster came to Biscoe, 'Sir, what can we do? All the boys are waiting in the compound. Please come Sir and speak to the lady doctor sahib.' He said, 'Poonoo, go back and give the boys a week's holiday, which will give us time to find another building to rent.' So the school shifted into a nearby house till Dr K.K. eventually found somewhere else and moved away – Habba Kadal School then returned to its own home. Biscoe and Dr K.K. never referred to the incident and remained very good friends for the rest of their lives. He realised what a tremendous struggle women had to face to become doctors at all. It was fight, fight, fight all along the line and Dr K.K. was a fighter, which he admired. She could of course have asked him for the use of the school for her hospital and he would have let her have it – as he did – but naturally she couldn't expect that, and her common sense said, seize it, and because she had always had to gain everything by show of force.

The fact that her dispensary was so closely associated with the Mission School and its Kashmiri teachers was an important factor in her success with the city women because they felt they could trust her. And her fluency now in Kashmiri was also an important factor in giving her access to the homes of her patients. She discovered some of the dreadful conditions in which women lived, especially the dire effects of early marriage, early widowhood, and inability to ever remarry. A world apart, into which no male doctor could ever enter. This was 20 years before Katherine Mayo's book, *Mother India*, exposed similar conditions in other parts of India (see Chapter 6).

When Biscoe learnt of these things from Knowles he called his staff together and chided them for having kept this from him for 17 years. With this knowledge they began the struggle to change the attitude of the boys in the schools towards their mothers and sisters, and in course of time to their wives. And to press for reform of the custom that forbade a widow from ever remarrying – it took until 1928 for the drive for widow remarriage to come to fruition in Kashmir.

Both Biscoe and Knowles saw the immediate need for a school for girls in the city and, with her experience of teaching in England, she was ready to start one. Biscoe would provide the school buildings at Habba Kadal, as well as some of his staff, to begin a mixed school, in which he 'left behind 100 small boys to act as tamers for the girls'. Both wrote to Ireland Jones in Lahore putting the case for mission support, as well as approval for her to take on this new role. One of their strong arguments was that the Theosophists were planning to start a girls' school with the help of Dya Kishen Koul:

> A certain American lady has been sent up by Mrs Besant and she intends starting her schools with éclat in April. Now it seems a thousand pities that she should capture the girls without a good try on our part. I find that girls come to a school run by my men, older ones of course, and in one of my schools I have 37 boys and 35 girls and if I liked to push it I could get a lot more. Now I am intending running two of my branch schools into one in order to centralise and bring down expenditure. This will leave one of my school buildings in the heart of the city (Habba Kadal which holds 400) free. I propose to hand this over to the girl department. Some of my old Persian masters will stay behind for the girls and my staff are keen that we should get the girls rather than Mrs Besant. The girls will come to schools under my control as their brothers and relations come. I suggest that Dr K. Knowles should run them and she has kindly consented to do so [...] You see it is important that something should be done at once and as my men are keen and the school can be run without extra expense to the CMS, as it comes under my budget, it seems to me to be a good opportunity not to be lost. I have long wanted a good Girls' school in the city for the sake of my boys and staff to find us future wives who will not hold back my boys. The matter requireth haste.[60]

Dr Knowles wrote in the same vein and Ireland Jones supported them. The girls' school began in November 1907 in the same buildings she had previously used as a dispensary. By February the next year it was going well when she wrote to London herself:

> I was so very glad to get your kind letter of sympathy and went on my way more light hearted in the knowledge of kind friends

at home. Life has indeed been full of the unexpected. I and others feel that God has spoken with no uncertain voice that he has kept me here because he has so much that I, *as teacher and doctor,* can do for the women and girls, Mr Biscoe's men opening the doors for me. They have sent in a petition claiming me for work here. You see, no qualified woman missionary, *knowing the language* has worked here since the days of Dr Fanny Butler. The men and boys have been well looked after, the better class women are uncatered for and it is for these the men want me for. The Neves *do not know* fully the awful murder and mutilation which is carried on by the native midwives. The purdah system shuts them out from this class and efforts to break thro' it is to be deplored in the present immoral condition of the country. I have already more medical work, with the dispensary and house to house visitation, than I had in Batala, and if the rate of increase last week goes on, the men's prophecy that I shall soon need a colleague will come true. It is for the women I am pleading when I ask to be allowed to stay. I hope to keep guard over my present girls and save them from the awful fate of so many of the women here.[61]

And Biscoe wrote as well:

I trust Dr KK will be allowed to remain for the present at her work in the city, which is most valuable, as she now has the entree to hundreds of houses, through her close connection with the School Staff and the scholars. She has such a nice way with her that she has 'caught on', the masters are proud to introduce her to their friends' houses. I hope this memo is what you want. Yours affectionately, CETB.[62]

Lahore approved the proposal in March, 'Dr Kate Knowles to continue her education work among girls during the summer in the hope that it may lead to useful medical work among women.'[63]

The next two years were a happy time for Kate Knowles: her school for girls flourished and was thoroughly approved of by the mission and her medical work in the city also continued with financial help from the Mission Hospital.[64] Later that year Lady Younghusband laid the foundation stone for the Rainawari Women's Hospital,[65] which for many years served the women of Srinagar city. Knowles also participated in the out of school activities of the boys' school. In April she joined the party that rowed across the Wular Lake and sailed back in a storm,[66] and in September acted as the medical officer for the annual swim across the Wular when 18 boys started but only one completed the swim because of the cold temperature. The next day she and Biscoe and his sister Frances drove from Baramula to Mahora where the Maharaja opened the electric power house.[67] They dined in a huge tent at Baramula and on their return they watched the Maharaja take a trip in the big steam tug given to his father by Queen Victoria.

The reason that Frances was in Kashmir at this time was because Blanche gave birth to a daughter on 30 July 1908, who was named Frances Irene. And, as so often happened in those days in Kashmir, her elder brother Donald died suddenly five months later at the age of 2 and a half.

In the summer of 1909 they all went to Nil Nag and it was while they were there that Biscoe and a young girl Pamela Nice had a very close encounter with a panther. They were returning from a walk in the forest and Eric had run ahead when they entered a clearing in which a large panther was playing as a cat before a mouse. When it saw them it stopped and for a long moment they stared at each other; Biscoe could not move because Pamela was clasping his leg in fear so he continued to stare at it until it leapt away into the forest. Then they rushed on to the hut where they were relieved to find Eric who had not seen the panther. Biscoe wrote, 'I would not have missed that experience for anything, but it was terribly alarming'.[68]

At the end of 1909 the Biscoe family left Kashmir for a year's leave in England. By the time they reached the plains of India, Eric was desperately ill with diphtheria but, unlike Donald the year before, he recovered and began his schooling in England – what he called the years of exile.

Two months after they had left Srinagar, Kate Knowles closed her dispensary and girls' school for the winter months and went to

Bannu on the north-west frontier. In Bannu, Dr Pennell had been ill with typhoid and there was need for a relief doctor until he recovered. However, within two months she also contracted the same disease and was very ill; Arthur Neve went to treat her and found her recovering but she was ordered to take leave to recuperate in England. Her school in Srinagar reopened in 1910,[69] being run by two new recruits, Violet Fitze and Frances McKay, and, over the next two years it grew and eventually in 1912 moved to new premises next door to the Central Boys' School, where it remained for the next 50 years. Tragically both these young women died a few years later, McKay of typhoid in 1912 and Fitze in 1921. Knowles returned to Kashmir in 1912 and concentrated on the medical work until 1915 when she left Kashmir for war service.

Having initiated the girls' school and the women's dispensary, which was succeeded by the Women's Hospital at Rainawari, Kate Knowles fades out of the picture. For a year or so she worked in Lahore in a military hospital and then went on leave to Australia where she founded St Lukes Hospital, Sydney.[70] Five years later in 1923, Biscoe received an anonymous donation of £400 from Australia[71] and the most likely donor of this substantial sum would have been Kate Knowles. She returned to Scotland in 1930 and retired to Crieff Hydro Hotel. She died in 1952 (aged 86) and bequeathed her body to the Anatomy Department, University College, Dundee.[72]

The hospital at Islamabad where she had originally hoped to work continued for many years under the care of Dr Gomery and Miss Newnham and Miss Coverdale.

5

War Years and the Aftermath, 1911–22

During the second decade of the century, three themes dominated Biscoe's life and work and were inextricably linked: he continued to be dogged by insufficient funds to support the work, which affected his less than robust health and his relations with his wife and family; he continued to develop his ideas on the paramount importance of social service in education; and he was caught up in the prevailing suspicions against educated Indians and political unrest.

His emphasis on social service was driven by the belief that the primary purpose of education is to prepare a boy for a future of service to his own community, and to enhance his self esteem; if that helps his self advancement that was secondary. He was not concerned about what a person said they believed but only in how they behaved towards other people. Hence he was not particularly interested in whether a person was a Hindu, a Muslim or a Christian and much more interested in how they conducted their life.

This emphasis and his failure to make converts to Christianity or to employ Christian staff put him at odds with senior members of the Church Missionary Society (CMS), both in India and London, so that financial support was never sufficient and he constantly had to seek financial aid from other sources. His best support was from other British people in India, who shared similar views and whom he assiduously cultivated by public displays of school activities for visiting dignitaries, and by his publications.

Because he was not impressed with education divorced from service he held educated Indians in low regard and by association their opinions about independence from British rule. In this he reflected the prevailing attitudes to Indian politics of the British in India who, throughout this decade were increasingly fearful of any hint of political unrest in the Indian population, which was conveniently termed sedition.

Funding Support from the Church Missionary Society and Biscoe's Health

Since 1905 Biscoe had had the loyal help of Frank Lucey and he was left in charge of the Mission Schools when the Biscoes went on furlough in January 1910. They took their two youngest children with them, Eric, aged 9, who nearly died of diphtheria on the first part of the journey, and Frances, aged 2. In England, Blanche established a home for the family and Biscoe visited schools and churches to speak about the work in Kashmir, reconnecting with his two older sons at school, and catching up with retired colleagues from former days in Kashmir. He took the boys to the British Museum and to the Naval Arsenal, where they watched huge 12-inch guns being made for the Dreadnought battleships that were such an important part of the arms race between Britain and Germany at the time.[1] Among former colleagues he met old Rev. T.R. Wade and his family, Dr Maxwell the second CMS doctor to Kashmir in 1871 and Dr Downes the third, and his old colleague, Hinton Knowles. He also met several ex Kashmir Residents: Col. Parry Nisbet (1883–90), Sir David Barr (1892–94), Sir Francis Younghusband (1906–09), and Sir Mackworth Young, late Lieutenant-Governor of the Punjab. And he picked up two ideas to introduce to the Kashmir schools: he saw firemen sliding down poles from an upper floor rather than coming down the stairs and decided to install similar poles for rapid evacuation of the school buildings in case of fire or earthquakes, and at the Albert Hall he saw Dr Barnado's children performing a show at the double and decided that the annual Prize Day would be conducted in the same manner.

His main task in Britain, however, was raising funds for the CMS, some of which would be available for his own work, like the hostel for boys from Ladakh and Gilgit. In all he gave 42 illustrated lectures, 55 drawing room meetings and preached in churches 37 times. In recognition of his efforts the Home Committee of the CMS in London promised to increase the grant to the Kashmir schools from the current level of 5,320 rupees per annum. While this only represented one-quarter of the running expenses of the Mission Schools, it was an essential component and the promised increase most welcome. In addition he was able to build up the funds for the proposed hostel, greatly helped by the decision of the managers of the Irene Petrie Fund to hand over the balance of the fund for this purpose.

However, when Blanche, Frances and he returned to India early in 1911 he was informed by the Punjab Secretary, Ireland Jones that the grant to the Kashmir schools was to be cut by 1,000 rupees and the funds go to the CMS School in Multan, and he did not want to discuss the matter. 'I told him that he was handing over the money to a man who never attempted to raise money for his school and that he was acting quite contrary to Our Lord's parable of the talents.'[2] In Kashmir the action against Biscoe was not forgotten; two years later Arthur Neve wrote to the then local Secretary, Canon Waller, to express his deep concern – as he had done ten years before:

> The grant made by the CMS to this school is in proportion to the total expenses exceedingly small. Fees are a relatively small source of income as the State Educational authorities have made their fees so low, and are prodigal in scholarships to lads who having studied in the CMS School and are ready for examinations. The result is that Biscoe has to make strenuous unceasing efforts to raise money from private sources. He spent his whole recent holiday in writing to subscribers and others and has come back very tired and unrefreshed […]

It is a most short-sighted policy to wear out a man like Biscoe prematurely. He cannot be replaced. If he goes the schools will lose half their scholars and most of their prestige. I think all of us feel that the reduction of his grant was a real injustice, accentuated in our view by the fact that it was the only reduction made in educational grants in the Punjab (1910) and almost simultaneously the grant to another school was increased by Rs700 or so. That is now past but Biscoe still has year by year to raise this big sum of Rs10,000 from private sources. No other educational missionary has such a yearly burden.[3]

Waller wrote to London:

Dr Neve's memo on the crushing burden now resting upon him has just gone home, and should shame some of those who profess to admire Mr Biscoe's work to come out to his rescue before it is too late [...] I entirely endorse all that is written in the letter and agree regarding his severe strictures upon the policy of curtailing Biscoe's grant so largely in the year 1910 [...] I think I am correct that it was cut down in that year from Rs 6,000 to Rs 4,000 and that this year we succeeded, when distributing the block grant, in restoring Rs 400 of the cut [...] I wish you could have copies of this made and put in the hands of the chief members of your Group Committee and also the Educational Secretary and Committee.[4]

A hundred years later it is difficult to understand the attitude of the CMS administration to Biscoe. The lack of financial support from London was consistent from the earliest years and persisted despite the obvious success of the work he was doing and the effort he put into fund raising while on leave. Apart from the lack of converts to Christianity among the Kashmiri staff and boys and his antipathy to employing non-Kashmiri Indian Christians on the staff, another less admirable reason may have been his high reputation among the senior British officials in India; unlike missionaries elsewhere, he enjoyed good relations with the Maharaja and with successive

British Residents in Kashmir; Provincial Governors and senior military men regularly visited the schools, as did every Viceroy who visited Kashmir. Did this perhaps rankle in the minds of administrators in London who felt that Biscoe should be brought down a peg or two by having his funds reduced? Or let him get his funds from his posh friends? Arthur Neve's veiled comments hint at something of the sort. Biscoe's original diaries might have provided an answer but he destroyed them. Whatever he felt about the injustice of the decision in 1911 he did not hold it against the principal of the school that was favoured because five months later Johnson-Smyth was on holiday with him at Nil Nag and he was teaching him to swim.[5] Two years later the CMS increased the grant to the Kashmir schools and in the log Biscoe wrote, 'Our thanks are due to the Maharaja for increasing the State grant; and to the Church Missionary Society for following His Highness' example!'[6]

As Arthur Neve pointed out, the need to meet the shortfall in funds was relentless; every evening after the day's work was done or when he was on holiday Biscoe had to write hundreds of letters to potential supporters, most of which brought no response. But without extra support he could not meet the monthly expenses of the schools, especially the salaries of his loyal Kashmiri staff. The constant stress affected his health, which was never robust. As previously mentioned he suffered a major breakdown in 1903–04, which was partly alleviated by the appointment of Frank Lucey as his assistant in 1905 but, after he was forced to leave because of the ill health of his wife in 1911, Biscoe had to rely on several short-term men who were not much use. Adding to the stress was Blanche's decision to return to England to be with her children.

When the Biscoes left Britain in February 1911 their three sons remained behind. Harold was now 19 and was at Cambridge studying forestry with the aim of joining the Woods and Forests Department of the Government of India, Julian, 16, was at secondary school and Eric, 10, had just begun as a boarder at a preparatory school, Seabrook Lodge. Their guardian in England was Blanche's elder sister, Sophie, and her clergyman husband – a very pious middleclass household where the nephews were not particularly welcome. For each of the boys their first seven years in Kashmir had been an idyllic life that changed abruptly and permanently when they were successively taken to England, placed in boarding schools and left with unsympathetic relatives in the holidays. For Blanche the enforced separation from her growing sons for years at a time must have been very difficult; she must have been acutely torn between wishing to see her boys grow to manhood and supporting her less than robust husband in his stressful work. Four years before she had made a brief visit to them and now she was facing the prospect of several years of separation again. It was too much; at the end of 1913 she took Frances and returned to England and remained there for the next six years. She made a home for the boys in their holidays and, after World War I began, she was there for Harold and Julian when they came home on leave.

A few days before she left Kashmir, Biscoe's brother Edward and his wife Ina came to stay with him for the next year just as brother George had done in the nineties. Like George they also trekked together along the Gilgit road as far as Astor, up Rupal Nalla and back to Bandipur[7] and they also helped in the school work, Ted designing a new cutter and Ina teaching.

While they were with him news came that Lucey's wife had died in England, which led to a flurry of correspondence between Lahore and London. Wigram wrote:

> I shall see CETB this afternoon and I have little doubt I shall be cabling 'Kashmir' tomorrow regarding Lucey. He is so obviously the man Biscoe really wants that even if it should mean risking Paterson I am sure we ought not to hesitate. CETB is 51, and can't go on for ever [...] But in the present distress is CMS prepared to throw so much force into one place?[8]

They did and Lucey returned to Kashmir at the end of 1914 when Biscoe was again nearing collapse. With Lucey now able to take charge of the schools, Biscoe was given three months leave to visit his wife and family in England and left on 19 November, cycling the first part of journey to the Indian plains.

Figure 15 Biscoe's immediate family in England, 1915. L to R, Julian, Eric, Frances, Blanche, Harold, Cecil

By then Julian was serving in the Royal Horse Artillery as a subaltern and would shortly be in action in France and Harold was training as a pilot in the newly formed Royal Naval Air Service and in 1915 would be flying solo missions over Turkey to support the Gallipoli campaign. The reunion of Biscoe with his family, after two years apart, was quite strange; Blanche and Harold met him in London and then went back home and he stayed at an hotel in London and joined them next day where Julian also joined them![9] Early in the new year he visited CMS House in London and was ordered to take a further three months sick leave by the CMS doctors – another bout of his chronic bad health. They later extended his leave to early 1916, during which time he spoke at many venues and raised money for the CMS, and then returned alone to Kashmir for the next three years, and Blanche remaining to support the family.

On the way he visited Ted and Ina in Delhi where Ted was now a military censor and as he approached Baramula he was met by seven cyclists who accompanied him to Srinagar, the whole school with band escorting him to Sheikh Bagh, where he was welcomed back by Frank Lucey and Arthur Neve.[10]

Because of the exigencies of his work and the constant need to raise sufficient funds to keep the schools solvent, Biscoe's relationship to his wife and family was fairly remote. While his life was wholly devoted to educating Kashmiri boys he was a stranger to his own sons through their adolescence and education. Harold and Eric suffered this acutely and it considerably affected their development; Julian was a more robust character – more similar to his father than the other two – and he seems to have developed more rapport through letters. While on active service between 1915 and 1918, he wrote to his father in Kashmir in a light-hearted vein, which contrasts markedly with other accounts of the horrors of Ypres and the Somme, even after he was seriously wounded and invalided back to England.[11] The first letter after he was wounded reached Biscoe a month later and merely said he was recovering in hospital in Oxford. A few days later, while Biscoe was conducting the annual Prize Day with a gathering of British notables, he was handed a telegram. Fearing the worst he did not open it until the show was over and then learnt that Julian had been awarded the Military Cross[12] for his action in August when he was wounded. When his longer letter arrived describing the Battle of the Somme and his experiences as a forward observation officer and how the shrapnel had passed through his lungs and just missed his heart, Biscoe was so thrilled by it that he called all the school staff to his house to read it to them.[13]

Social Service in the Mission Schools

The immediate effect in 1911 of the severe rebuff from the CMS was for Biscoe to appeal yet more strongly to his support base among the British in India and England. Wherever he had spoken in Britain in 1910 he would have encountered the scouting movement; Baden-Powell had launched his book *Scouting for Boys* in 1908 and a revised version was reprinted in 1909 and another in 1910. The movement was phenomenally successful especially among boys in English Public Schools, which were where Biscoe spoke. His ideas meshed so closely with those of scouting that when he spoke at Epsom College in July the publisher Mr Seeley of

Seeley Service & Co. Ltd, London offered to advance him £200 if he would write a book for him to publish. Biscoe refused saying if he wrote a true book he would be turned out of Kashmir.[14] Nevertheless, 10 years later he did oblige Mr Seeley. Although there is no mention in his diary that he met Baden-Powell in 1910, he was sufficiently affected by the new movement in England that, on his return to Kashmir he entitled the 1911 log *Scouting in Kashmir*, and the 1912 log *Scouts in the Making in Kashmir*.

Baden-Powell's intention was to:

> instil into every boy and encourage an idea of self improvement. A fair average standard of proficiency is therefore all that is required. If you try higher than that you get a few brilliant boys qualified, but you dishearten a large number of others who fail, and you teach them the elements of hopelessness and helplessness, which is exactly what we want to avoid.[15]

This view was very similar to Biscoe's, who always encouraged the less able boys by rewarding the whole class or whole crew rather than giving a prize to the best boy. Indeed, he called the annual event the non-Prize Day. However, he did honour those boys who displayed outstanding courage, such as swimming six miles across the Wular Lake, or unselfishness by risking or even giving their lives for others. Their names were inscribed on one of the four honours boards and, as he wrote, 'These boards are a continual sermon to the boys and help implant in their hearts a desire to do plucky and noble deeds.'

But while he adopted 'scouting' in the title of the Logs what he recounted in them was very different from the activities that English boys undertook. Biscoe did not adopt the patrol structure of the Scouting movement or the winning of badges, nor were his schools affiliated to the Scout Movement in Britain. Indeed, they could not have been had he wished it because Baden-Powell envisaged scouting as being an activity only for British boys with the class structure maintained – Public School boys would be patrol leaders and working class boys would not –and he did not favour any but white boys being scouts. When African, Indian and coloured boys in South Africa wished to join they were placed in separate organisations, called the Pathfinders under wholly separate management.[16] And later in India the Scout movement separated from the British movement when it was clear that they were to be debarred on racial grounds.

So, why did Biscoe adopt this new label for the activities that he had already been developing in Kashmir for 20 years? The reason was that the annual logs were written for a specific audience – the upper and middle class people in Britain and the British in India, who were his main supporters and who were now well acquainted with Baden-Powell's Scout movement. So, in 1911 and thereafter all the boys in the CMS Schools were called scouts and all the teachers were scoutmasters, although none wore Scout uniform or followed the strict regulations of the movement in Britain. His British supporters in India were fully aware of the fact that his ideas long predated the Scout movement, as was explicitly stated by the British Resident in Kashmir, the Hon. Mr Stuart Fraser, when he conferred on Biscoe the Kaiser-i-Hind Gold Medal in 1912:

> Practical morality is his principle, and long before the Boy Scout movement had taught thousands of boys in England and the Colonies the ambition of doing some one a good turn if possible every day, Mr Biscoe had been teaching his boys here in Srinagar by example as well as by precept the dignity of service. His boys save lives from drowning, they assist at putting out fires in the city, they help the weak and decrepit in the streets, they take out convalescents from the hospitals for outings on the river and lake, and they are imbibing from their master his righteous intolerance of cruelty to animals.[17]

By 1912 these voluntary activities of social service by the 70 teachers and 1,380 boys of the six schools had become a regular part of school life alongside normal school work, and continued to be so thereafter, as shown in the table for 1911–14.

Social Services by Teachers and Boys

Activity	1911[18]	1912[19]	1913[20]	1914[21]
People saved from drowning	4	6	7	15
People saved from cholera	–	–	–	73
House fires attended	6	8	7	7
Boat trips for hospital patients	45	23	46	60
Number of patients taken on boats	201	134	230	299
Cases of good turns to townsfolk	88	126	99	112
Labour gangs of 10–100 boys for poor fund	25	36	9	35

These are astonishing figures of activities that are not normally associated with schools anywhere; and the individual stories behind the figures are equally remarkable. For instance, the cholera epidemic in 1914 reached the city in August and continued until November keeping all the doctors in Srinagar busy. All schools were closed except the five Mission Schools in the city, which remained open day and night with a good supply of medicine; those attacked could send for aid at all times and receive prompt attention, which was the single most important factor in surviving the disease. Potassium permanganate was quite sufficient to save those patients who were attended to at once, but if there was a delay of an hour or more medical aid was needed. So boys with cycles became despatch riders. Directed by Dr Kate Knowles, the schools saved 73 out of 103 people that they attended.

Or another instance of an outing for patients that Biscoe came upon and described in the 1914 log:

I heard music as I was passing a village and went in search of it. The School Drum and Fife Band were in front with a crowd of 29 bandaged and sick folk and almost 50 boys forming the crews of the fleet who had just returned with their cargoes of hospital patients from a pleasant afternoon paddle on the lake, the Band discoursing sweet music the while. Among the crowd

Figure 16 Patients from the State Women's Hospital taken for an outing in school shikaras

was a lame man with white bandages supported under the arms by two boys who were helping him to walk; there was a strong boy with another cripple on his back; there were men with bandaged eyes being led by others. This school party which was for the most part composed of Brahmins were helping Muslims.

Now why do these boys spend their afternoons with the sick, striving to brighten up the lives of those who need cheering? Are they paid for it? No. Is it done to win my approval? Possibly some may do so for this reason. Is it done because it is part of the Mission School effort? Yes, partly. There are no doubt many mixed motives but there is something more. They have learnt to be sorry for those in trouble; they see the difference between their school spirit and the spirit of the city. They have realised that superstition, ignorance and stupid customs has drowned the nobler spirit, they realise that their country is down and needs lifting and they will have their try at changing everlasting custom and the like.[22]

To the sceptics Biscoe wrote in the 1911 log:

Job's comforters have even reached Kashmir and done me the honour to call on me and tell me that the teachers and boys will no doubt do acts of chivalry and scouting in general when I lead them on but whenever I am not there they will do as the rest of the crowd do. Well, Mr Job's comforter I should like to tell you personally and your connections generally that I have not myself been present at one of the fires or drowning during the year, so put that in your pipe and smoke it![23]

On the same theme five years later he observed that he had not heard of a single case of the boys being given any reward for their services from those who owe to them the safety of their homes and goods but he received several letters of thanks from those who appreciated their work:

To Padre Biscoe Sahib Bahadur (the treasure of kindness), Protector of the poor may you be in peace. With hundred respects I beg to state at 1.15 am there broke out a great fire near my house on account of which all my neighbours were in great consternation. In the meantime Pandit Samsar Chandji, who is a master on your staff, climbed over the wall and with great sympathy and bravery supplied water with other helpers and put out the fire. I pray for the British Government from the core of my heart, who have sent Padre Sahib who infuses such noble practical education, has created thoughts of helping and of kindness in masters and boys; for this I thank Padre Sahib from the bottom of my heart.[24]

But while he was in India he received another letter: 'We know that devil Biscoe [...] Warn him that if he puts foot into our sacred Kashmir he would be driven out bare foot in his shirt and would be drawn with wild horses.'

Return to Kashmir, 1911

After the disagreeable encounter with Ireland Jones, the Biscoe's return to Kashmir in March 1911 was a happy affair.[25] They were

Figure 17 Chief Judge of Srinagar High Court, Rishibal Mukerji, 1912

met at Baramula by some staff and boys and at Srinagar they were
met by the whole school with flags and band and a reception at the
Central School, accompanied by Frank Lucey, who had held the
fort through 1910, and Violet Fitze and Frances MacKay, who were
maintaining the girls' school. A week later he and Blanche and
Frances were entertained at the Rainawari School by their friend
the headmaster Amar Chand.[26] The boys had made the trees and
plants to flower with coloured paper – very realistic. Amar Chand
had copied the Mogul Amir of long ago, who had ordered the
Kashmiris to have spring flowers in bloom when they arrived on

their elephants otherwise they would be slain. So coolies were sent to bring snow from the mountains with which to bury the tree roots and flowers, which retarded their flowering.

A day later Biscoe was back in business putting matters to rights in Srinagar.[27] He discovered that a man he knew well, Nabira, had been in Khoti Bagh Prison for six months without trial and nearly died with brutal treatment. Back in 1901 this man had been the President of the Srinagar Sodomite Club whom Biscoe, after a long fight, had been responsible for convicting and gaoling (see Chapter 3). When his two year sentence ended he came to Biscoe repentant and wished to serve him in any capacity, which he did. While Biscoe was on furlough in England he was charged by the police with stealing a tablecloth and imprisoned without trial, the police making money out of prostitution and sodomy. In anger Biscoe went to the Chief Judge, Rishibal Mukerji, and asked for justice. The judge arranged for Nabira to be tried by his colleague Surij Bal three days later. But Biscoe sent Amar Chand and another member of staff to watch the trial for him. When the judge discovered who they were he ordered them out of the court and sent Nabira back to gaol. Biscoe:

> I visit Mukerji and demand justice as a Britisher; he promises to try him himself. Result, Nabira is released but given no compensation for the grave injustice done to him! Miscarriage of justice put right by Chief Judge Mukerji, an honest judge![28]

Conversely, when he discovered that the school registers had been tampered with and burnt he offered the two culprits, Rago Koul and Tara Chand, like Nathan of old the choice of three punishments: 1) faces blackened for a month while visiting all the schools; 2) march to Gilgit and back carrying loads; 3) expulsion. They chose Gilgit but Arthur Neve judged Rago unfit for such an arduous task so they had to bring hockey sticks from Nil Nag for a month.[29]

A month later there was a state visit by the Maharaja of Ulwar and as the State Barge passed the Mission School the boys jumped off the roof. The Maharaja of Kashmir asked him if he would like to see Regatta. He said he would, so Dr Mitra was ordered to make

Regatta for a week hence.[30] It did not go well; Biscoe had learnt that Ulwar's Private Secretary was none other than his erstwhile foe, Dya Kishen Koul, Kashmir's former Private Secretary to the Maharaja, who had been expelled from the State in 1908 by the British Resident Younghusband. Biscoe told Stuart Fraser, the current Resident, of this and he stopped Dya Kishen Koul entering Kashmir. This had incensed the Maharaja of Ulwur and humiliated the Maharaja of Kashmir, who knew who was behind the action. So when the Mission School boats won the boat race, he ordered the race to be run again. When they again won it was too much for him; he said he was sick of seeing boys race, he ordered the Governor to take charge of the regatta and the boat men must race. This ended in a free fight with both crews rushing to the Maharaja screaming and shouting in their blood-stained and torn clothes. The Maharaja of Kashmir gave them 60 rupees to go away and gave 200 rupees prize to the defeated school crews for the honour of having been defeated by the Mission School!

The fact that the Mission School crews won was not surprising because boating and swimming were so much a part of school activities, but not of the State Schools for some years to come. In 1912 Biscoe had a floating boathouse built near the Dal Lake, which could accommodate seven boats[31] and a year later was able to build a permanent one on land given by a local landowner, Shamsundra Lal Dhar; the teachers and boys preparing the site by removing rocks. He also bought a motor boat that had been built in Peshawar and had it brought up the 200 miles cart road on a bullock cart;[32] and early in 1914 he had a new 12-oared cutter built to the design of his sailor brother Ted, who was staying with him that year. They chose a deodar log from the depot at Parauni [old] Channi, watched it being sawn up,[33] and then watched Salama the carpenter build it on the hostel ground.[34] It served the school for more than 70 years. Also by 1912 the April excursion of boys and staff to the Wular Lake to sail and swim across had become an annual event.

In October 1912 the Viceroy and Lady Hardinge visited Kashmir and Biscoe had the idea to put on a very special event by the school – a living welcome – during the State entry to Srinagar

Figure 18 Living 'Welcome' to Viceroy and Lady Hardinge, 1912

city.[35] Three days before they were due to arrive he borrowed a steel hawser from Colonel J. de-Lotbiniere, the State Engineer, and with the help of his friend Cecil Hadow fixed it across the river from the top of the school building to a winch on the other side. Dr Mitra the City Medical Officer opposed the plan because of the danger to the boys so Biscoe went to the British Resident who told him to carry on. Finally, 40 minutes before the great arrival 16 boys, with the help of rope ladders and an aerial trolley, were swung up into position on the hawser to spell out 'Welcome'. As the living letters were clothed in the colours, red white and blue they were mistaken for flags, but as soon as the State Barge passed the State guests were undeceived as all the boys dropped into the water before the crowd of boats in the rear and swam ashore. In the State Barge the Maharaja would not look at the event until the Viceroy urged him do so. Biscoe thought it was because he did not like the Mission School – or its principal – but it may have been because he agreed with his medical officer that it was a dangerous risk to the boys and those beneath and he was offended that the Kashmir Government's authority had again been overruled by the British Resident. Whatever he thought then, the next day he put on a palace banquet at which Biscoe was invested with the Kaiser-i-Hind medal he had

Figure 19 Gymnastic display at the Central School for the Viceroy's party

been awarded some months before, and the following day the Vice Regal Party visited the Mission School by boat.

Hostel Development

For several years there had been a need for a place of residence for boys from Ladakh and Gilgit who had no relatives in Srinagar and in 1909, with the support of his friend Diwan Badri Nath, who had succeeded Dya Kishen Koul as the Maharaja's Private Secretary (see Chapter 4), permission was granted to build a hostel on land adjacent to the Sheikh Bagh for a cost of 19,948 rupees. While in Britain in 1910 Biscoe had been permitted to appeal for additional funds from supporters for this purpose. In this he was helped by several Kashmir friends who lent their names to the appeal – Francis Younghusband, Henry Cobb, Walter Lawrence and the

Bishop of Lahore. The trustees of the Irene Petrie Fund also agreed to support it so a start was made on the Biscoes' return in 1911 when Blanche cut the first sod on 22 June 1911.[36] The following January the Prime Minister, Diwan Amar Nath granted 1,000 feet of *kairoo*[37] wood for hostel building as for religious purposes and the boys hauled 17 *kairoo* logs from the river to the hostel ground,[38] where they were sawn into planks and beams. By April 1912 the new building was up with the third floor unfinished and it had two boarders from Ladakh, Dechan and Chimed Gergan, illustrated in the annual log.[39] All went well for the next year; more boys joined the hostel and a warden, Thakur Das, was appointed who lived in an adjacent house.

In October 1913 Biscoe was approached by a Colonel in Peshawar who had charge of an Abyssinian boy that he could not control, and Biscoe agreed to put him in the hostel. Within a month of Samuel's arrival all the boys in the hostel had money stolen from their boxes. Meanwhile he was giving sweets and cigarettes to all of them and was warmly thanked for his generosity. Biscoe managed to get him to own up to 25 of the 26 articles stolen, but until he could remember the twenty-sixth he had to sit in the big mulberry tree at the corner of the garden with Biscoe's tame monkey Hasham Khan tied to the bottom of the tree and there he remained for a week because he was afraid of Hasham Khan. When this failed to convince him Biscoe gave him a thrashing.

> He took his thrashing very well so I congratulated him on his pluck but I saw fire in his eyes, so-called Thakur Das and warned him not to let Samuel out of his sight for he meant mischief. While we were just finishing our dinner the servants rushed in shouting the Hostel is on fire!![40]

The flames sky high from the roof, a fire having been lit in the shavings in the unfinished third floor. Thirty soldiers poured in from the barracks under General Bhagwan Singh, four fire engines came and Biscoe and his dinner guests in their evening dresses worked hard with buckets, so that the fire was brought under control by 2 am. Samuel was nowhere to be found but was later discovered under the warden's bed.

Two days later he confessed to having fired the hostel and threatened to murder Thakur Das's children and to fire Biscoe's house so he was handed over to the police and was put in gaol. When Biscoe and his brother Ted visited him there two days later he was quite cheerful and said he was comfortable and that the food was much better than at the hostel. The court decided not to prosecute him and instead he was sent to the Salvation Army Reformatory House in India. Damage to the hostel was covered by insurance and repaired and it continued without more trouble for the next 40 years.

Food Shortages in Srinagar City, 1917–22

As the war in Europe ground on the traditions of social service in the Mission Schools were turned to a new purpose in Kashmir. In 1917 severe food shortages occurred due to hoarding by grain merchants, particularly for rice, the staple food.[41] The Governor was a fearless Kashmiri, Pandit Narendra Nath Koul, who at once grasped the situation and acted promptly by fixing fair prices for foodstuffs. To see that his orders were carried out, he recruited a Vigilance Corps, composed of some 20 of Cecil Hadow's carpet factory headmen and 50 Mission School teachers. These 70 vigilantes, Muslim and Hindu helpers, willingly gave their work and spare time and their best services to help the weak against the strong and to enforce obedience to State orders by systematically patrolling the entire city and reporting to the Governor cases of rice hording, extortionate and unauthorised prices and other malpractices. Many of the thwarted dealers closed their doors so the Governor opened shops of his own in which the Vigilance Corps sold rice to the poor until the rice dealers came to reason. The helpers were blessed by the poor and cursed by the dealers; on one occasion a certain baker was overheard to say, 'there go the fiends of Hell let loose upon our city by Padre Biscoe'.

The Governor apologised to Biscoe for this, a measure of the relationship that had developed between them in the past year.

Governor Narendra Nath was an able man who had been educated in England and aspired to join the Indian Civil Service to which a small number of Indians were then being recruited. But he was passed over and returned to Kashmir a very bitter man against the British. When he became Governor he hated the Mission Schools but he changed right round as a result of the unselfish work rendered by the school staff during the food shortages.

Cooperation continued into the next year, as the artificial shortages continued:

> Some of our men were sent up and down the river for many miles searching for boats of rice and fuel which were hiding in quiet places, while waiting for a rise of prices in the city. Others went into the villages to discover those who were hoarding rice and also those who were smuggling it out of the country, as the law forbids the export of rice. They also made themselves useful by selling the rice which the Governor collected, preserving order among the crowds of impatient townsfolk waiting to purchase grain and seeing that the women and the poor folk were not done down by the strong and the rich. It was work requiring much tact and perseverance and sometimes the use of muscles, for often women and weak persons were pushed into the river during the struggle for food, and a few were drowned.[42]

However, the food profiteers had some very powerful allies in the Maharaja's Court who were opposed to what the Governor and his supporters were doing and the consequences of thwarting them were dire. In May 1918 the Maharaja's Private Secretary and a supporter of the Governor and good friend of Biscoe, Diwan Badri Nath, aged 45, died suddenly at Jammu while in the train, probably poisoned.[43] And in August of the same year the Governor was sacked[44] and no longer had control over food prices and so for a time the Vigilance Corp was disbanded.

Two months later the Viceroy, Lord Chelmsford, visited Kashmir and to allay any thoughts he might have about food shortages, officials had lined both banks of the river with boats filled with rice or fuel before his State entry by boat. However, the next Sunday Biscoe got a different message to him from the pulpit: 'I preached on "Bear ye one another's burdens" as I wished to bring before His Excellency the food troubles, although some in the congregation disapproved of me using the church for a political message.'[45] His message got through because at the State Banquet a few days later the Viceroy in his speech told the Maharaja that he expected him to resolve the rice trouble.[46]

This nicely demonstrates the political realities of the times; while the Maharaja and his court were ostensibly autonomous in civil matters such as food distribution they could be overridden by the British Government in India, especially if its supreme officer was listening to British residents and then publicly humiliating the Maharaja. It is little wonder that Biscoe and Hadow were disliked by the Kashmir Government and were thwarted whenever possible.

For Kashmiris, however, it was more difficult to get a message to the Viceroy. A week later while Biscoe was holding a teachers' meeting in his garden two old boys rushed in asking for protection for themselves and another student who had been seized by the police and taken to gaol for having sent a telegram to the Viceroy about the food conditions in the city. Immediately Biscoe cycled off to Judge Mukerji at his house to ask him the meaning of this *zulum* and told him, 'I, not those boys, should go to gaol as I told Lord Chelmsford *in his ear* what these boys had telegraphed, therefore mine was the greater crime.' When the judge said, 'Don't lose your temper.' Biscoe answered, 'I am a Britisher and have a right to be angry.' The judge then promised to release the boys, which he did next morning into Biscoe's garden, where they were very grateful.[47]

However, as the next winter began the situation became even worse than the previous year, notwithstanding the bumper harvest; the profiteers having increased in numbers and boldness. As the situation demanded promptness, Biscoe closed the schools so that all the staff might be able to throw themselves into the work:

> We considered that feeding a city was more important than teaching boys. Incidentally, it is giving us plenty of opportunities for social service beyond the actual work of selling rice from

11am to 5pm at thirty distributing places. We are able to show that we are no respecter of persons so that when we see a rich man come in gay clothing we do not allow him to put the poor widow aside in order to be served first or permit the strong to steal from the weak [...] Our men had some amusing experiences also for several people who wished to be served first or to receive more than their share [and] thought that our men were out for bribes like the rest of their brethren. One of our men accepted the coin put in his hand and then, holding it out to the crowd to show what a fortunate man he was, threw good money straight into the river. The crowd just opened their mouths![48]

Because of his bad health, Biscoe usually spent the winter in India and in January 1919 he was in Delhi and was invited to dine at Vice Regal Lodge, when he sat next to Lord Chelmsford and talked with him on two matters relating to Kashmir politics.[49] He brought the Viceroy up to date on the rice troubles since his visit three months before and especially on the wickedness of Sir Daljit Singh, a senior member of the Maharaja's Court. He noticed that the red and gold suited waiters were listening to their conversation so he spoke louder so that they might hear and report direct to Sir Daljit Singh what Biscoe thought of him; he knew that Maharajas and such rich folk bribed the Viceroy's servants heavily to spy for their benefit.

Biscoe also raised another matter concerning the young heir to the Gadi in Kashmir, Raja Hari Singh. He had taken an interest in Hari Singh for the past ten years, since he had been asked by the Prime Minister to be his tutor (see Chapter 4). At the outbreak of the war in Europe Hari Singh had been appointed commander of the Kashmiri troops who were offered to Britain and great hopes were held for the future when he should become Maharaja. However, his uncle Maharaja Pratap Singh did not want him to succeed him but was constrained by the British Government to do him no harm – as he had done by poisoning Hari Singh's father, his own brother, Raja Amar Singh. Nevertheless, he continued to favour the son of the Raja of Poonch, a more distant relation, and they both conspired to get rid of Hari Singh by other means.

In September 1918 Raja Baldur Singh had an iron goddess brought to his private temple at Poonch from India, a very expensive job but no matter if Hari Singh's death was accomplished.[50] This goddess demanded a shirt of Hari Singh's to wear plus the parings of his finger and toe nails and hair, all of which was duly collected and placed on the goddess. Then the lady demanded slippers of gold plus many rupees night and morning when the Raja came to worship, which increased as the appointed day arrived. The Raja naturally begged the priest to hurry up the goddess as the expenses were increasing so rapidly. At last the day arrived and the Angel of Death arrived. But alas! There was some great error somewhere for the Angel of Death grasped Raja Baldur Singh himself instead of young Raja Hari Singh!

Now Biscoe was much concerned by a very different threat to the young Raja; a certain Captain Arthur had inveigled himself into being appointed the Aid-de-Camp to Hari Singh, aged 25, on his first visit to Europe and Biscoe urged the Viceroy to revoke the appointment because he distrusted Arthur's motives and considered him to be 'a first class devil'. But matters of much greater moment were occupying the Viceroy's mind at the beginning of 1919 – the public reaction to the Rowlatt Bill (see below) – and unfortunately Biscoe's advice was not heeded. Biscoe continued to press for action when he was in England later that year by calling on Sir James Dunlop Smith at the India Office, still to no avail.[51]

However, his fears for Hari Singh were soon realised. Arthur introduced Hari Singh to a socialite woman and then arranged for them to meet in Paris, a standard set up; he gave her a silver razor and they flew there in a private plane. While they were in bed together the hotel door burst open and an 'outraged husband' entered and demanded £25,000 for his silence.[52] Hari Singh paid and returned to India in March 1920. Biscoe was on the same ship and he noted that 'he spends all his days at accounts on deck. He had need for looking into his accounts as he had parted with £25,000 to the husband of Mrs Roberts, blackmail. Led into this trap by Captain Arthur, the devil'.[53]

Four years later the blackmailers fell out and went to court; the victim of the blackmail was referred to as 'Mr A.' but his true identity was soon known.[54] When this happened Hari Singh felt deeply humiliated and became a very bitter man, who henceforth distrusted British people and, when in 1925 he became the Maharaja, he got rid of most of his British advisers and appointed Hindus from Kashmir and Jammu.

But back in Kashmir, before the humiliation, he developed a good relationship with Biscoe; he attended a gymnastic display at the school[55] and they worked together on the food troubles that continued to beset Kashmir. The postwar food shortages around the world made it highly profitable for powerful people in the State to export Kashmiri grains illegally. Early in 1921 the old Maharaja was given full powers to deal with this[56] and Narendra Nath Koul was back in Kashmir in the higher post of Revenue Minister. He at once called round him his old friends and held councils of war and was soon at the attack on the enemy, not on the *Zamindars* and agriculturalists, but upon the middlemen and interlopers called *galladars*. His scheme was to create a Citizen Co-operative Society which would purchase grain from farmers, oust the middlemen, and distribute it to the city people at a fair price.[57]

Much to the disgust of the Maharaja, Hari Singh joined those who were opposing the food profiteers and called a public meeting which went from 3 pm to midnight and heard 19 witnesses. Biscoe wrote to London:

> Raja Hari Singh's Great Committee meeting re rice profiteering. I sat solid with him and three others on Committee. He was splendid!! He talked just like a young sahib saying how he would like to punch their heads etc, it was great! When he asked me, as one of the witnesses, how I would deal with the profiteers I answered, 'Have them up and give them a sound thrashing.' 'Yes,' said he, 'You as a school master could do that but I fear I could not.'[58]

The Co-op Society was formed in August with a board of 16 directors and a management committee, which included Shenker Koul the headmaster of the Mission Schools. Cecil Hadow was elected Director and Samuel Bakkal was made Executive Officer to oversee the distribution of grain.[59] Staff and boys of the schools were deployed in fast boats to find barges of grain hidden in backwaters, and to help with food distribution as previously and to outwit those who opposed them.

In October the new Viceroy, Lord Reading, who had succeeded Chelmsford earlier in the year, made a State visit to Kashmir. As with Hardinge's visit in 1912 Biscoe organised for the school to give him a living welcome.[60]

Three days later Hadow and Biscoe were ordered to be at the Residency to meet the Viceroy for an update on the food shortages in Kashmir.[61] They told him that senior officials were at the bottom of it, money making. He said he guessed this and hence a law was needed to meet the situation. He invited them to smoke his cigars while he and Sir Grimwood Mears drafted a new law. On his return he read, 'Anyone caught profiteering shall be fined Rs1,000 and imprisoned with hard labour for one year.' 'I thank you for your help but I must ask you to come again this evening when I shall have all officials present.' Hadow says, 'Sir, may I tell you this when you ask the Governor the cause of the shortage of food he will tell you on account of the shortage of transport.' At the evening meeting the Governor did indeed say that the shortages were due to lack of transport but the Viceroy then asked Narendra Nath the Revenue Minister who contradicted the Governor.

At the State Banquet ten days later the Maharaja had to read out the new law against food profiteers composed by the Viceroy; nominate the new council, Hari Singh being Chief with Narendra Nath; and dismiss Diwan Bishen Das and his brother.

Tragically, six weeks later Narendra Nath died from internal haemorrhage as a result of complications after surgery. Biscoe went to his house at 10.30 am and spoke to the mourners all sitting on the floor in silence.[62] At 2 pm the funeral started. In front of the bier walked priests and his eldest son, aged 12 years; thousands of people followed among them the British Resident. The slow march took one and a half hours to the burning *ghat*; women all along the route wailing, 'our friend has gone'. A few days later a great gathering was held in the school compound to raise a memorial to him and Biscoe spoke:

Our friend is not dead, he lives and his spirit will remain with us to help us in the fight against oppression and wrong; for wrong and oppression it is when a country is allowed to be under the power of a handful of scoundrels who starve a city in order that they themselves may be rich.[63]

Raja Hari Singh voiced similar sentiments at another public meeting called by him.[64]

The Viceroy's law and the co-op grain stores brought the crisis to a close. Samuel Bakkal worked tirelessly as the Executive Officer until his own death in 1926.

During his leave in England in 1919 Biscoe's great friend and colleague, Arthur Neve died suddenly from the scourge of influenza that swept the world, killing more people than all those who died in World War I. Neve had just returned to his work in Kashmir after serving with Indian troops in France for the past three years. Henry Holland, who was in Kashmir at the time, wrote to London:

It is with a very heavy heart that I write to tell you about dear Arthur Neve's home call. He contracted influenza on Saturday 30 August and passed away on 5 September. His brain was affected very early on in his illness and for the last 20 hours he was quite un-conscious, recognising no one. His wife, Ernest and Miss Neve were with him at the last. All through the dear fellow never complained in any way and was always thinking of his work and of others. Poor Mrs Neve is naturally very bowled over. We laid dear Arthur to rest on Saturday at 6 pm. He was given a military funeral and I have never seen such universal sympathy and sorrow. There must have been a crowd of over 2000 at the graveside.[65]

Publication of Two Books

While in England renewing his ties with his wife and family, Biscoe wrote two books on Kashmir. He wrote *Kashmir in Sunlight and Shade*, which had been requested by Seeley Service in 1910 and it

179

was published by them in 1922. He also expanded and brought up to date the pamphlet he had published in 1909, *Character Building in Kashmir*, which followed the same format as the earlier pamphlet by comparing the conditions in Kashmir when he first went there in 1890 with the changes that had occurred in the 28 years since then. It particularly emphasised the social services that the staff and boys undertook in Srinagar city and in Islamabad and, in the new edition he described the work that the schools did during the artificial food shortages in the city during 1917 and 1918 caused by the hoarding of grain by food profiteers. The new edition was published in 1920 in London by the CMS as a small book with the same title and it carried a foreword by Baden-Powell. It was reviewed by E.M. Forster, along with two other books by missionaries, in October of that year.[66]

At the time when he wrote his review Forster had spent a total of three months in India in 1912, as the guest of a minor Raja, Dewas Senior, in Central India, and was planning to visit him again in 1921 with the hope that he would there be inspired to complete the novel on India that he had begun in 1912. This he did with the publication of *A Passage to India* in 1924,[67] recognised as his greatest book and a classic commentary on India in the time of the British Raj. His review of the three books in the *Athanaeum* began with an overview of missionary endeavour in China, India and Africa. Its rise, he wrote, coincided with the Industrial Revolution and the development of a leisured middle class who, mindful of the Gospel injunction, prepared to evangelise the heathen, especially in the expanding British Empire. Much unselfishness and heroism went to the growth of missions but they also met a home need. There was surplus money in England seeking a sentimental outlet and much of it was spent trying to alter the opinions and habits of people whom they had not seen. In the aftermath of World War I, Forster foresaw the demise of foreign missionary endeavour because of the drastic decline in available resources to fund it and the profound loss of credibility of the Christian message in the wake of the dreadful conflict between Christian countries in Europe. After extolling the virtues of the first two books Forster turns to the third:

But now it is time, yea high time to turn to the Rev C.E. Tyndale-Biscoe MA, headmaster of the CMS School at Srinagar and to the deeds for the Empire and Christianity that he has wrought in that city. There is no rubbish about sympathy now. Take the Kashmiri by the scruff of his neck; that is the only way you can strengthen his backbone. Kick him about until he has learned Boy Scout methods. Srinagar was a cesspool, moral and physical, when Mr Tyndale-Biscoe arrived – Brahmanism and corruption, early marriages, cruelty to animals, nor did the population wash. Not boys were his pupils but jelly-fish: he can only call them jelly-fish, bundles of dirty linen; and he started their education by throwing them into the River Jhelum, then he caned and fined them and bullied them into breaking caste, and mocked their religious observances, also thwarting and insulting their parents whenever opportunity occurred, for he knew that whatever Indians think right is bound to be wrong and that the British Raj exists in order that missionaries may drive this home.

Mr Biscoe's success in passing on his knowledge is immense. Srinagar totters under his blows: he tells us so and missionaries always tell the truth, especially when they are schoolmasters. And even if he exaggerated, his book remains valuable, for it indicates the sort of person who is still trotting about in India. The Indian climate has much to answer for but it can seldom have produced anything quite so odd as *Character Building in Kashmir* – anything quite so noisy, meddlesome and self righteous, so heartless and brainless, so full of racial and religious swank. What is the aim of such a book? As the Rev. C.E. Tyndale-Biscoe MA himself puts it, 'Qui bono?' And why has the Church Missionary Society published it? For it is bound to create grave prejudices against their other workers in the Foreign Field.

Amid such varied efforts does the labour go forward, the labour of imposing a single religion upon the terrestrial globe. It is an extraordinary ideal, whatever one's personal sympathies, and it will bulk more largely than we realise in our history when that history comes to be written. To what extent

Christians still hope for their universal harvest it is not easy to say. They think it right not to give up hope, but that is rather different. They can scarcely ignore the double blow that the war has dealt to Missions – cutting off their funds and discrediting the Gospel of Peace at its source.[68]

How much of the book did Forster read? Certainly he read Biscoe's early experiences but these were nearly 30 years ago and presented in the book, as in many of his other writings, to contrast with the present in 1920. There is no acknowledgement that it was the Kashmiri masters and boys who were engaged in the various activities – fighting fires, saving animals, taking patients from the hospital on trips on the lake and making grain available at affordable prices. It is the style of the book, pitched to the main body of supporters who were old India hands, which seems to have particularly offended Forster. But the venom of his criticism has a deeper significance. Biscoe had an abiding hatred of homosexuality that began with his own experiences at Bradford College as a small boy about to be raped by an older boy. He fought against paedophiles in Srinagar when they attempted to attract young boys in the school and he used all his influence with the British Resident to get foreigners seeking young Kashmiris for sex expelled from the State. Because of his own experience as a boy he did not differentiate between paedophilia and homosexuality. Forster was a covert homosexual in Britain who felt liberated when he visited India in 1912 and was accepted sympathetically by the Raja of Dewas Senior.[69] In 1920 he had recently experienced a deep and passionate relationship with an Egyptian man and was planning to revisit Dewas Senior the next year to resume his long-standing friendship with Syed Ross Masood. He would have clearly detected Biscoe's prejudices against his own sexual preferences, which were then illegal in Britain, and his strong reaction to this may have coloured his opinion of the book. Biscoe did not 'trot around India' and he actually had very good relationships with many Kashmiris, both Brahmin and Muslim. None of the things he described in the book could have been achieved without the wholehearted support of the Kashmiri staff themselves. He did not impose his ideas on them and more significantly he never pressured anyone to convert to Christianity, quite the reverse; he was far more interested in what a person did than what he professed to believe.

There is no evidence that Biscoe, or for that matter the CMS, were ever aware of Forster's review. Had he read it, it is quite likely he would have quoted from it. He had a saying he posted in the school, 'They say, what do they say? Let them say what they say.' After his later book, *Kashmir in Sunlight and Shade*, was published in 1922 it received a critical review from the *New York Times*, which Biscoe always included in the selection of reviews:

> We know the kidney of the writer of this book, the Britisher who sits in his easy chair all day eating beef steaks and drinking whisky pegs [...] The writer of this book knows nothing of the soul of the people and lacks the one saving grace of humour. This last, I guess, is some Review!![70]

Certainly I never heard of it during the life of my father and only became aware of it recently in the1976 book on Forster by G.K. Das.[71]

By contrast with Forster, A.S.N. Wadia, a professor from Elphinstone College, Bombay, visited Kashmir in 1919 and wrote about the Mission School while Biscoe was in England:

> But more striking still was the institution I visited next day. It was a missionary school established and conducted by one who, having been imbued from his youth with the highest Christian ideals burned to realise them as well and as fully as he could in the youth he found around him in his own limited sphere of life [...]
>
> The only sure way of doing permanent good to a suffering people was to make the people themselves the regenerators of their own decayed manhood and the menders of their own misfortunes, natural and otherwise. With this idea our young Christian enthusiast thought of helping the people by teaching them to help themselves. He knew of course that he could not hope to do much with the grown up. They were a hopeless and

irreclaimable lot and any time and effort spent on them would be so much time and effort wasted. But with their children it would be otherwise. They were plastic and impressionable and if caught early enough and persevered with could certainly be moulded and made to respond to better influences [...] Biscoe was aware that merely pumping into minds of the young sound principles of Christian conduct and great ideals of Christian life without at the same time giving them opportunities to put these principles into practice in their day to day life would only end in turning the youths into mere enthusiastic bores and insufferable little prigs. So the first thing he made the boys do was to go out into the streets and work out amid the immediate limitations discouragements and disappointments of actual life the great things they were taught in school.

To cut a long story short the grand result of this noble idea and Christian endeavour carried over a period of thirty long years in face of strong opposition and caste prejudices is – the Biscoe Boy, who is now the pride of Srinagar and the hope of Kashmir. Many a noble tale of his chivalry and manhood are told in the streets of Srinagar and even in the far off valleys. [I]f ever I came across a Kashmiri upright in bearing and conduct he invariably turned out to be an old Biscoe Boy.[72]

With the hindsight of 60 years Mangan, in his book *The Games Ethic and Imperialism*, supports Wadia's assessment, while recognising the strictures expressed by Forster. He considers Biscoe to be, 'the preux chevalier of imperial Christian knights [...] a man of astounding tenacity, courage and compassion', but 'there can be no denying Tyndale-Biscoe's bigotry, ruthlessness and occasional insensitivity in striving to achieve these aims'.[73]

The Amritsar Massacre of 13 April 1919

But to return to Forster: he wrote his review 18 months after the horrific events of April 1919 in Amritsar when over 300 people were shot to death in the Jallianwala Garden on the orders of the British military commander and which event only gradually became known in England during the subsequent months. The experience of one English woman was published in May 1920, which Forster drew on for a major scene in *A Passage to India*. Forster's views of the British administration in India were deeply affected by those events and he wrote two articles on the subject early in 1920; he would have seen Biscoe as a representative of the people responsible for Amritsar, and he would have been correct to draw that inference but it is necessary to go back a few years to put it in context.

Baden-Powell and Biscoe were in full accord on the primacy of the British Empire and its beneficial effects for all subject races. While it was important to encourage education to produce good citizens who were honest, courageous and socially aware, they abhorred educated Indians who sought independence from Britain. In this they were with the majority of British people in India who treated all attempts by educated Indians for a greater share in the Government of India and, ultimately, full independence, as seditious.

Biscoe expressed his views on the importance of discipline in the 1912 log:

I especially bring out this point now as the Commission on the Civil Service is now travelling round India. Englishmen and Indians are being asked their reasons for or against giving Indians a greater share in the administration of this country. How are undisciplined men to become able administrators and leaders of men?

I notice that many advocate Indians going to the Universities in England to be trained, but surely that is too late. If they are ever to become men in the true sense of the word they will need a little knocking about in a public school and above all for administration honesty is needed. How is this to be learnt or ingrained?

Everyone agrees that most if not all English boys need the rough and tumble of school life if they are to be leaders of men; why then should Indian boys be an exception? They are not exceptions and that is why the disease of swelled head is an epidemic among the educated class. It is discipline they need and hence the importance of schools which believe in discipline.[74]

This view was prevalent before the outbreak of World War I but was muted during hostilities because 1.3 million Indians offered their service to Britain and fought against the Germans in France and against the Turks in the Middle East; of these, 70,000 lost their lives. The Lieutenant-Governor of the Punjab, Sir Michael O'Dwyer, was particularly successful in recruiting Punjabi men to serve but he was also a firm believer in not giving Indians more power to govern and in condign punishment for those who disagreed with him. Early in 1916 as a result of political troubles he established a Special Tribunal which condemned 24 men to death for sedition. The Viceroy, Lord Hardinge, was appalled by the severity of the sentences and made a special visit to Lahore where he categorically declined to endorse the sentences. O'Dwyer offered to commute six of the sentences but Hardinge said he would only allow the six actually convicted of murder to be executed. For his leniency he was attacked in the Anglo-Indian press,[75] which expressed the prevailing views of the British in India who deeply feared any hint of uprising by Indians.

Shortly after he had made these awful decisions the Viceroy, at a Vice Regal Garden Party in Delhi, unburdened himself to Biscoe who wrote in his diary, 'Lord Hardinge called me for a talk and told me much interesting matter, re keeping India quiet, he had had to hang several babus.'[76] Later that year O'Dwyer was in Kashmir and visited the Mission Schools[77] where he presented a Challenge Cup for drill.

It is clear that Biscoe's sympathies lay firmly with the British establishment. In a church service for British volunteers of the Indian Defence Force that September, Biscoe preached the sermon based on the words of Psalm 115 2–9, 'Where is now their God?' the taunt of enemies to exiles and to those building the city wall. 'I likened our efforts of Church building to building a city, our material rubble, our enemies etc. and asked for their help.'[78] The words of the Psalm refer to those who worship idols, so the enemy he alludes to is not Germany with which they were at war, but Hindus.

When the India Defence League was founded in 1933 by Winston Churchill and other British people opposed to relinquishing political power to Indians, Biscoe joined it.[79] In this he was not unusual as many missionaries in India also expressed revulsion at Hindu beliefs and practices and were convinced that Indians would not be ready for self government for a very long time to come.[80]

The Indian National Congress under the leadership of Mohandas Gandhi supported the war effort but with the expectation that after hostilities ceased India would move to full independence. It was not to be. Within months of the Armistice the government in India introduced new regulations in the form of the Rowlatt Act, which retained emergency wartime measures and curtailed any expression of independence. To Congress and educated Indians this was a flagrant betrayal of India's record in the war just ended. When the bill was debated in the Legislative Council the Indian members unanimously condemned it and Mohammad Ali Jinnah the leader of the Muslim League said:

> If these measures are passed you will create in the country from one end to the other a discontent and agitation the like of which you have not witnessed, and it will have a most disastrous effect on the good relations that have existed between the Government and the people.[81]

When it was passed in March 1919 Jinnah and several other members resigned and Gandhi called a *hartal* or general strike across India as a peaceful protest against the new Act.

In Amritsar the protest was led by two distinguished lawyers, who supported the movement for self government: Dr Saif-ud-Din Kitchlow was a Kashmiri Muslim, who had been educated at Cambridge at the same time as Pundit Jawaharlal Nehru, obtained a PhD from Munster University and had been a member of Lincoln's Inn, London; Dr Satyapal was a Hindu who had been educated at Lahore where he had been an outstanding medical student and during the war had served with the Indian Medical Service. The protest on 30 March 1919 went off peacefully and a second protest called for 6 April was also peaceful with Hindus and Muslims in amicable unity. This show of unity alarmed O'Dwyer and he threatened dire consequences for anyone opposing the Rowlatt Act; he gave orders to prevent Gandhi entering the Punjab and he ordered Drs Kitchlow and Satyapal to be deported from Amritsar to a remote location.

The civil administrator of Amritsar, Miles Irvine, decided to do this by inviting the two men to his house and then secretly removing them with the hope that the protest would fizzle out. Unfortunately his deception had the reverse effect; it provoked widespread anger in the city and many thousands came on to the streets to protest at the illegal arrest of their leaders. When they refused to disperse, the frightened and severely outnumbered forces opened fire and several protesters were killed and injured. This infuriated the crowd which began to attack British buildings and people and to chant, '*Hindu Mussulman ki jai!*' (long live Hindus and Muslims). First, two Banks in Amritsar were attacked and the British managers were bludgeoned to death and then burnt on piles of bank furniture; then the Women's Hospital was attacked but the English doctor was bravely protected by her Indian colleague and escaped; then a missionary teacher, Marcella Sherwood, who had worked in Amritsar for 15 years and was cycling to her girls' school to close it, was beaten to the ground and left for dead. She only survived when frightened Indians nearby took her into their house and protected her from the angry crowd.

Realising that the city was out of control, Irvine called on the Lieutenant-Governor in Lahore for help and O'Dwyer ordered an army unit to Amritsar under the command of General Reginald Dyer and it arrived on the night of 11 April. On the morning of 12 April, Dyer declared martial law throughout the whole city and refused to allow more than four people to accompany each funeral of those killed two days before. On the morning of 13 April, he led a procession of troops through the city with a town crier declaring that he had imposed military control and forbidding any assembly of people and a curfew at night. But he did not cover the whole city and particularly did not go near the Sikh Golden Temple or the Jallianwala Bagh where country folk were gathering for the Hindu festival of Baisakhi, and where a public meeting had been called for that afternoon; under the newly promulgated regulations that was now illegal. Unaware of the order an estimated 40,000 people were in the enclosed Jallianwala Bagh that afternoon from which there was only one exit. At 5.15 pm General Dyer arrived with 50 armed soldiers who he immediately ordered to open fire on the people and continue to fire into them until they had expended 1,650 rounds of .303 ammunition. He then ordered the troops to return to their barracks and himself drove away, leaving about 300 dead and 10,000 injured. Although he was at the time the commanding officer in the city he did nothing for the casualties of the ten-minute carnage. In subsequent inquiries that were held into the events of that afternoon there was a strong suspicion that the whole action had been deliberately set up by O'Dwyer to deliver a severe and exemplary punishment on the people of Amritsar and so avert worse troubles in the Punjab.

Certainly Dyer thought he had performed a necessary and effective response to the events of two days before and avenged the deaths of the British men. He was especially outraged by the assault on Miss Sherwood and the attempted assault of the woman doctor and set in motion a whole series of orders designed to humiliate the Indian populace. Every Indian was ordered to bow low when passing any British person, and in the narrow street where Miss Sherwood was assaulted all Indians had to crawl on their stomachs thereby fouling their clothes and person; no one was exempt, even the Hindu family who had protected her. Those who had assaulted her were whipped in the same street. When the shopkeepers in Amritsar and in Lahore closed their shops in protest they were ordered to open up or face public whipping. The crawling order was too much for O'Dwyer who countermanded it after several days but other humiliating orders were enforced.

News of what had happened in the Punjab was slow to reach Delhi, because O'Dwyer controlled the news outlets, but a week after the massacre when C.F. Andrews learnt from an eye witness of the public whippings administered to shopkeepers who kept up the *hartal* and to others he was incensed.[82] On 21 April he fired off two angry letters to the Viceroy, Chelmsford. 'Of all the insults and humiliations this is the one which will rankle most and will never be forgiven. Do you realise the loathing, the hatred against the oppressor that it engendered?' He concluded, 'I know the provocation of the outrages on Europeans in Amritsar but this public whipping is being done in cold blood.' India's great poet, Rabindranath Tagore was so outraged that he publicly returned his Knighthood to the Viceroy.

Reaction of Biscoe and Other Missionaries

At the time of these events Biscoe was in Kashmir preparing to leave for furlough in Britain; he travelled through Lahore on 30 April en route to a ship in Bombay but makes no mention in his diary of what is happening there. However, he had been in Lahore the previous January when he had met the Vice Chancellor of the University of the Punjab and the military commander, Colonel Frank Johnson, who had been a partner with Biscoe's brother Ted in a Mashonaland gold mine during 1890–1910. As they discussed the current unrest over the proposed Rowlatt Bill, Johnson had said, 'what the natives need is the jambock'. Biscoe commented in his diary:

> His words were prophetic for within a few months he was in command of Lahore in the days of mutiny and with his triangle and cat-o-nine tails brought the city to law and order in a marvellous short time. And when he left he was the most popular man among the populace for he reduced the food crisis with the help of the triangle and cat.[83]

Biscoe's attitude, reflected in these comments, was not exceptional among the missionary community in Lahore and Amritsar. A week after the massacre the head of the CMS in Lahore wrote to London:

> Seditious rioting in the Punjab
> It was found necessary to put Amritsar under strict martial law and a gathering which took place on Sunday 13th in

defiance of military orders and refused to disperse was fired upon by troops and several hundreds were killed and wounded. This seems to have had a salutary effect and many ringleaders in Amritsar have been arrested. The shops are now open and everything is said to be quiet, under martial law which is being strictly enforced. Most of the Europeans are still in the Fort, but the girls of the Alexandra and Middle schools and the ladies in charge of them are now in the Alexandra school buildings under protection [...]

No one can say how long the present state of affairs will continue. The result must inevitably be much hindrance to missionary work and also bitterness of feeling between Europeans and Indians. Even Mr Gandhi now sees that he has made a mistake and has aroused passions which he cannot control. He is now advising the cessation of all resistance to authority at all events for the present and Mrs Besant is also giving the same advice. We are fortunate in having so strong a Lieut. Governor as Sir Michael O'Dwyer at the head of the Punjab Government at such a crisis.[84]

A year later the assessment of the Lahore Mission headquarters was sombre:

If anything the country folk seem to be more friendly than ever. Never before did we receive such a hearty welcome back [...] The danger is of course the villagers becoming disaffected by contact with the people of the cities. Great efforts are being made by the extremists to poison their minds against the Government and all its ways.

The people of the towns, especially those of Amritsar, are most hostile, and seem to have a deadly hatred for the English. I very much doubt if it will be safe for English ladies ever to work in the city of Amritsar again. I have heard that it has been said that as they have been made to suffer so much for the assault on one English lady they will see to it that when the next chance offers they will make a bigger job of it and give the English something to remember, or words to that effect.[85]

Dyer was generally commended for his action by the British authorities and British people in India. Indeed, many thought his action had prevented wholesale mutiny and, as time passed he also came to believe that. However, when the events of April–May 1919 reached Britain the government set up a Royal Commission on which British and Indian judges sat and it condemned the actions of Dyer and O'Dwyer. When he was questioned by the Indian judges, Sir Chimanlal Setalvad and Pandit Jagat Narayan, of the commission, Dyer was unable to defend his actions adequately and was condemned out of his own mouth to the acute embarrassment of his colleagues.[86] A year later in Kashmir the Maharaja gave a Garden Party at Nishat Bagh. Col. C.F. Johnson was there and he told Biscoe of the trial of General Dyer. 'The babu lawyer who gave him such trouble was sitting at the next table.'[87]

Dyer was retired from the army and invalided to England where he did not long survive. O'Dwyer, who had reached the end of his tenure as Lieutenant-Governor also retired to England where he maintained a campaign to vindicate himself and Dyer, without success; he was shot in 1940 by a young Sikh while attending a meeting in London. His killer was hanged but after Indian independence his remains were returned to India, where he was regarded as a national hero, and interred in Amritsar.

With the hindsight of a century, it is easy to see the folly and wanton cruelty of the British administration that opposed the demands of the educated Indian population for the right to govern themselves and their growing frustration at being denied it; and then a seemingly minor action by an unprepared administrator flared up into a terrible massacre of unsuspecting people. While a very few British people, like Andrews and Forster saw what was happening and where it was leading, the great majority, which included Biscoe, were trapped in the immediate circumstances and events and reacted accordingly. Forster scorned Biscoe because he saw him as a representative of the order that he deplored and which his book later helped to abolish. However, between 1920 and 1924 he may have changed his views about what Biscoe was doing in Kashmir and his good relationship with his staff and students because the character in *A Passage to India* that most resembles

Biscoe is Fielding, the Principal of the College, rather than the ineffectual missionaries.

Whether or not Biscoe would have been swayed by Forster's strictures if he had read them cannot be known, but he certainly did not change his ways and the next decade saw him tackle another social problem in Srinagar – the remarriage of Hindu widows and the subjugation of young girls and women that it represented. This had its beginning in Kate Knowles dispensary and school at Habba Kadal in 1907 and Violet Fitze's school that succeeded it but only came to fruition 20 years later.

6

Succession and Success, 1923–33

A wonderful thing has happened […] Widows are at last emancipated! This has been worth living for.[1]

Cecil Tyndale-Biscoe turned 60 in February 1923 and his succession was being discussed in the Church Missionary Society (CMS) in London.[2] In 1927, when he was 64, his son Eric joined him and thereafter was the de facto principal, although never acknowledged as such. His views on Indian independence were far more in tune with public events than Biscoe's and his influence on the development in the schools prepared the staff for the profound transition to Indian independence, the severing of the ties with the CMS in London and the long-term viability of the institution.

The place of women and girls in Kashmir society had exercised Biscoe since Kate Knowles' work from 1907 to 1912 but it truly came to fruition in the mid-twenties with the arrival of Muriel Mallinson to run the girls' school and the first successful remarriage of two Hindu widows.

This decade also saw the rise of political awareness among the Muslim population in Kashmir, which coincided with the collapse of the world economic system after 1929, and the demand for freedom from Dogra rule which was perceived to be illegitimate.

While all these matters occurred concurrently they are treated here sequentially.

Succession – Eric Tyndale-Biscoe

While he was at Haileybury College, Eric had become alienated from his father, who was absent for most of those four years. He was close to his mother who made a home for the family in England so that when he completed his university course at Cambridge he had determined to migrate to Australia to take up farming. He had studied Agriculture at Cambridge and he had no interest in being associated with any sort of educational institution and not much interest in conventional religion or missionaries. He had little in common with his father and less interest in his work. By this time both his parents were back in Kashmir and at the end of 1923 he decided to visit them, primarily to see his mother, before migrating to Australia. He arrived in Srinagar in January 1924 and was soon overwhelmed by the Kashmir spring; he painted lovely watercolours of the familiar birds in his parent's garden – the bulbul, the myna, the bee-eater and the kingfisher – and sketched the waters of the Wular Lake and later Nil Nag. But more importantly he learnt that his father was not the doctrinaire missionary he feared he was but was a true social reformer, who worked with the men and boys that looked to him as their leader. Biscoe soon had him teaching the senior science classes and participating in all the unconventional activities of the schools. He was won over and by mid year asked his father whether he could join him in the work.

This posed a problem for Biscoe; earlier that year he had floated the idea with CMS that his second son might succeed him, 'Julian has his thoughts towards Kashmir re relieving me later on. He possesses the go and pluck that is needed and would I know make a splendid 2nd to Jack Dugdale'.[3] In reality this would not happen; Julian was too much like his father[4] to ever be his subordinate and he made his life in Africa. On the other hand Eric would willingly follow him, despite knowing that Julian was the favoured son.

Biscoe's colleague at the time was Jack Dugdale, who had been in Kashmir since Frank Lucey left in 1921, so there was no hope that the CMS would fund a third missionary for the Kashmir schools and Eric could only join him if additional funds could be raised to support his salary. By the end of 1924 Biscoe had found two parishes, one in England and one in Ireland, which were willing to support Eric if he was accepted by the CMS. Unexpectedly, Eric received an offer of a teaching position at a private school in New Zealand that was looking for an Oxford or Cambridge man to teach agriculture to the sons of farmers; Biscoe encouraged him to accept the job for two years as it would give him good experience for teaching in Kashmir later. So in January 1925 Eric sailed for New Zealand, rather than Australia, where he taught for two years at the Wanganui Collegiate School and where he met Phyllis Long, also a Cambridge graduate teaching at the nearby Nga Tawa School for Girls.[5] They both returned to England in 1927 where he was accepted as a missionary by the CMS and they became engaged to be married. However, a young missionary was not allowed to marry until he had passed his first language exam, so he left for Kashmir in August 1927 and she waited in England for another year.

Meanwhile in Kashmir Jack Dugdale's health had deteriorated and he was unable to stay in Kashmir. Biscoe was hoping to be able to recruit another person to take his place but the CMS decided that Eric would fulfil that need. However, the old antipathy in local missionary circles to Biscoe and his unconventional ideas was again expressed by Force Jones, the Lahore Secretary in a letter to London:

> I hear rumours that Eric Tyndale-Biscoe has been accepted for Kashmir. I do not know whether this is true or not. The future of the school there needs careful consideration. One wonders whether when a change of headship becomes necessary a possible change of methods may not be desirable. Tyndale-Biscoe has done magnificently and much that he has done will stand and bring fruit, but India is changing and the methods which have done so well in the past are not necessarily the methods which ought or could be adopted today.[6]

The 'careful consideration' he referred to was the imminent closure of the schools in Kashmir because they did not produce Christians and Biscoe would not employ Indian Christian staff, preferring Kashmiris of whatever religion. Neither the very considerable achievement of remarriage of Hindu widows nor the remarkable record of social service by the staff and students of the Mission Schools, to be described below, carried any weight for the officers of the CMS in Lahore. But far from proving to be out of date Biscoe's methods would soon be shown to be more relevant in the emerging India as Eric and Phyllis introduced new ideas and attitudes to the established traditions of the institution.

The New Partnership

Eric joined the school staff in Kashmir in September 1927 at the same time as Douglas Barton was appointed to the Kashmir Mission Hospital as a junior doctor under Earnest Neve. Both were the sons of missionaries and had been born in Kashmir and both were sent to Haileybury College but had very different experiences because they were in different houses; so much depended on the housemaster and how he controlled the boys in his care. Unlike Eric, Douglas had thoroughly enjoyed his time at school.

For their first year they lived with the Biscoes while they were learning Urdu and Kashmiri and found that they shared similar views on religion and society. After passing their first Urdu exams a year later, both married accomplished women. Mary Barton was a medical doctor and joined the Women's Hospital at Rainawari and Phyllis (Phil) was soon participating in the junior school and the girls' school. The two couples shared holidays together at Nil Nag, and both doctors helped with school events in a medical capacity. Eric and Douglas were each working with men who had become used to unquestioned acceptance of their own authority and points of view, and while Eric and his father seemed to have had a good relationship, few junior doctors stayed long under Ernest Neve. The last one had been Charlie McLean in 1924 who had lasted less than two years.[7] Douglas lasted five years and had some very critical things to say about medical missions at the end; Eric and Phil remained in Kashmir for 20 years and much later returned twice, in 1960-62 and 1968.

While always acknowledging the originality and force of his father's ideas and achievements, Eric quietly moved the emphasis away from the imperial trappings that had featured prominently under Biscoe towards more emphasis on sound education and social equality; less confrontation and more mutual respect. In this he was greatly supported by Phil who was determined from the beginning to get to know the Kashmiri staff and their wives as friends.

In the 1928 log – for which Douglas Barton drew the cover – Eric contrasted his experiences of teaching in a traditional British school in New Zealand with the very different ethos of the Mission Schools in Kashmir. He wrote:

On the walls of the Upper School Hall are large boards on which are lists of boys' names. In early years the head of the school used to have his name written on a board. Now that is gone; after all it is a gift to be clever and there is no great honour in becoming top of the class or for that matter excelling in sport. So now that board has the name of the boy who by his fellows is voted to be the finest character. Now in spite of our school being a mixture of Hindus and Muslims, we never find the voting goes on communal lines, so in that way we seem to be ahead of the legislative assemblies of India.

A second board is for athletics. Athletics may be looked upon as an end in themselves i.e. pot hunting, or they may be looked upon as a means of becoming strong and plucky and quiet and self-reliant in order to be of service to others; therefore we do not put on the board the highest jumper or the fastest runner but only those feats which need pluck or grit, eg jumping from the school roof, 50 feet into the river or swimming five miles across the dreaded Wular Lake.

There are yet more important boards however. Those in which boys have shown that they have soul – deeds of kindness and pluck to save others. Here each year we put up the bravest deed in saving life out of the many that occur, and on another board we put the kindest deed to animals during the year. This latter perhaps deserves a moment's consideration for one sees the claims of religion being overridden by the claims of love. A Hindu boy carries the load for a lame donkey (a donkey is unclean to him); a Muslim boy takes a bone out of the throat of a pariah dog. Imagine the pluck needed for this; a half wild dog in pain and above all he must not touch a dog as it is unclean. Finally we come to the last and noblest board of all, those who have given their lives for others [...] Every day when the school assembles for roll call they face that board [...] and without any words the message of love is shown to them in deeds.[8]

Very much on his mind when he wrote that would have been the death of Samuel Bakkal a year earlier.[9] Twenty years before Samuel had been Biscoe's first convert from Islam to Christianity (see Chapter 4) and later served in the Middle East during the war; he came back to Kashmir and because he was incorruptible he was made Chief Controller of Grains for the Kashmir Government and the strain of that work lowered his resistance to pneumonia and he died at the age of 38. Two thousand Muslims attended the funeral.

Six months later another valiant old boy of the Mission School met his death, because he refused to accept bribes.[10] Chimed Gergan came from Leh; his father, who was the leader of a small group of Ladakhi Christians, sent him to the Mission School where he lived in the hostel and was a leader in school activities. After completing school he got a job with the Kashmir Forest Department and was given the task of preventing the illicit trade in *kuth*.[11] This plant grows wild at high altitude and the root was collected and exported through Bombay to China where it was much prized for incense. It was a State monopoly but because of its great value much of it was smuggled out of Kashmir by well organised thieves who bribed the officials. Chimed captured five *kuth* thieves in Baltistan and brought them safely to Kargil where the *Tehsildar* let them go. Chimed wrote to Biscoe about this, thanked him for his kindness and wished him farewell, knowing that on his return the men would try to kill him. He captured 35 smugglers and their loot and when he refused to accept their large bribes he was murdered by them.

On the Mission School's main playing field two mulberry trees were planted at one end as the goal posts and on each was fixed a brass plate with the name of Samuel Bakkal on one and Chimed Gergan on the other.[12] Biscoe chose mulberry trees because they live for 200 years but twelve years later the trees were cut down and the plaques lost during the school's lowest point.

To commemorate the Mission School's Jubilee, Eric expanded his account into a book, *Fifty Years Against the Stream*, which was published in India at the end of 1930. It described the condition of Kashmir in 1880 and its recent history and later chapters treated the different aspects of the School and what it had achieved in social service and education in its first 50 years. It was similar to the smaller book published by Biscoe ten years earlier and like it carried a somewhat condescending foreword by Baden-Powell. Unlike the earlier book, which was published in London, it was not reviewed by E.M. Forster.

Like his father before him (see Chapter 1), Eric sought permission from the CMS to advance the time of his marriage on the grounds that he had fulfilled the probationary period by taking into account the year he spent in Kashmir in 1924, that he had completed his first Urdu exam, that the school would be short staffed when the Dugdales left and that his fiancé was a Cambridge graduate with three years teaching experience and so would attract an additional State Government Grant. London approved as a special case,[13] so Phil travelled to India and they were married at Jhelum in the Punjab on 16 November 1928. Douglas Barton was the best man, Lilian Underhill gave the bride away and they were married by Biscoe. Apart from Blanche and Lilian's husband the only other witnesses were two Kashmiris: Kallak Dar who became their house servant and Tara Chand Zalpuri, who was Biscoe's motor launch driver who had never been out of Kashmir before. Like Blanche and Cecil 37 years before they travelled up the Jhelum Valley road to Baramula and spent their honeymoon in a houseboat on the Wular Lake.

Phil had a fair idea of what to expect because she had heard Eric talk about Kashmir and his father's work a great deal in New Zealand, and she was attracted to what she heard as well as to Eric himself. Although a devout Christian she was not a missionary in the conventional sense, nor was she interested in the life of an

English memsahib in India; she was deeply interested in people and threw herself wholeheartedly into getting to know the Kashmiri staff of the Mission Schools, especially their wives and families. Eric and she set up home in a large house built on the same plan as the Biscoe's house in the Sheikh Bagh that had been built 30 years before for Douglas Barton's parents and was called Barton House. They occupied the first floor and offered the ground floor to another family. To the Kashmiris it was extraordinary that on marriage Eric would leave his parent's house and set up separately with his wife, for to them Phil's role was to serve her mother-in-law and how could she do this in another house? With her bobbed hair, athletic lifestyle and unconventional relationship with her in-laws she aroused the curiosity of the womenfolk she never met. When Nand Lal Munshi and Shenker Koul told Eric that their wives would like to meet her, a discrete meeting was arranged in a public park. She suggested to them that next time they should invite Eric as well, as it is not the English custom to do things separately. Eventually one or two were willing for both of them to visit their homes. He wrote:

> So it came about that we began to meet the families of our school staff. In some cases, we entered homes where my father had never been. Of course, at first, they would serve us only, plying us with *Moghul chai* – green tea boiling hot from the samovar, sweet and spiced with cinnamon, cardamoms and crushed almonds among other flavours. We had to learn how to drink this boiling hot tea from brass cups without handles. But they never partook themselves.
>
> The women became thrilled when Phil began to be able to speak to them in Kashmiri; for they were all illiterate, and knew no other language. In fact they became quite intimate, as when Shenker Koul's wife patted her on the tum in front of us all, and said anything inside here yet?[14]

In April she took part in the annual Wular Lake camp with the party of about 40 masters and boys, and in early July she and Eric led the first school party to climb Mahadeo, the 13,000 feet peak

Figure 20 Eric and Phil Tyndale-Biscoe, 1943

that overlooks the Dal Lake. By then she had acquired the nick name 'Bulbul' from the friendly little bird that frequents the gardens and verandas of Srinagar all year round. Two months later Nand Lal Munshi and Samsar Chand, with their wives and families spent a weekend with them in their brand new *doonga* at a secluded place called Nagin Bagh.[15] But still the women would not leave their homes and venture out to her home at Sheikh Bagh, which was understandable because some had never left their own homes since their marriage as young girls (see next section). What finally enticed them out was the arrival of Phil's son – yes, there was something inside – and eventually two wives came heavily veiled in completely covered tongas to see the baby. Phil had dug a sunken garden that provided the shy women with seclusion and from then on others came in larger numbers openly and without veils.[16]

During the next four years Phil and Eric initiated more encounters with the Hindu and Muslim masters and their wives. The July climb of Mahadeo became an annual event at which everyone had to carry their own bedding and they camped together in the unoccupied hill shelters built by the goat herders known as *Gujars*. At first Hindus and Muslims would not eat together and Phil and Eric had to eat separately. But by 1933 that restriction had broken down and everyone ate together.[17] This was all the more significant because Srinagar had been wracked by communal riots for the past two years (see below).

At the end of 1930 the Biscoes went to England on a year's furlough and Eric was left in charge of the schools. While Eric and Phil were growing into the work and initiating their own ideas with the support of Biscoe, the Bartons were not so fortunate and in 1932 they resigned from the Mission Hospital and left Kashmir. Douglas could not subscribe to the prevailing attitude that preaching the Gospel to Kashmiris who came to the hospital was more important than practising modern medicine– in this he was similar to Kate Knowles a generation before him. He offered his views to the CMS when he resigned but the response from Lahore was that there was no reason to listen to the views of someone who had a 'great theological unsettlement' and was departing after five years service![18] However, they probably should have listened to him for he summarises the real dilemmas facing the society in a fast changing world:

It must be clear to anyone who is interested in missions in general and the CMS in particular [...] that the position today is precarious. The financial situation is serious enough as everybody knows. This is in part due to the world wide economic depression but there is more to it than that. People are not supporting the CMS in the way they did. Why? Because the CMS falls theologically between two stools. It cannot take up the uncompromising attitude of the Bible Churchmen's Missionary Society, which still largely attracts the crudely minded; neither can they make a frank appeal to the modernist, who is prepared to shelve doctrine and concentrate on service.

The same thing exactly applies to candidates. They dare not accept young men and women who do not conform to the orthodox pattern for fear that if their heretical tendencies were made known CMS would lose many of the supporters they still have. And in this connection I may add that even when a candidate has successfully passed the soul-searching examinations and questionnaires of Committees at home and reaches the mission field, he still finds himself regarded as suspect by the older generation, who feel themselves called upon to act in loco parentis to his every action.

As regards the work in India [...] the more I see of evangelisation as such without education the more I feel that it is not only useless but worse than useless. The mind of the average Indian, born and bred in ignorance and superstition, has a fatal tendency to single out what is worst and meanest in orthodoxy and leave out all that is finest and best. They adopt the form of our services but not the spirit. They are willing to be saved by Christ but make no attempt to follow him. They accept the Old Testament picture of God rather than the New, and there is a notable difference between the two. Evangelisation without education is a waste of time money and effort.

Finally about medical work. When at home I was considering coming out as a missionary, the argument which had most weight with me was the need of the people out here. I was given to understand that it was only the mission hospitals which stood between these people and suffering and death. I have not found it so. It is true that the need is great, but that need is being met more thoroughly and more scientifically by the civil and military hospitals. The mission hospitals handicapped as they are by lack of funds, lack of equipment and lack of staff, cannot hope to compete. Here and there the hospital has a name behind it which goes back thirty or forty years, like Neve or Holland, but a hospital cannot be indefinitely supported on the reputation of a single man [...] If the Government hospitals can meet the physical needs of the people, and year by year they show themselves capable of doing so, it is far better that they should.[19]

His views expressed in this farewell letter reflect the dilemmas that had also plagued Biscoe throughout his career and probably reflected the conversations that Douglas and Mary had shared with Eric and Phil.

Relations with the Church Missionary Society in Lahore

As Douglas Barton had pointed out, the administrative centre of the CMS in Lahore was wrestling with how to maintain its many activities across northern India and Kashmir in the face of diminishing support from Britain for missionary work, as predicted nine years before by Forster,[20] and the impact in India of the global economic crisis. Faced with too little money to support all its educational institutions it resolved to apply its accepted policy and only support those of its schools that were fully staffed with Christian masters. When this criterion was applied the Kashmir schools failed and were recommended for closure to London.[21] The members of the council were acutely aware of the likely response from Kashmir, which was not represented at the meeting, and Force Jones wrote an explanation to head office, London:

I know it will be a bomb and will be said to be preposterous. We all know the splendid work that Biscoe has done and is doing. We are conscious that it is work which appeals to many outside the missionary circles but it is largely personal and Biscoe is not likely to be able to carry on many more years. What will happen then? The uplift work is beyond praise.

The European staff is a good one. They are doing a lot of good to the Kashmiris and are helped excellently by the Kashmiri masters (very nearly all non-Christian). The Resolution was not quite unanimous. Some suggested that Biscoe was so well known and his work so much appreciated that in the event of withdrawal he would raise enough to pay all the cost of the Kashmir schools himself. On the other hand Dugdale who felt the suggestion a mistake thought that Biscoe could not raise the extra money. He uses every spare moment to write letters now to supporters and could do no more.[22]

Biscoe's response was to show that the funds lost (66,000 rupees) would be four times more than would be saved (16,000 rupees) by the closure,[23] and the proposal lapsed. Nevertheless, for 1929 the Kashmir schools received no support from CMS but kept going on the State grant and the 25,000 rupees of private donations that Biscoe raised himself. London considered raising an endowment to make the Kashmir schools permanently self-supporting and five years later an appeal was launched for this purpose but meanwhile no action was taken.

When Force Jones died in 1931 Wigram replaced him in Lahore and re-assessed the educational work, including the Kashmir schools. He began by cutting the annual grant from 4,800 rupees to 1,200 rupees,[24] and then recommended that in 1933 the grant be discontinued altogether on the ground that practically no Christian teachers are employed and that therefore the missionary purpose of the schools cannot be adequately fulfilled.[25] Biscoe was offended by the reason for the decision and wrote:

> With regard to the proposal to cut our grant next year, we are of course only too glad to be in a position to help the Society during these times of stringency by not calling on them for financial help. If the proposal had been based on the grounds of economy pure and simple, we should have nothing to say, but we deeply regret the wording used in connection with the proposal.
>
> While appreciating the fact that opinions may differ on various subjects, we feel that the Committee at Lahore should

at least be prepared to admit that any line of action we may adopt, is adopted because we feel it to be the best line to take for the advancement of God's Kingdom. The wording of the proposal is in effect a vote of censure on all the CMS educational work in Kashmir and as such is a sorry return for our unconditional sacrifices in the past on behalf of the Mission as a whole.

We would also point out that the remark about the amount we have applied for during the coming year gives a most erroneous impression. It looks on the face of it as if we were asking for more than usual during these times of stress. Actually we have always indented for about the same amount (Rs 6000) though we have never received that sum.

We would request that a copy of this letter be forwarded to the Parent Committee as we feel that the Minutes as they stand, which were passed in the absence of any missionary from Kashmir, are unfair to us.[26]

Wigram did that[27] and mentioned that Biscoe had written another letter saying what a failure and bad lot most of the Christian teachers he had tried had been and the Christian atmosphere in the school was better without them. The committee at Lahore felt that it had become the settled policy in the schools of employing their own pupils and making no effort to get good Christian masters, and so a protest in this way was made. But if the Parent Committee in London felt a grant should be given would they add it to the budget. Others in Lahore thought it excellent that Biscoe and his son were being brought into line.[28] London replied that, in view of the strategic importance of the Kashmir schools, the Parent Committee cannot approve of the complete withdrawal of grants from the Kashmir schools for the purpose of strengthening other work in the mission.

Wigram wrote to tell Biscoe this but reiterated his view that the schools lacked Christian influence because they had so few Indian Christians on the staff[29] and followed it by sending a missionary from Lahore to explain his concerns. As will be seen later, she arrived just a week after the fiercest communal riots ever experienced in Srinagar during which the recipients of her message had spent every day saving staff and boys from attack and sheltering many families at Sheikh Bagh. It is small wonder that she got a cool reception! 'Poor Miss Cocks!! Had to pass on their humbug to us missionary lepers, Blanche, Eric, Phil, Muriel.'[30]

Matters took a better turn a month later when George Barnes was enthroned as Bishop of Lahore on 1 November 1932. At the garden party that followed he invited Biscoe to accept the honorific title of Canon of Lahore Cathedral, a clear indication of his view of the work in Kashmir. On opening his first meeting of the CMS Executive Committee the next day,[31] he asked Wigram to read the Minute recording the vote of censure on the Kashmir schools; he then ordered him to delete it before any other business. It was replaced with the resolution that:

> The grant be continued on the basis of 1931 grant and to meet the difficulty emphasised by Biscoe of obtaining suitable Christian masters for Kashmir, the managers of the Punjab and Frontier schools are asked to put before their Christian masters the challenge of missionary service in Kashmir. In this way it is hoped that the much desired link with the Indian Church may be strengthened.[32]

George Barnes recognised the importance of Biscoe's approach to social reform and six years later, when opening the new school building, he said:

> To be a Biscoe boy is a claim to distinction. They have stood for the Brahmin widow and for removing her cruel disabilities; they have stood out against child-marriage and succoured many poor little victims; they have fought prostitution and saved many lives from enforced shame and degradation; they have espoused the cause of animals; they have again and again proved themselves unbribable; they have gone to prison for their honesty, preferring four walls to selling the pass; they have preferred death, Chimed is the classic example who fell

riddled with bullets rather than take a bribe. Did Our Lord not
say, 'by their fruits ye shall know them?'[33]

In this he specifically recognised the two greatest achievements of
the Mission Schools in Kashmir during the previous 15 years;
improving the lot of Muslim and Hindu girls and women through
reform of the laws on the minimum age of marriage and the rights
of widows to remarry, and on the education of girls.

Success – The Remarriage of Young Widows

At the beginning of the twentieth century the condition of Hindu
women in India was dominated by the age-old teachings that the
only proper influences for a girl came from her own family and
later that of her husband's. For this reason no system of school or
college education would suit their requirements; girls got sufficient
moral and practical training in the household and that was far
more important than the type of education that schools could
give.[34] As a consequence very few women could read or write and
those that could would pretend not to be able to. Far more
significant was the belief that a girl must be married by the time
she reaches puberty and to ensure this, the girl's family would often
arrange her betrothal much earlier and sometimes to a much older
man whose previous wife, or wives, had died. Thus throughout
India, including Kashmir, great numbers of girls were married in
infancy and were pregnant at 12 years of age, sometimes even
younger. The Census for British India of 1922 gives the stark
figures: in a total population of 350 million people there were
329,000 wives under the age of five, 2.8 million under ten and
8.7 million between the ages of ten and 15.[35] Thousands of these
young girls became widows before the age of 15 because their
much older husbands had died. In Kashmir in 1929 there were still
3,000 widows under the age of 15, although by then it was illegal
for a girl to be married before the age of 14.

The knowledge of this profound abuse of Hindu girls was slow to
emerge; in Kashmir, Kate Knowles discovered it in 1908 through
the dispensary she set up at Habba Kadal School and her ability as

a woman doctor to enter the homes of Kashmiris and treat the women themselves. She brought to light the real consequences of the prevailing Hindu belief in the propriety of early marriage: girls became pregnant at a very young age and, if married to an older man, became widowed also at a young age. While a Hindu man could remarry if his wife died, a Hindu woman never could. These were unintended consequences of the abolition of suttee in British India in 1840 and in Kashmir in 1857; while a widow no longer had to die on her husband's funeral pyre she was instead condemned to a life of servitude and prostitution in the home of her deceased husband's family. If she became pregnant to one of the men in the household, the baby would be killed at birth. Likewise girl babies were far more likely to die early than boy babies. Kate Knowles learnt how this was done by exposing the baby to the carbon monoxide fumes that came from the *kangri*[36] that every woman held under her clothes, or by putting the first finger of each hand down the baby's throat and giving the fingers a quick jerk. The body was disposed of by being thrown into the Jhelum River and ended up at the weir below the Seventh Bridge in the city. Biscoe said that he had personally seen scores of these murdered babies when the weir was cleared each month.[37]

One consequence of these practices, especially among the Hindus, was the highly unbalanced sex ratio revealed in the first census in Kashmir in 1891.[38] For every 1,000 Hindu males there were only 817 Hindu females in the city and 721 in the country; that is to say, between a quarter and a fifth of Hindu girls were killed at birth or died young. For Muslims the sex ratios were nearer to parity with 916 females to 1,000 males in the city and 895 females to 1,000 males in the country.

Kate Knowles also learnt from the women she treated of the terrible effects of pregnancy on the very young girls. The first was that the mother-in-law would starve the young girl so that the baby would be small and more easily delivered and the second was the practice of not allowing the young girl outside the house. This in many cases resulted in softening of the bones or osteomalacia. Knowles wrote a brief paper on this in the *British Medical Journal* for 1914[39] and her findings were later confirmed by two other women doctors, Janet Vaughan who worked as a missionary doctor at the Rainawari Women's Hospital and Kathleen Vaughan who worked at the Kashmir State Women's Hospital and published a much more detailed account in 1926.[40] They found that this condition never occurred in men and was most prevalent in high-class Hindu families where the young women were permanently confined to the family home and only ever left the house enclosed in a burkha that entirely covered them with two mesh squares for their vision; it was especially bad after the long winter months when the women lived in the lowest floor of the house where there were no windows at all. It was very rare among young Muslim boatwomen who were exposed to the sun and worked in the open with the menfolk and were better fed. In the worst cases that the doctors saw the young woman's limbs were so badly affected that she was unable to stand or walk at all. As the Hindu families began to trust the foreign women doctors, they would bring their women to the hospitals when the delivery went wrong so that the baby could be delivered surgically. A consequence of Caesarean delivery, however, was that the subsequent pregnancies would be difficult and painful.

Another missionary nurse, Lilian Underhill,[41] published a pamphlet in which she described the case of a Brahmin priest who brought his young wife to the hospital for delivery of her second child by Caesarean because she was so deformed by osteomalacia. He was warned that if she became pregnant again the only way she could survive would be another Caesarean delivery. As his wife had produced two daughters he was indifferent and when her third confinement began he called the local midwife and unable to bear his wife's screams he went on the lake for three days to be out of the sound. When she was dying they took her to the hospital but he refused to admit that she had been mistreated because he knew it was only a third girl baby. Lilian's reply to him was that she would like to be the Chief Judge and condemn him to death and even be the hangman but, since she could do neither she would pray that in his next life he be born a woman to learn what suffering means. Could words suggest a greater insult than that – to be born a woman!

But it was not only Hindus who were indifferent to the suffering of their women; the Maulvi who taught Urdu at the Rainawari School was dismissed by Biscoe for neglecting his pregnant wife, not bringing her to the hospital and allowing the baby to die because he thought it was another girl.[42]

Lilian's pamphlet, published locally in 1926 and distributed to English women visiting Kashmir, was hard hitting. Its medical evidence was based on the article published in the *British Medical Journal* by Kathleen Vaughan in the same year and it described in brutal detail the condition of osteomalacia in young Hindu girls that English women on holiday in Kashmir would never encounter.

> I have seen a girl of about 24 who could only crawl by using arms and legs together in a sitting position. The expectant mother even three or four months before the child is born cannot sit stand or walk without severe pain and sometimes is completely crippled by osteomalacia.[43]

Her pamphlet was effective in one respect; the new Maharaja Hari Singh in this first year of his reign raised the marriageable age for girls from 10 to 12 years.[44]

A year later, on 14 April 1928, in response to pleas from Hindu men, including Shenker Koul, he went further and promulgated a new law, 'In future no girl under the age of 14 years of age and no boy under the age of 18 years may be married, under the penalty of four years imprisonment to all concerned in the marriage, priests and guests as well as the parents.'[45]

Meanwhile in India an American woman was collecting evidence on the plight of young girls subjected to the age-old customs of Hindu belief. During 1924–25 Katherine Mayo travelled throughout India interviewing all manner of people from untouchables in the villages, priests in temples, educated Indians and British civil servants. As an American her sympathies at the start were pro-Indian and critical of the British administration and she was welcomed by the Indian political elite. But what she found and what she published in her book, *Mother India*,[46] roused their fury. The book was published in America in May 1927 and in

England two months later; the British Government banned its publication in India but reviews reached there in August. When they did she was fiercely criticised as a foreigner who had no understanding of Indian culture and society and had no business to come on a short visit and criticise people she knew nothing about. One thing that particularly riled the political leaders was that her findings would adversely affect American opinion towards Indian aspirations for independence. What she found and described in much detail was similar to the Kashmiri conditions of young Hindu girls already described in the Underhill pamphlet but not widely known: married far too young to men much older than them, starved of food to keep them small and producing small and undernourished babies. She had gone to India with a mind favourable to Indians and prejudiced against the British administration but, as she travelled throughout the country she became appalled at the plight of young Hindu women and the dire consequences for the undernourished babies that they produced. Part of her message was an eugenic one that Indians were small and weak because they were produced by severely undernourished young girls who should not be pregnant. Opposition to her book came not only from educated Indians but also from English people who felt that she was demeaning Hindu culture. C.F. Andrews was particularly critical of her on these grounds[47] and, while he in no way condoned early pregnancy and the ban on widow remarriage, he deplored her depiction of Hindu culture as debased and preoccupied with sex. He also emphasised the point that successful reform can only come from within the community and not be imposed by government. By the time his book was published in 1939 early marriage in Kashmir was illegal and widows were free to remarry precisely because this approach had been taken.

First Widow Remarriage in Kashmir

These things were thus known in Kashmir years before the furore provoked by *Mother India* but change was very slow as it had to come from influential Hindus themselves rather than from the missionaries. When Biscoe had first become aware of these matters from Kate Knowles in 1908 he tried to raise the age of marriage for girls by discouraging the boys in the Mission Schools from early marriage. He did this by charging higher fees for boys who were married and by impressing on the boys the importance of their sisters growing to adulthood before marriage. In 1891 almost all the boys in the Mission School were married, by 1905 this was down to half, by 1915 to one-quarter and by 1924 only a tenth of the boys were married.[48] This was also the main motive for starting the girls' school in 1912. While these moves began to have an effect within the Mission Schools, the orthodox Hindu hierarchy in Srinagar were not prepared to be criticised by foreigners on such intimate matters as how they treated their daughters.

However, in 1918 an opportunity did occur when a particularly disagreeable form of venereal disease came to the city and frightened the men so much that the Dharam Sabha invited Dr Kathleen Vaughan to the Rago Nath Temple to tell them how to combat it. She was happy to accept as she realised it would give her an opportunity to speak directly to the most influential Brahmins in Srinagar about another disease, which had evidently being going on for untold years and was far more deadly than the new disease in which they were so interested: the constant murdering of baby girls that she knew about from her work in the State Women's Hospital and the terrible suffering of very young girls undergoing pregnancy and labour. She asked Biscoe to accompany her to the meeting, which was attended by a large gathering of Brahmin men, and he recorded how she spoke for nearly two hours:

> KOV fairly scared them with her home truths. She not only used her tongue but by action how these extra holy people took the lives of their babies. It was really great!! They put their *chaddars* or blankets in their mouths and looked anywhere, so ashamed were they. Har Gopal, President of the Dharam Sabha and the greatest enemy of our schools saw us into our boat and asked KOV to come again, the hypocrite![49]

Five years later senior Brahmins still continued to resist any change to their customs regarding girls and women. When Biscoe sought the help of the Chief Judge, Pandit Radha Kishen Koul, to prevent the continuing slaughter of baby girls, he became very angry and said women in England have worse treatment than those in India, the Indian return students tell him so, and that Biscoe, as a foreigner, had no business to interfere in these matters.[50] This reaction from someone Biscoe had expected to be an ally made him realise that no reform of such a sensitive matter could be achieved except by Brahmins themselves and that the heart of the problem was forbidding widows to remarry; if one Brahmin would consent to marry a widow under full Hindu rites others would follow.

By the early 1920s many of the Hindu teachers in the Mission Schools had imbibed Biscoe's ideas on postponing the marriage of girls until their late teens and it was to these men that he turned for leadership in this much more fraught matter of widow remarriage. As in so many of the reforms he initiated in Srinagar the key person was Pandit Shenker Koul, the headmaster, himself a respected Sanskrit scholar and devout Hindu, who had been striving for years to help widows in Srinagar. And there were several other senior masters who supported him, such as Pandit Bagwan Das, Pandit Shrida Butt the headmaster of the Islamabad School, Nand Lal Munshi, the school Bursar and Pandit Samsar Chand, the naturalist and writer. The first widow willing to remarry came forward in 1922 but under pressure she was unable to go through with it.[51] Six more years passed before two Hindu men were prepared to marry widows and two widows were found who were prepared to marry them. The joint weddings were set for 16 May 1928.[52]

Shenker Koul and staff of the Mission Schools plus some 200 old boys and other Brahmin guests assembled to witness the first remarriage of Hindu widows in Kashmir under full Hindu rites and at a place holy to Hindus near Islamabad. They marched to a certain house to fetch the bridegrooms and brought them to the house of the two waiting brides at 6.30 am. When all were assembled the three priests, who had agreed to conduct the wedding ceremonies, reneged. But Shenker had anticipated this and called on three of the school staff who taught Sanskrit and were also priests and they immediately took charge and the marriage was completed. Photographers were at hand to record the event so that no one could later say it had not happened.

It is important to emphasise that neither Biscoe, Eric nor any other foreigner was present at the ceremony; it was a Kashmiri ceremony conducted by Kashmiris for Kashmiris.

The three priests then became the target of the enraged Dharam Sabha; four days later the faithful were called to attend a monster meeting at the Rago Nath Temple in order to excommunicate Shenker and all the Mission School staff. Biscoe, Lilian Underhill and Eric went by boat to watch the meeting from the river but it did not take place;[53] an old boy of the Mission School in a high position in the State had persuaded the Governor to intervene and the High Priest of the Temple was told to provide surety of 20,000 rupees, which would be forfeited if there was a disturbance. When another meeting was called at the same temple two weeks later the faithful arrived to find a policeman at the door who told them that anyone who attempted to enter the temple precincts would be taken to the lock-up. So again the excommunication did not take place.

As Biscoe later wrote:

We hear that there are now a number of Brahmin widows and bridegrooms ready and wishing to be married; so the chains have been cracked if not broken. And this day before Ascension Day, 16 May 1928 will ever be a day of rejoicing for the Kashmir Brahmin widows.[54]

And to his son Julian in Africa he wrote:

The City seems to be settling down to the accepted fact that the holy Hindu religion has been outraged by the remarriage of Brahman widows but another catastrophy has befallen these holy bipeds; before he sailed for England His Highness actually signed the new law regarding marriage of children, for now, marriage of girls under 14 has been forbidden under the penalty of 4 years quad and a heavy fine on not only the parents of the child and bridegroom but on the priests and anyone attending the wedding, and a still heavier punishment on those who marry a child to an old man which these holy bipeds delight to do.[55]

The new law did not come into effect for three months after promulgation so that there was a rush on marriages, but only among the Muslims; for Hindus the stars were not propitious so they could not avail themselves of this last opportunity to marry their under-age daughters.

A year later the Mission Schools had a holiday to commemorate the first widows remarried in Kashmir and by then two more widows had remarried,[56] by 1933, 48 widows had remarried[57] and after ten years 80 had done so.[58] In 1931 the Maharaja, in his first public proclamation after his return from Europe, formally legalised Hindu widow remarriage[59] but the Dharam Sabha held out for another ten years. Biscoe wrote to Julian on 21 October 1941:

A wonderful thing has happened. The Brahmin religious assembly Dharam Sabha has at last passed the law that Hindu widows may remarry. It is almost too wonderful to be true [...] Widows are at last emancipated! Our school was given a whole holiday to honour the occasion. This has been worth living for.

The new Maharaja, Hari Singh, played an important role in this reform. When serious proposals for reform were brought to him in the first years of his reign he supported them; he successively raised the minimum age of marriage and he confirmed in law the right of Hindu widows to remarry. He was then a bold and progressive ruler but as the big challenges of the 1930s and 1940s came he unfortunately became indifferent to the well being of his State and spent his time in idle pleasure and his reign ended ignominiously (see Chapter 8).

The First School for Girls in Kashmir

The first serious attempt to educate Kashmiri girls was made by Dr Kate Knowles with Biscoe's strong support in 1907 (see Chapter 4) and was continued by her until she fell ill with typhoid in 1910 and on recovery went on leave to England. Her school was continued in her absence by Violet Fitze and Frances McKay. Biscoe had first met Violet Fitze in 1903 when he visited her father, a business man in Calcutta.[60] Presumably she had financial support from her father, since she was not supported financially by the CMS as a missionary. When Kate Knowles returned to Kashmir in October 1911 she resumed charge of the girls' school at Habba Kadal, along with her dispensary for women. Frances McKay then accepted a post in Gilgit, much to the disappointment of Kate Knowles, and soon after she contracted typhoid there and died. The following year Violet Fitze moved the school to a building adjacent to the Central Mission School at Fateh Kadal and named it the Frances Aberigh McKay Memorial School for Girls and it has continued to function ever since, celebrating its centenary in 2012.

The Memorial School for Girls was a grand title for the reality of a small Kashmiri dwelling overlooking the Jhelum River. The assembly hall was a loft at the top of the building with windows on three sides, covered with paper because none had glass; about 60 young girls sat on the floor trying to write with ink made from white clay on black boards. None was older than 14 yet some had babies with them and all were eager to learn. Most were Muslim girls but there were also a few Hindu girls. The latter were known as *purdah nashi* meaning caged birds because they were not allowed outside and coming to school was their only escape from their dreary life and they yearned to spread their wings and be free. It grieved Violet Fitze that, while the girls were eager to learn, their parents were indifferent or angry; this was presumably because they knew that there was only one fate awaiting a girl and it was useless to raise her expectations. In 1917 she described the tragic case of a bright young girl, the younger daughter of a widow, who was taken from school to be married to a man of 25, at the same time as her 16-year-old sister to save the cost of two weddings. 'The horrid tale was told me when it was too late to interfere and nothing could save her. Now my little song bird sits in a mother-in-law's cage, never allowed to speak unless spoken to.'[61] Despite discouragement the numbers attending the school increased to 100 by 1919 when Fitze

Figure 21 Muriel Mallinson, Principal of the Mission School for Girls, Srinagar, 1922–62

went on leave to England. There she was accepted as a full member of the CMS, having previously been an honorary missionary.

She returned in December 1920 looking fit and full of joy at being back at her beloved work but somewhat dismayed by the deterioration of the school in her absence. Three weeks later she suddenly collapsed in mind and body. The mission nurses, Lucy McCormick and Elizabeth Newman nursed her and Drs Kathleen and Janet Vaughan attended her. It was of no avail and after four days she just slipped away. Biscoe suspected poisoning but the doctors thought she had been infected before her return to Kashmir. The funeral was impressive. A white coffin covered with wreaths and the school Union Jack given by the Viceroy. The pall bearers were Shenker Koul and Mahanand Razdan (masters who loved to help Violet); Dulchen, a Ladakhi Christian boy; Cecil and Ken Hadow; and Biscoe – East and West paying the last honours.

Biscoe wrote to London:

> We feel very deeply the loss of our dear friend and fellow helper, as she was in many ways unique, selfless to a degree and we all admired and loved her greatly. The work she accomplished was wonderful she was so wise and broadminded. We all want her work to go on, not simply the school to continue, but Violet Fitze's work, she was out for the future and laying foundations on which others could build without fear of collapse. It is such a lady who will follow her method we need. We want one who can be a mother, sister and teacher to the girls in one. We want to make good wives and good mothers, real helpmates for our boys. So if you can help us to find such a helper we shall be grateful.[62]

Frank Lucey, on furlough in England in 1921, spoke at a flourishing preparatory school in Eastbourne where, among other things he mentioned the importance of educating the girls if the educational work of the CMS was to be effective. On the staff was a young assistant mistress, who came forward after the lecture and asked Lucey whether he thought that she would be any use.

Muriel Mallinson was of that generation of young women who came to maturity after World War I when the partners they might have had were dead in the fields of France; they had to make their way through life on their own in a world still dominated by men, and they had to be tough. Muriel was a formidable person, unusually tall, direct in speech and very self contained but quite shy. When she approached Frank Lucey she was 26 and a qualified teacher, having graduated from St Andrew's University, Glasgow, like Kate Knowles before her. And like Kate, she had a yearning to do more than lead a quiet life in England; a girls' school in Kashmir must have seemed much more challenging than Eastbourne. Her offer coincided with another urgent letter from Biscoe for a suitable replacement for Violet Fitze:

> Blanche says that she is ready to receive the lady into our house and I think we can make her happy. All the people we have had in our house, and it runs into three figures, have all turned out to be angels so we can look confidently to this one being like the rest. To be like dear Violet she will have to be an archangel. Don't tell her this for it might frighten her and she would fly elsewhere. Jack Dugdale is of the archangel type as you know.[63]

The CMS accepted her and she travelled out to Kashmir with Ernest Neve and his wife in October 1922 to begin her life's work.[64] How different was her first encounter with her new school from the Eastbourne she had left. Eric wrote:

> Going down the narrow winding lanes, past the heaps of garbage thrown out from the windows, where numberless hordes of pariah dogs fought for their living in the heart of Srinagar city she came to a narrow cleft between the houses which led into a filthy little courtyard ten to fifteen feet square. Up a few rough steps she passed through a low doorway into a typical Kashmiri house, with small mud-floored rooms, low ceilings, lattice windows without glass, pasted over with paper in winter to keep out the cold. Here huddled together on the floor were 80 girls, teachers and babies. None of the teachers

was qualified or had read beyond middle standard though all were married and had to bring their babies to school. Many of the pupils also had babies with them for in those days there were no laws against child marriage. When a baby cried or needed attention everyone would cease whatever lesson was supposed to be in progress and crowd round the baby with a great deal of shouting and advice.[65]

Within a year she had appointed the first qualified teacher, Miss Ahmed Shah, the daughter of a Kashmiri Christian convert from Islam, who remained her close assistant for the next 30 years. They soon had the girls playing netball and attending a picnic in the secluded garden of the British Resident and the number in the school rose to 130. In 1926 she introduced Girl Guides to school, which also helped to encourage the girls' self assurance and independence without disturbing their parents; and numbers continued to rise to 155 Muslim and 30 Hindu girls.

Muriel went on leave in 1928, and Marion Price, who had visited Kashmir about six times for summer holidays, offered to run the girls' school in her absence. She wrote, 'how affectionate, how humorous and how thoroughly human they are; how pathetic though life often is for them'. She was thinking of the arbitrary manner in which a young girl would be taken away from school at the demand of her family for her marriage or of her husband who no longer wished her to attend school.

After Muriel returned in 1929, she gradually increased the scope of activities through Guiding without disturbing the parents of the girls, and the numbers continued to rise to 200. By providing uniforms for the guides she introduced the concept of cleanliness and through camping out for several days, greater independence. 'It is difficult to describe the spirit of freedom but not licence that pervades the camp for with it goes obedience, self-control, courtesy and cleanliness.'[66] She also introduced a school clinic run by the mission doctor Marion Smyth who visited every week and kept a record of the health of every girl. To appreciate the importance of this recall the condition of young girls in Srinagar described four years before by Lilian Underhill in her pamphlet.[67]

With funds from the family of Violet Fitze she was able in 1930 to enlarge the school buildings with six new classrooms, a large hall, a dispensary and an office, with a veranda along the river side of the compound to which most of the girls arrived each day by boat. Boys from the Mission School next door had provided most of the labour to prepare the site for the new building and one of the senior teachers, Pundit Suraj Baliya acted as architect, contractor and clerk of works during its construction, even during the summer holidays.[68]

With the new building, numbers continued to rise to 350 by 1932 and each year the experience of camping away from home became more adventurous. As Muriel wrote in the 1931 school log:

> Thus through guiding and through everything in connection with the school we aim at driving out the spirit of fear which still has far too strong a hold on the women and girls; but they are beginning to realise that God has given them the spirit of power, of love and of a sound judgement.[69]

And in 1932:

> The girls have developed tremendously in thoughtfulness and carefulness and self reliance since they have been Guides and have been out hiking and camping.[70]

In 1934 they also began to learn to swim, something they had never been able to do before. This was greatly helped when the boys and masters excavated a site for the construction of a swimming bath on land adjacent to the school.[71] This was funded by Fred Jacob, recently retired from being headmaster of a junior school in England, who volunteered to help Biscoe in the Mission Schools and remained for the next 12 years. Biscoe wrote to Eric in England:

> You will be interested to hear that the girls' school bath is finished and full of water. It is really a very fine swimming bath, waiting for Muriel and Phil to show the girls the joy of

swimming. Some day I hope the girls will rival the boys in saving life, which is quite possible, for they will be going with their women relations to the river after dark to bathe in the river when they are apt to get into difficulties.[72]

His reference to Phil was because the year before she had been the first woman to swim across the Wular Lake,[73] setting an example that in later years was followed by the girls swimming across the Dal Lake and climbing the surrounding peaks, including in 1936 the first ascent by five girls of Mahadeo.

As Eric wrote at the 50-year Jubilee of the school:

In these new surroundings, the girls blossomed like seedlings when planted out from the seed-bed. Muriel led them out from the shackles of their strict seclusion: she took them out into camp; climbing in the mountains; swimming in the lakes. From this school came the first girls in Kashmir to enter University. Now, all over the country are Muriel's old girls in positions of authority. The present head of the Kashmir University College for women is an old girl; many old girls are qualified doctors; others have gone overseas to study.[74]

Political Awakening in Kashmir

Maharaja Pratap Singh died in September 1925 ending a 40-year reign and Hari Singh, the nephew he detested, became the fourth and last Maharaja of Jammu and Kashmir. The succession marked the beginning of the end of the Dogra autocracy that Kashmir had endured for 80 years; there was no representation of the people in the governance of the State, especially for the Muslim majority, and the wealth of the State was exceedingly unevenly distributed. To put this in context, 5 rupees was just sufficient for a widow to feed herself for a month.[75] At the same time the Maharaja took out of the revenue of the country 150,000 rupees per month, a sum sufficient to support 30,000 of his poverty-stricken subjects, or fund the Mission Schools for two years! The plight of ordinary workers was little better. The government-owned silk factory, founded 20 years before, employed 5,000 Muslim workers on a daily wage of 4.5 annas, equivalent to 8 rupees per month. Early in 1924 the first signs of political awakening among Kashmiris began when the factory workers went on strike for higher pay.[76] The Kashmir Government reacted with considerable violence and suppressed the strike, which enraged the Muslim community so that when the Viceroy, Lord Reading, visited Srinagar in October 1924, he was presented with a Memorandum that outlined their many grievances against the Hindu-dominated government. It called for increased employment opportunities for Muslims in State service, land reform and a State Constitution with a Legislative Assembly with representation of all communities.

While there was no response to this under Pratap Singh, high hopes were held for his successor, Hari Singh. He had already shown leadership during the food shortages a few years before (see Chapter 5) and in the first year of his reign he responded to public demand to raise the age of marriage for girls to 12, and two years later to 14, as already described. When Srinagar city suffered a major flood in August–September 1929 he himself worked for three days and nights cheering on his sepoys and coolies at their work on the embankment. When the trouble was over and the city saved, he ordered the Minister of Education to gather together at his office the Director, Inspector, Sub-Inspector, headmasters and all the promoters of learning in Kashmir to listen to his orders:

> Whereas during these days of danger I was visiting all parts of the city I observed Mission School boys at work quietly on the embankments but Government School boys were conspicuous by their absence. Therefore I command that all officers connected with Education go to the Mission School to learn their system of education whereby they can put the spirit of service into their boys and copy them at once.[77]

With the aim of cleaning up the administration of the State the Maharaja in 1927 appointed a distinguished Indian administrator, Sir Albion Bannerjee, as Prime Minister. Unfortunately this was a bigger task than one person could achieve and less than two years later he resigned, stating that:

> There is no touch between the Government and the people, no suitable opportunity for representing grievances and the administrative machinery itself requires overhauling from top to bottom to bring it up to the modern conditions of efficiency.[78]

He was replaced by G.E.C. Wakefield who had served Hari Singh in other capacities for several years before he became Maharaja. In his memoir of this final period he records a less favourable side of the new Maharaja;[79] during the annual migration of thousands of waterfowl through Kashmir Hari Singh decided to conduct the world's largest duck shoot and, with Wakefield's help seven guns in five hours shot 2,136 birds off his private estates.

As the political ferment in India grew and Hari Singh was unable to reform his State he became convinced that the British were plotting against him and that Wakefield was their agent. There may have been some truth in this because at the First London Round Table Conference in 1930 Hari Singh spoke in favour of Indian aspirations for independence, saying that the Princes supported it.[80] Some British officials thought these views on Britain's future in India were dangerously radical and may have asked Wakefield to watch him. While he was in London Hari Singh dined with Sir Walter Lawrence, who had known his father, Raja Amar Singh, in Jammu and Kashmir 30 years before. He asked Lawrence to persuade the Indian Government to abolish British Residents; they were expensive and the Rajas could manage without their help. Lawrence replied:

> Let me tell you a bit of history. I was in Jammu long before your birth when the Kashmir troops wished to kill your father. What did he do? He went for help to the British Resident and a regiment of cavalry galloped from Sialkot and saved your father's life. History may repeat itself, so I advise you not to ask for removal of British Residents. Listen! There are three chief sins into which Rajas fall: love of vengeance, love of money

Figure 22 Hari Singh, Maharaja of Jammu and Kashmir, 1925–47

and love of self. The worst of these is love of self and that Hari Singh is your sin. If you love yourself you cannot love your people.[81]

History did repeat itself later that year but Hari Singh's deficiencies were not as simple as Lawrence portrayed. On his return to Kashmir in April 1931, the Maharaja defied tradition by entering the city in his ceremonial barge with the Maharani beside him, instead of hidden in purdah; and shortly after he legalised the remarriage of widows in the State,[82] two matters that would have deeply offended the powerful Hindu Dharam Sabha. While he was forward thinking in these respects he did not sense the political forces at play in Kashmir that would within months embroil its people in the worst communal riots that the State had experienced and lead to the first public demands for an end to Dogra rule.

While the State administration remained recalcitrant to reform, greater forces were at work in India that began to influence Kashmir affairs. Students from Jammu and Kashmir, who went to the Punjab University in Lahore, became aware of the freedom struggle in India, inspired by Lala Lajpat Rai, met earlier in 1907, and saw more clearly the deficiencies of the State administration compared to British India.[83] However, the key event was Gandhi's Salt March when he and his followers defied the Indian Government's imposition of a tax on salt by collecting salt from the sea on 6 May 1930. This was Gandhi's first powerful demonstration of *satyagraha* or soul force, which galvanised the people of India and totally out foxed the British administration. Gandhi was first arrested but then released and called to negotiations with the Viceroy, Lord Irvine.[84] Many British people in India and some in London, led by Winston Churchill, strongly disapproved of this response by the Viceroy which they thought showed weakness and encouraged civil disobedience, a view reflected in the Mission School log at the end of that year:

> When Gandhi was arrested on 6 May for the first and at any rate for this year, the last time, Srinagar experienced a slight attack of the malady that has intermittently affected other parts of India to a greater or lesser extent. A procession was formed, composed mostly of foreign elements from India which marched through the city forcing shops to close; passers by wearing garments made of English cloth were stopped, their clothing confiscated and destroyed. Several of our boys lost their puggarees in this effusion of patriotism, and for a few days persons not attired in the 'nationalist uniform' were liable to abuse.[85]

This was written by Eric but it reflected his father's opinions; Biscoe would not allow boys in the Mission Schools to wear the 'nationalist uniform' of *khadi*, or homespun cloth, or the white Congress cap. He argued that, since the schools were supported in large part by donations from British people, if they wished to follow the nationalist path they should go to a state school. While Eric went along with this at the time, his views would take a different turn the following year after his first encounter with the young Kashmiri nationalist leader, Sheikh Mohammed Abdullah.

Sheikh Abdullah was born in 1905 into a typical Kashmiri family; originally Brahmin but converted to Islam in the eighteenth century. His father was a trader in Kashmiri shawls but died when he was a child, leaving the family well-connected but poor. Nevertheless, his young son received a good education, culminating in a MSc in Chemistry from the Aligarh Muslim University where he was exposed to the ideas of Marx and Engels as well as the growing movement for Indian independence. As he wrote later, 'It was during this period that the whole of India was shaken into a new awakening following the civil disobedience movement of 1931 and had its own psychological influence upon us.'[86]

He returned to Srinagar early in 1931 but, despite his excellent qualifications, failed to get an appointment in the State Government because he was Muslim. Instead he got a teaching job (not at the Mission School) and started the Fateh Kadal Reading Room as a place for young men to discuss politics, and the problems of the day, discretely. Discretion was necessary as the State Government took a hard line against political activity of any sort; it banned political publications and forbade the entry of Congress leaders, such as Gandhi and the young Pandit Nehru, to the State. Sheikh Abdullah became a close ally of the new *Mirwaiz-i-Kashmir* (head of the Kashmir Islamic community), Mohammed Yusuf Shah. Between the religious prestige of the one and the charismatic and organising ability of the other they made a formidable team[87] and were the main instigators of the public protests in Srinagar against the State Government and for more representation of the majority Muslim population.

Early in the year Mirwaiz Yusuf Shah spoke strongly in Srinagar against the demolition of a mosque in Riasi, a small town in Jammu, and the disruptions of Muslim worship by the Maharaja's forces in Jammu and this encouraged others to speak out; one man from Lahore, who had entered Srinagar as the private servant of a British visitor, made a vehement speech advocating violence against the Maharaja's rule and was promptly arrested. This further provoked public protest and the man's trial on 6 July had to be postponed because of the huge demonstration of Muslims around the courthouse. When the trial reopened outside the gaol a week later, 13 July 1931, another large crowd assembled, and when they heard that he was to undergo imprisonment, they besieged the jail, and tried to rescue him. The police baton charged the crowd, which responded by throwing stones; the police then opened fire, killing 22 demonstrators and one policeman. The mob then broke up, and returned to the city, bareheaded and infuriated. They attacked Hindus, and looted their shops, and declared a *hartal* – a kind of general strike. It also provoked Muslim protests and clashes with police throughout the valley and in Jammu. Thereafter this date became known as Martyrs' Day.

Martyrs' Day

Biscoe was on furlough in England at this time and Eric was in charge of the Mission Schools.[88] He got a call at midday from the Central School to say that they were besieged by an angry mob and would he come quickly to rescue the Hindu boys. Not knowing what to expect he recalled his father telling him how he had calmed a hostile mob by lighting a cigar and letting it go out several times until the mob were more interested in seeing whether the cigar would stay alight or not, than in the cause of their wrath, which went off the boil.

So Eric put a couple of Burma cheroots in his pocket, got on his bike, and set off for the three mile ride through the city to Fateh Kadal. The streets were ominously empty, except for the odd solitary cow looking for a vegetable seller's stall, and the ubiquitous pi-dogs, which could now sleep in peace without any cart wheels to menace them. Most of the shops were shuttered, and on those that were not, the men who sat there were sullen. Occasionally someone would call out and advise him not to proceed. At the school he banged on the big gates and when they heard his voice the gates were opened. The compound was littered with bricks and stones, but no damage had been done. Huddled under the shelter of the covered way in front of the main school building were the Hindu staff and boys looking very scared. He assured them that the menacing mob had dispersed, so the boys were divided into groups according to localities, and put under the escort of masters.

One group under Shenker Koul came face to face with a mob, and had to turn round and take refuge in a police station. The police everywhere had run away and locked themselves into their stations; in this particular station some of the policemen had hidden themselves in the big chests in which their uniforms were stored.

Another group would have to pass close to the great Shah-i-Hamdan Mosque, in order to get to their homes; and no one seemed keen on going through that area. Fortunately on the staff was a Muslim ex-army band-master. So Qutub Din and Eric marshalled their group of about 40 boys, and warned them that on no account were they to panic or scatter. Eric went in front and as he reached the street he lit his Burma cheroot; Qutub Din brought up the rear. All along the route Muslims were begging them not to proceed, while Hindus asked to come in under their protection so that their numbers finally swelled to a couple of hundred. They passed through a Hindu area that had been sacked; a motor with its bonnet lifted had a pile of rocks smashed down on its engine. On turning a corner they came upon a mob engaged in plundering. On seeing the procession led by a tall Englishman smoking a cigar, the looters dropped their 'swag' and bolted, leaving the road clear. A lorry full of armed police now appeared but they wisely declined to descend from the lorry – it had a good strong roof – but offered to go slowly along with them. The road, however, was so blocked with debris that the lorry could not proceed so the police asked the boys to clear it for them. Thus the tables were turned, and unarmed school boys enabled the law to pass in triumph and safety.

Forty-four years later when Eric was visiting Kashmir a Hindu man accosted him and said, 'Mr Eric, you do not remember me but once you saved my life. It was on Martyrs' Day and I joined the party you were leading through the streets with a revolver in your hand.'[89] So in his memory the cigar was so potent it had become a revolver! More likely it was Eric's mere presence that curbed the looters for at that time any Englishman, official or not, carried extraordinary authority. Nevertheless, his courage was remembered by a member of the Maharaja's council three years later.[90]

By the evening quiet was restored as troops were picketed all over the city, martial law was proclaimed and a sullen calm descended on the city. The Maharaja was much disturbed by what had happened; he suspected Wakefield of plotting the recent troubles on behalf of the British Government, so he was promptly sacked and Raja Hari Kishen Koul was appointed the first Prime Minister of Jammu and Kashmir. He was the brother of Dya Kishen Koul, who figured earlier in this account (Chapter 4). And to placate the Muslim community in Srinagar the Maharaja appointed a Muslim lawyer from India as Home Minister responsible for education and schools.

Some Muslim parents thought this concession meant that education would now be free and told their sons to refuse to pay fees. The State schools acceded to this but the Mission Schools did not and the boys were ordered to pay or be marked absent and incur a fine. Their parents appealed to the new Home Minister who ordered Eric to re-instate all the Muslim boys without penalty, or issue them with discharge certificates. When he refused to do either he was called to the Minister's office where he pointed out that it was against the inter-school rules of the State for boys to change school in the middle of the year without adequate reason. The Minister argued that in these anxious times the State should be more conciliatory since all over India boys were taking part in politics. Eric said:

> Is the State really frightened of a band of school boys? Rather than have a school in which boys dictate to the masters and where there is no discipline, we will close down. But if you are really anxious for the inter-school rules to be broken for the sake of these boys, you may do it yourself on your own responsibility for we never shall do so.[91]

When the Minister issued orders for the boys to be admitted to other schools without permission rioting started afresh; he had emboldened the whole city to have another try to get their grievances redressed.

Meeting Sheikh Abdullah

A few days later the Muslim leadership intervened;[92] Sheikh Abdullah, accompanied by a former student of the Mission School, Ghulam Bakshi, and some other followers of his, visited the Central School to speak with Eric. He was surprised to see Bakshi, who two years before had been pretending to be a Christian among missionaries and a Muslim at home and was now dressed in khadi and Congress cap; but Eric was most apprehensive at a confrontation with the well known radical leader. However, Sheikh Abdullah disarmed him with his opening words:

> 'I feel I must first of all apologise to you, Mr. Biscoe for taking up your time. I, along with all the Muslims appreciate the great service that your father and you have given to us over the years; and therefore I hope you will excuse me for coming to see you on the matter of the Muslim students of your school, who are roaming the streets at present.'
> 'Well I am ready to take them back as soon as they pay their dues.'
> 'Yes, I quite understand that; and realise that they are at fault. But the fines are excessive, and the boys are poor, and they have been misled.'
> 'Well, what about asking those who misled them, to pay the fines for them?'[93]

Whereupon, they both laughed, for they knew that was an utter impossibility. So they finally compromised on the understanding that Eric would look into the matter, find out which were the really poor boys, and make concessions where necessary. This was a formative event; the beginning of a life long friendship between the two men based on mutual respect and shared aspirations for Kashmir. Both had been born in Kashmir at the turn of the century, each had a traditional conservative upbringing, one Muslim and one Christian, each chose a scientific path at university and developed secular socialist views of how society should be. As the troubles in Kashmir continued through the next decade they maintained close contact.

Twenty years later when Sheikh Abdullah was Prime Minister of the State with a special relationship in the Indian Union, Eric wrote to encourage him to keep Kashmir independent of India, as Switzerland is in Europe. Whether or not this influenced Sheikh Abdullah, his own advocacy of independence led to his arrest and imprisonment by the Indian Government in 1953. His erstwhile colleague, G.M. Bakshi, supplanted him as a more pliant and renamed Chief Minister.

For the Maharaja the events of Martyrs Day had wider repercussions;[94] in India leading Muslims formed a Kashmir Committee to press the Government of India to hold a commission of inquiry into the cause of the crisis and to declare throughout India 14 August as 'Kashmir Day'. Despite prohibitions of the Maharaja, it produced a rally of 50,000 people outside the Jama Masjid mosque in Srinagar. Then on 24 September Sheikh Abdullah was arrested for speaking against the State[95] and Muslims who protested were fired upon, which only infuriated them more. A day or so later the authorities tried to arrest some other leaders, but were prevented by the mob. Muslims were instructed to arm themselves, and crowds of villagers also came into the city armed with axes, spears and all sorts of improvised weapons, and a challenge was sent to the Maharaja that he could send his army, as they were ready for him. It was a definite attack on the State and no Hindus where molested.[96]

After vacillating for two or three days, the authorities decided to show strength. State troops were sent in force into the city and everyone was made to salute the flag and shout, 'Maharaja ki jai!' (Long Live the Maharaja). People were encouraged to lay charges of disloyalty against their neighbours a great opportunity for paying off old scores. For about ten days there was military rule, the first few days of which proved a veritable reign of terror. Wretched men were summarily condemned to cruel floggings. The Dogra soldiers, mainly Hindus, became completely out of hand, looting shops and beating up innocent passers-by. At last the nightmare came to an end with a general amnesty on the Maharaja's birthday.

However, the dreadful doings in Srinagar and other towns in the valley caused such a wave of indignation among Muslims in India, that they began sending in gangs of men to help their co-religionists in the State. Things became so serious in Jammu and other parts of the State adjoining British territory that at last the Maharaja was forced to ask for the aid of British troops, precisely what Lawrence had predicted six months earlier.[97]

At one period, during the height of the disturbances, a curfew was imposed on Srinagar city from dusk to dawn. A gun was fired each evening from Hari Parbat Fort to mark the beginning of curfew, after which anyone found outside on the streets would be liable to arrest. On every evening, when that gun boomed, suddenly and spontaneously, from all around – it seemed as if from nearly every housetop in the city – came the shout '*Sher-i-Kashmir Zindabad!*' (Long live the Lion of Kashmir) over and over again. This was the first time this title was bestowed on Sheikh Abdullah by which he was known thereafter. Kashmiri Muslims believed he had magical powers by which he could thwart the Maharaja's efforts to control the people. And in a sense he did because he had challenged the power of the State, as Gandhi was doing in British India.

Unable to control the new power of the people, in November 1931 the Maharaja was obliged to appoint, under pressure from the Government of India, a Commission of Enquiry, chaired by Sir Bertram Glancy, of the Indian Political Department. It included two Kashmiri Muslims and two Kashmiri Hindus and it obliged the Maharaja to grant the State a Constitution supported by a degree of freedom of speech and association. It came into effect in 1934 and included a Legislative Assembly in which there were 33 elected seats (10 Hindu, 21 Muslim, two Sikh) and 42 appointed by the Maharaja. Soon after Hari Kishen Koul was replaced as Prime Minister until 1936 by E.J.D. Colvin, a British member of the Indian Political Department.

In anticipation of the first elections ever to be held in the State the Muslims, led by Mirwaiz Yusuf Shah and Sheikh Abdullah, formed the All Jammu and Kashmir Muslim Conference, which became the main focus of opposition to the Maharaja. When the elections took place in 1934 they won 19 of the 21 seats reserved for Muslims. And of the ten seats reserved for Hindus, six were won by old boys of the Mission School.[98]

The collaboration between the two Muslim leaders was, however, short-lived; the Mirwaiz wanted the movement to be wholly Muslim whereas Sheikh Abdullah wanted to include the Hindu minority in the movement for self government in the State. He publicly stated that the sale of the State by the British to Maharaja Gulab Singh in 1846 was illegal and should be abrogated in favour of self government by universal suffrage. This reflected to some extent what was occurring in India where Jinnah was advocating a separate Muslim State and Congress was advocating one secular country. In Kashmir the Mirwaiz moved closer to the Muslim League and later supported the incorporation of Kashmir into Pakistan, while Sheikh Abdullah favoured closer links with Congress. When the split occurred in 1933 he formed the Kashmir National Congress which was open to all Kashmiris.

This led to the Battle of the Match Boxes between the followers of Sher-i-Kashmir, whose enemies called him *Garda Kala*, which means fish head, and the followers of the Mirwaiz, whose enemies referred to as *Bakr* meaning the Goat. There were two popular brands of matches on sale in Srinagar. One had a prancing unicorn on it, which rather resembled a goat; and the other had a picture of a fish. People used to display one or other of the match boxes to their foes, and shout 'Yah! Fish head!' and hold up the picture of the fish; or the unicorn would be held up when taunting followers of the Mirwaiz.

The Biscoes returned to Srinagar from furlough at the end of 1931 and he was soon back in the turmoils of the city; Sheikh Abdullah called on him, following up on his earlier visit to Eric, and Biscoe and Eric visited Bertram Glancy the Chairman of the Commission of Enquiry.[99] Throughout the troubles Biscoe and Sheikh Abdullah maintained a respectful correspondence one example of which survives:

> Many thanks for your kind letter which has touched me. I take
> courage, even under adverse conditions, from expressions of

sympathy and appreciation for my humble services that I may render for the long oppressed people. I take your valuable advice to heart and will try my best to launch a campaign for reform against social customs.[100]

Biscoe was delighted that at the inaugural meeting of the Legislative Assembly the first piece of legislation enacted was aimed at stopping the traffic in young girls to the brothels of India.

Despite his 69 years Biscoe was still vigorous.[101] While riding to Ranawari his cycle skidded on the wet road, as he tried to avoid a Pandit, and he was pitched head first over a wall, leaving him hanging upside down above a sunken market garden. 'There's old Brown upside down. The passers by had a good laugh until I kicked myself free and fell among the cabbages.' When an old boy, now college student, would not salute his old teachers Biscoe made him run to school and there learn his manners again.[102]

Fearing to lose their privileges from the concessions made by the State to the Muslim community, in 1931 the Hindu community began to protest in the new year. They were encouraged in this by Congress party activists from India and, when six pundits were arrested in May 1932 a *hartal* of government services was declared in the city. Through the summer months from June to September 1932 there was turmoil in the city between Hindus and Muslims and between the two Muslim parties.

The trigger for violence when it began on 22 September 1932 was a decision by the Director of Education, Balwant Singh, to hold a procession through the city of all the school and college students, many to be in Scout uniform; this was to encourage the populace to clean up the city streets and compounds as a mark of respect for the Maharaja's birthday. Shenker Koul, who had been put in charge of the procession, urged postponement because of the dangerous tension in the city, but he was overruled.[103]

As the procession began Shenker noticed that some school contingents were rather small though the Mission School mustered in full force. It turned out that some Hindu boys from other schools were boycotting the procession but when it went ahead anyway they decided to hold a rival procession. When, as was inevitable in such a charged situation, some of these Hindu boys from Sri Pratap School insulted Muslim boys in the official procession, it set the city ablaze, as described later in the 1932 log:

> By the evening the whole city was in an uproar. Any stragglers from either community who were unfortunate enough to be in a hostile area were lucky to escape with their lives. For three nightmare days this storm raged in the city of Srinagar and even spread to the town of Islamabad. It was terrible to see the mobs possessed with the spirit of murder and destruction. Regardless of age they attacked old men and boys and the pitiable sight of grey hairs bowed to the blood-soaked earth made no appeal to their mercy; from different parts of the City one would hear the confused roar of angry mobs, while other parts seemed completely deserted and a feeling of furtive malevolence was in the atmosphere. The Hindus being the minor community were practically besieged in their quarters. Having systematically set out to defy authority they now began to complain that the State did not use its forces in their protection; having cried 'Long live revolution!' they were only too glad to welcome any protection from the Government.[104]

Most of the Mission School boys, being at the front of the procession, completed it and were able to go home safely but a few were not and in the afternoon Biscoe set out with Bal Govind from Islamabad to escort them through the city, as Eric had done a year before. But this time it was different and they found themselves in the midst of a battle raging and were at once attacked by stones and clubs, a very bloody affair. One of the young masters, Naranjan Nath Misri who had already been assaulted and was bleeding profusely from head wounds, saw Vishnu Hakim's son, a boy of 12 in scouts' uniform, being clubbed as he lay on the road. He rushed to save him and bent over him receiving fresh blows on his back that could have killed him. With difficulty Biscoe was able to get them into a house although the owners were reluctant to open their doors. Another one of the party, Goongoo, was thrown for dead under a shop and Nand Lal Munshi was wounded. But one old man defended Biscoe against the blows of his fellow Muslims. They gave first aid to the wounded and when it was dark got them secretly to the canal and with difficulty commandeered boats and took them to hospital.

Elsewhere in the city the homes of two teachers, Suraj Baliya, already met as the builder of the girls' school, and Rago Koul, were wrecked but the women of the two households were protected by a neighbour, a Muslim carpenter. But he was reluctant to protect them after dark so Eric and Biscoe brought them all to Sheikh Bagh. In the Mission Hospital there were about 400 wounded, Hindus and Muslims in equal numbers. Eric piloted the hospital assistants to their homes.

Because of the danger for staff and students travelling the streets or the Jhelum River, it was difficult to keep the Mission Schools open and on the day after the riots only three teachers and 20 students attended.[105] In the following days Biscoe ferried people in his motor boat but as they passed under the bridges opponents of those in the boat would pelt them with stones, so he then always carried Hindus and Muslims together.[106] Regular school routine was difficult or impossible so classes were held in Biscoe's garden.

After a week the city quietened down with only occasional violence. Biscoe escorted Suraj Baliya and Rago Koul to school and visited Nanda Lal still unable to walk.[107]

After the rioting was over the State Officials asked Biscoe to provide the names of those who deserved recognition. He recommended the old Muslim who took the blows intended for him, the Muslim carpenter who saved the households of Rago Koul and Suraj Baliya, and Naranjan Nath Misri. The two Muslims received *sanats* within two weeks but after a few months the Governor wrote to Misri, a Hindu, asking him to write an account of his own gallantry. Biscoe gave the Governor a suitable answer to his insult and put Naranjan's name forward for the Viceroy's Silver Medal for Gallantry, which he eventually received three years later.[108]

Throughout the three years of communal unrest and rioting the Mission School boys and teachers continued to provide voluntary social service in the city as in former years. In 1931 the boys saved

15 lives from drowning, took 1,300 patients for rides in the school boats, helped at 14 fires including one in the Women's Hospital and performed numerous acts of kindness and help to women, children, old men, blind people and strangers. In the 1931 log is a group photograph, not of a sporting team but of 'The Most Honourable Class for 1931'.[109] Similarly in 1932, at the height of the communal troubles, the boys saved 19 lives, took 276 patients for rides, helped at 29 fires and numerous other acts of help.[110] As previously mentioned they were also preparing the ground for the swimming bath in the girls' school. At the branch school at Islamabad the boys were the town's only fire brigade and attended every fire with a fire fighting pump which the headmaster, Shrida Butt, had persuaded the townsfolk to buy some years before. Such a record of voluntary service would be remarkable in any other school and yet by the early 1930s Biscoe had so inculcated the ethos of social service into his Kashmiri students that they continued to behave in this way even during those tumultuous times. The log for 1933 also describes the many acts of help given by boys of the schools, including 14 lives saved from drowning. Twelve boys were given medals for their act but two did not receive a medal because they had reported the deed themselves. In reporting the details of the many acts by the boys, the 1932 log concludes:

Just after the September riots a big fire broke out in the city and two prominent leaders, one from each of the communities came to help in fighting the flames. This shows that the spirit of citizenship is the only way in which the spirit of communalism can be eradicated; therefore it is now more than ever incumbent on us to encourage our boys to learn good citizenship through social service.

Thus we see year by year the boys learning by practical experience the joys of service which when once sampled prove the truth of Christ's promise to all who try to follow in His footsteps, 'I am come that they might have life and that they might have it more abundantly.' Through the joys of service life becomes really worth living, as it does by no other means.[111]

This sentence is the only one in the 1932 log that refers explicitly to Jesus and there is one other mention of the same quotation; it is not therefore surprising that conventional missionaries were unsympathetic to the work of the Kashmir schools. Recall that it was in those same months of 1932 that Biscoe was being criticised by the CMS in Lahore for not fostering Christian teaching in the Kashmir schools and they were being recommended for closure! In marked contrast, Sheikh Abdullah wrote to Biscoe:

> I, on behalf of the Muslims of Kashmir, offer my heartfelt thanks for the strenuous efforts by you and your school in helping our wounded to hospital. You have shown us all what true Christianity means.[112]

At the end of 1933, Eric had completed six years service with the CMS and was due for furlough in Britain. Muriel Mallinson would also be on furlough in 1934, so Biscoe at 70 would have no assistance. However, early in 1933 he received an unexpected and very timely offer of help from Fred Jacob to come out at his own expense. Jacob was then 60 having just retired from being Headmaster of Felsted Preparatory School in England. He had heard Biscoe speaking on his last furlough in 1931 about the Kashmir schools and volunteered his services on retirement. A widower with two adult step-daughters, his offer was most timely; he arrived in October 1933 and contributed a very great deal to the schools during the next 12 years, including a period when he acted as principal. As previously mentioned his first activity was to provide the means to build a swimming bath for the girls' school and lead the boys in excavating the site. During the tragic events that occurred the next year, while Eric and Phil were away, he played a major part in supporting Biscoe.

7

Victory After Defeat, 1934–39

God meant it for good.[1]

Missionaries and Indian Christians

In November 1933 Eric and Phil left for their first furlough in England as did Muriel Mallinson, so Biscoe, now 70, resumed full responsibility for the six boys' schools and the girls' school as well. He and Eric wrote to each other every week and it is clear from their letters, which have survived, that Eric was now much more familiar with the enterprise and the staff than Biscoe and he would be sorely missed. While Biscoe had the timely support of Fred Jacob, and Marion Price took charge of the girls' school, he was also beset by parochial troubles in the Indian Christian community in Srinagar and some of the English missionaries.

One elderly missionary, Aggie Churchill-Taylor, ran a small school for girls under the auspices of the Church of England *Zenana* Mission Society (CEZMS) and she had several Indian Christian teachers who lived in an annex to her house. One of her Kashmiri servants told her that he was interested in becoming Christian and read the Bible with her. She had written about him in her missionary magazine as a potential convert. Biscoe and Eric had suspected his motives in 1933 and early in 1934 Biscoe wrote to Eric in England:

Re Aggie's swine of a motor driver. I find the reason of her love
for him is that he is an inquirer!!! I also have now discovered
that the CEZ Christian teachers' quarters have been a Brothel
for three years or more, her servants making a good living out
of it. When shall we get these damned fools of Missionary
Societies to learn common sense? As you know I have had to
see during my time in Kashmir so much scandalous wickedness
which would never have been, had missionaries not been such
idiots and fools, embracing with both arms the rascals who say
they want to go Christian. No wonder that few people support
missionary work.[2]

One of the women teachers was diagnosed with advanced syphilis
and was treated at the Mission Hospital; Ernest Neve was very
angry and said he would charge the CEZ for the expensive drugs
she would need. However, she died soon after. Wigram in Lahore
ordered a committee of Neve, Biscoe and Marion Smyth (doctor at
the Women's Hospital) to close down the school forthwith and sack
the servants, despite the protests of Aggie, who insisted that the
driver was innocent and the woman caught the disease from her
parents.

The repercussions of this were that the little school was absorbed
into the Mission Girls' School[3] and strained relations between
Biscoe and the Indian Christian congregation increased. They felt
he was responsible for exposing their shame and he was reinforced
in his view that most of them were not genuine in their Christian
beliefs. This was doubly difficult because he was the only ordained
priest to serve their church. The strain on Biscoe was evident in his
chronic and severe indigestion and his increasing irascibility that
would become acute two months later.

The other ever present worry for Biscoe was the shortage of
funds to support the whole enterprise. Since 1930 support from the
Church Missionary Society (CMS) had declined to less than half of
its former level and continued to fall, and State support, which now
was the main source of funds, was always uncertain because of the
protracted bureaucracy. In February 1934, he had to dismiss seven
teachers, and the others offered to take a 10 per cent cut in salary,

in order to cut expenditure by 800 rupees per month. 'It is most noble of the staff! And shows their Christian spirit which certain people at Lahore would call their heathen offer.'[4]

In 1930 he and Eric had floated the idea of appealing for an endowment fund – the interest from which would provide the running expenses of the schools and so make them financially independent. This was launched at the end of 1933 with a forcefully expressed pamphlet, written by Eric that was distributed to 5,000 names in India, England and the USA.

> What's the good of Education? We cram a lot of useless facts into a child's head and give him mental indigestion. Do the successful candidates in examinations always prove equally successful in after life?
>
> What is good education? Certainly it is better than the foregoing. True education is character building, the development of the whole child in soul, in mind and in body.
>
> For fifty years an educational experiment has been conducted in Kashmir, India, for turning jellyfish into men of character.
>
> Do you believe in the Christian Standards of life and conduct? Loyalty to King and empire? The chivalrous treatment of women? Practical help and courtesy to the aged and weak? The humane treatment of animals? If so help the school which includes all these as an integral part of the education it gives.
>
> The school educates about 1500 boys and 300 girls in Kashmir. For many years it has been living a hand to mouth existence, and now urgently needs at least £40000 in order to endow it and ensure that its work may be carried on for the benefit of Kashmir, India and the World.

The pamphlet concluded with a list of 23 distinguished people who had all visited the schools and agreed to lend their names as references – 'ask any of them' – and a bank order form.

Biscoe enclosed a copy with every letter he wrote, Eric gave them out at all the meetings he had in Britain during 1934 and others were distributed in America. The endowment fund was singularly unsuccessful. In the next six years it raised £665 before being closed. By then Eric was instigating another plan to make the institution self-supporting, which it eventually did.

The Tragedy at the Wular Lake

Every April since 1893 Biscoe had taken a party of teachers and boys into camp by the Wular Lake where they sailed, and climbed the surrounding mountains. The purpose was to allay the fears of the local people of the dangers of the lake as well as to bond the staff and boys in outdoor activities. The lake is dangerous for the flat-bottomed boats that Kashmiris use because the sudden strong winds that blow from one of three directions can rapidly whip up waves that will easily swamp them. The most feared wind blows from the north – the *Nag Kawn* or One-eyed Wind; so-called because Kashmiris believed that one must always be careful of those who are one-eyed or squint with one eye. The second wind blows from Baramula in the south-west and the third from Bandipur in the east. Indeed the name Wular is Sanskrit for high waves. Round-hulled sailing boats are much more buoyant and Biscoe had English designed boats built for these expeditions, but even they could get into difficulties, as he described in 1923:

> Off Zurimanz we were struck by the Nag Kawn just as if a hand had spanked the water, the wind vertical. The 12-oar sails blown away, all the crew's pugarrees blown off. The launch all but expired. I made for Watlab harbour but the screw stuck fast in the weeds, with difficulty got the ladies ashore, then made for Zurimanz beach.[5]

For the previous five years the responsibility for the Wular camp in April had been Eric's, but in 1934 Biscoe, now 71 and stressed by the recent events in Srinagar, had full charge again. Immediately prior to the trip he had attended a farewell party for Ernest Neve's retirement, followed by one for Aggie Churchill-Taylor which had been stressful. In order to have a few days rest along the way to the lake he and Blanche and daughter Frances set off down the Jhelum River in their houseboat ahead of the main party on 5 April. Biscoe spent most of the time in bed with bad indigestion. This was

Figure 23 Cecil Biscoe at the Wular Lake, aged 70

probably aggravated by the knowledge that he had to return to Srinagar three days later to take the Sunday service for the Indian congregation. The account that follows is taken largely from the four letters that Biscoe wrote to Eric in England on 16, 24 and 30 April and on 6 May 1934 as the tragedy unfolded.

Flowing north, the waters of the Jhelum River enter the Wular Lake through a large delta where there are two small villages called Mukdanyari and Banyari where the people made their living by fishing, and by harvesting the edible water chestnut called *singhara* that grows around the edge of the lake.[6] The party comprising about 40 teachers and boys assembled at Banyari and then travelled westwards along the southern edge of the lake to a large camping spot at Ningal. The crossing was rough so the flat-bottomed boats were towed by either the launch or the cutter to safe moorings at Ningal nullah.

The fleet comprised Biscoe's houseboat, *Shotover*, and several *doongas*, all flat-bottomed local designed craft. The round-hulled boats comprised four sailing boats – the naval cutter or 12-oar, two six-oar boats, one light double scull skiff – and the motor launch. Apart from Biscoe the most experienced men were Nand Lal Bakaya who captained the cutter, Nanak Chand Koul who captained one of the six-oar boats and Tara Chand Zalpuri who drove the launch – he had attended the wedding of Eric and Phil six years before. As well as Blanche and Frances on the houseboat four English visitors accompanied the party – Fred Jacob and his daughter Mary in one *doonga*, and Edmund Wigram (the son of Marcus Wigram the CMS Lahore Secretary) and Daphne Douglas in the houseboat. Tara Chand had his own *doonga* which accommodated 14 members of his family, including three young boys who attended the school; his son Narian Joo (14) and two nephews Triloki Nath (9) and Dwarka Nath (3) the latter being the adopted son of Nanak Chand. The events that follow made such a strong impression on young Triloki Nath that 70 years later he wrote from memory a vivid account which was published in 2004.[7]

The first excursion from the camp began on 11 April when the four sailing boats crossed the lake to the north-west point called Zurimanz. The cutter left early so that the crew could climb the hills behind Zurimanz to the tomb of a revered saint, Babr Shukr-u-Din, while the other three boats followed later and all were due back at camp in the late afternoon. Biscoe was still ill and did not go on the trip.

At 3.30 pm a sudden very strong squall from Baramula struck the camp at Ningal, followed by the Nag Kawn from the north, which caused a cargo boat and two fishing boats near Banyari to sink and blew roofs off houses in Srinagar city 30 miles away. Three of the sailing boats returned soon after but Nanak Chand's boat did not return. At 5 pm Biscoe, who had been ill in bed all day got up and with Frances and Tara Chand set out in the launch to search for the missing boat. The first two squalls had blown themselves out but then a third squall from the east hit the launch and almost swamped it so that the engine almost stopped, 'I had never experienced such a dusting in the launch,' wrote Biscoe to

Eric in England. For several hours they searched the coast around Zurimanz and called to villagers who said they had seen sails to the north, so they followed that lead to no avail. As evening came on those at Ningal became anxious for the return of the launch and Nanak Chand's boat. Young Triloki Nath and his cousin watched the houseboat from a discrete distance and could see Jacob and Bakaya with other teachers on the rooftop platform of the houseboat holding a gas light, blowing a bugle and calling with a megaphone into the darkness. Blanche also joined them on the roof and she must have been especially worried because she knew Biscoe was not well and probably should not have gone out on the search. Eventually the launch returned near midnight, the crew exhausted and worried with still no sign of the missing boat and its crew of seven men. Triloki Nath wrote:

> Rev Biscoe came out of the launch and joined the party on the roof of the house boat. He was very furious. It appeared he was terribly annoyed with Mrs Biscoe as he had wrong impression that she did not show anxiety for their return from the lake and made no attempts for their return. More so it was a real shock to Rev Biscoe as there was no trace of the six-oared boat even after a thorough search. So high pitched was his rebuke that all present there heard him in dead silence. From Tara Chand we came to know later, when he returned to our *Doonga* for that night's rest, that Rev Biscoe was so perturbed and frustrated that he used un-parliamentary language when he spoke to his wife, which Tara Chand had never heard during his long service with Rev Biscoe.[8]

Early next morning the houseboat occupants left; Wigram to catch a bus to Peshawar and Blanche, Frances and Daphne Douglas returned to Srinagar. Only Jacob and his daughter remained with Biscoe and the staff. Until Triloki Nath wrote his account it was unclear why Blanche and Frances left so suddenly before the fate of the crew was known, but it is now. Blanche must have been acutely distressed at Biscoe's response to her concern for his well being; all her married life she had had to deal with his poor health and she would have been understandably worried at him going out while ill in an open boat in stormy weather. His public outburst at her was deeply humiliating and unreasonable and is indicative of the stress he had been under beforehand, now increased by the worry of the missing crew and boat.

Since Nanak Chand's boat had still not returned on that first morning the hope was that, as had happened before, they had run before the Nag Kawn to Bandipur on the eastern shore and were staying there with friends. All day they waited anxiously for a telegram from Bandipur and they enquired of every boatman that came from the lake, but none had seen the boat.

Early the next morning (13 April) the search resumed. Bakaya and Jacob in the cutter left for Bandipur while Biscoe and Tara Chand with Mary Jacob returned to Zurimanz in the launch. There they learnt from the villagers that all seven had drowned. The cutter found the boat near Mukdanyari, missing its oars and sail and containing only the bodies of Nanak Chand and Dina Nath. This was devastating news; how had they perished and where were the remaining five bodies? The two bodies found on the boat had no water in their lungs; therefore they had not drowned but had died of exhaustion on the land. Also Nanak Chand's watch carried around his neck had stopped at 4 o'clock but on which day was not clear.

Bakaya and Suraj Baliya, the senior teacher who had been responsible for the new building at the girls' school three years before, offered to take the bodies to Srinagar and break the news to the families, while Biscoe and Jacob began to organise the search for the other five. The school camp was abandoned, the 40 teachers and boys going back to Srinagar; the houseboat and Tara Chand's *doonga*, with his family, moved to Banyari to be closer to the site of the wreck as the search continued.

As news of the tragedy spread many people joined the search. Ken Hadow cycled out from Srinagar having asked the Governor to help. The *Lambadar* of Bandipur arrived with boats and men; the Forests Department offered help and the Inspector of Police, an old boy, came from Srinagar. He was especially helpful in finding out from the frightened villagers what they knew and organising boats to search the lake. A week after the disappearance three more bodies were found and taken to Srinagar for cremation and the last two bodies were found two days later.

Piecing together all the evidence from the position and state of the bodies and the condition of the boat it seemed that it had been swamped by the fierce winds on the first afternoon and all seven men lost contact with the boat in the maelstrom. Five of them drowned and only the two strongest swimmers were able to reach the shore, but in an exhausted state where they later died of exposure. At some time on the second day the abandoned boat was found by local men who stole its contents and then placed it and the two bodies near Mukdanyari, where the search party found them.

Nanak Chand was an outstanding and enthusiastic swimmer and he loved the Wular camps, so for him to have died as he did the conditions they faced must have been extreme. He had shown his fine qualities six years before in the big flood of 1928 when he rescued more than 20 women and children trapped in the military barracks when no boatman would go to their help. 'He successfully carried all the boats to the barracks at a great risk to himself, amidst the applause and wonder of the people assembled there.'[9]

His was the greatest loss as Biscoe wrote in the log at the end of the year:

> He was just the sort of man we need on our staff to encourage the boys to forget that they are 'high-born gentlemen.' He had a complete disregard for the taboos of orthodoxy. He was the first Brahmin to lead us in the matter of killing mad dogs for which he was boycotted. He was the first scout master in Kashmir to persuade his Hindu and Muslim scouts to give up the nonsense of separate cooking and feeding while in camp. His love of the water was phenomenal in a Kashmiri. In camp he was always up to some sort of 'rag' and kept us all lively with his good humour [...] He turned his love of carpentry to good use by starting a carpenter's shop in the school and exchanged the genteel position of a teacher for the menial position of a technical instructor, but he did not care a rap for these

distinctions. He soon had the technical department going splendidly with all sorts of plans for the future. However, it was not to be and the Wular which he loved so well claimed him for its own.[10]

With the search over and the many searchers paid, Biscoe, the Jacobs, Bakaya and Tara Chand could return to the city.

Response of the Dharam Sabha

When Bakaya and Suraj Baliya had taken the first two bodies to the city a relative of Nanak Chand called together about 300 Brahmins in order to carry the bodies in procession through the city to show how 'Biscoe kills his teachers'.[11] But before they could do so an extraordinary thing happened. The President of the Dharam Sabha, Pandit Jia Lal Kilam (later to become the Chief Justice of the High Court of Jammu and Kashmir), who had previously been an implacable enemy of all that Biscoe had tried to do, heard about the planned procession and with a party of supporters appeared at the scene and prevented it. He then wrote an article in the Hindu newspaper, *Martund*, explaining the tragedy and praising Biscoe for making men of the Kashmiris, and gave away 3,000 copies in the city. He then joined the mourners at the burning *ghat*, a symbolic gesture of approval from the highest leader of the Hindu community.

The next day, 14 April, he and the Secretary of the Dharam Sabha, Pandit Kashyap Bandhu came to Banyari to offer Biscoe their condolences.

> We come to thank you for having striven for 40 years to turn Kashmiris into men and those who you have lost you had made like British men to face dangers as in the great storm. I hope you will not allow this accident to prevent you taking your staff and boys to the Wular again, for those Wular trips help our people to become men and we should not be deterred by this year's disaster. We have not always seen eye to eye in the school's efforts for social uplift but now we understand and intend to work with you.[12]

Young Triloki Nath saw them arrive and recalled the encounter:

> So gloomy and shocked was Rev Biscoe that he used to roam
> about on the roof of his houseboat anchored near Banyari.
> He used to observe closely the Wular Lake waters with his
> binoculars in the hope that just per chance a gallant drowned
> swimmer's corpse may surface from the Lake [...] I noticed
> Rev Biscoe coming down from his house boat to receive his
> unexpected visitors. A word went round later that they offered
> Rev Biscoe their sincere condolences on behalf of the Kashmiri
> Pandits' Santam Dharam Sabha and on their own behalf.
> This touching and welcome gesture of the K.P. leaders proved
> a healing touch for the gloomy Rev Biscoe.[13]

The remarkable change in attitude of the orthodox Hindus
continued through the weeks that followed. On his return to the
city Biscoe wrote to Eric on 24 April and 6 May:

> It's wonderful how Kilam has taken up the matter, collecting
> funds for the families bereaved. I met him just come from the
> Prime Minister from whom he had got fifty rupees. The people
> generally have taken the blow remarkably well. After addressing
> Central and Sheikh Bagh schools I visited the Resident who
> was very sympathetic and asked me to come and see him often.
> The Governor visited me yesterday and said that he hoped to
> get some help from State funds. It really looks as if something
> more than talk will come out of this catastrophe.
>
> When the Mirwaiz's Muslim party [Goats] published an
> opposite opinion in their paper *Islam* the *Martund* countered
> with the question, 'Is anyone blamed because adventurers
> attempt Everest and other mountains and die in the attempt,
> are they not honoured? We look upon our men as heroes!'
> Sheikh Abdullah also called to offer his sympathy and
> support.[14]

Eric was astounded by Jia Lal Kilam's response because Jia Lal
Kilam had been so opposed to the remarriage of Hindu widows

since the first two in 1928 and had pursued the Hindu teachers responsible. Eric thought he would have been much more likely to exploit the disaster. As for the opinion in the *Islam* he wrote:

> I am relieved to know for certain that it was the Goats that wrote that article against us, for it counts for nothing. The Goats are obviously State puppets and were told to write that in order to bolster up the cuts so that the State might be able to say they had public support for their action.[15]

Three weeks later Biscoe learnt that the Dharam Sabha in Gilgit had already collected and sent 400 rupees for the widows of the drowned men and were sending another 200 rupees, other towns were also subscribing. He wrote to Eric, 'This tragedy has touched them, for I have never known them to be in the least generous before.'[16]

Even more astonishing in the turn around was a visit to Biscoe two months later of Kashyap Bandhu, the Secretary of Dharam Sabha, who had gone to the Wular Lake immediately after the disaster.[17] He called to say that a pregnant widow came to his house late at night and asked him to procure a doctor to do an abortion. He instead persuaded her to have her baby in his house and later returned with her to her village, talked her family over, and secured her remarriage!

Equally astonishing was the reaction to holding the annual swim across the Wular Lake in September.[18] Twenty boys wished to swim but the parents of 12 forbade them, so the remaining eight swam accompanied by five European visitors and Ralph Moan (introduced later on in this chapter) on the staff. All the boys made the full crossing, a record for this event and remarkable after the tragedy five months earlier.

It was these actions that decided Biscoe to title the 1934 log *Victory after Defeat.* In it he wrote:

> Now through the loss of our seven brave fellows, salvation for the women has dawned, for these men who were against us are for us. The younger spirits among the Brahmins had been for

the last year or so trying to alter the custom of ages, and it is they who were able to see in our lake tragedy something inspiring, viz. seven Brahmin youths who went forth to conquer the Wular storm [...]

In 1928 our Headmaster, Shenker Koul with 300 old boys carried out a double wedding and in consequence for more than a year they had to endure the curses of the orthodox and much else. Now we hope that ere long the Hindu women will be emancipated. Since that first wedding 46 more widows have been given the chance to live a lawful married life through the efforts of our school staff and old boys.[19]

In England Eric and Phil were especially concerned for the family of Nanak Chand and his little adopted son, Dwarka Nath. They sent him toys and his mother clothes and other support.[20] In later years Eric and Phil invited them to Sheikh Bagh and Dwarka Nath played with me and my sister Ann. In 1975 he and I renewed our friendship in Srinagar when our respective families got to know each other. When they had to flee Kashmir in 1989 we helped them establish a home in Delhi and since 2014 the association of our families, begun 80 years ago, is continuing through our respective daughters and their children. It was of course Dwarka Nath who introduced me to Triloki Nath and his vivid account of the Wular events.

Biscoe's Conflict with the School Staff

Despite the wonderful support that he received after the Wular tragedy, Biscoe's relations with the school staff deteriorated in the following three months. As already mentioned he had, earlier in the year, been obliged for financial reasons to sack seven of the teachers. Apart from one they were the most recent appointments and accepted their lot. However, Isher Koul was not happy as he felt a younger teacher, Balbadar Sapru (nicknamed Balji), had been preferred over him and so he made life difficult for Biscoe. Not surprisingly, several other teachers were sympathetic to Isher Koul because he was a jolly, good humoured man with many friends.

All was still well in May when Frances was married because there is a group photo of all the staff with the bridal party in the 1934 log. Something must have come to a head in mid July but Biscoe chose not to tell Eric in England; Eric's first intimation of disloyalty among the staff came in a letter from Blanche's sister Helen so he wrote to his father, 'What is it this time? Is it serious and therefore you don't want to worry me? I should prefer to know the full details rather than being left to imagine possibilities.'[21] Then Shenker Koul, the headmaster, wrote to him that Bakaya had resigned and 'You will have had full details from your father.'[22] But he had not. A month later he received the details:

As you ask about the trouble in the school staff, it has been the trouble you expected on account of some younger members of the staff throwing off punditom etc. and resented by certain seniors. It started off actually after I dismissed Isher Koul for refusing to play the game, preferring punditom to his school. It started off by bullying Balji by setting his wife's family against him, a long story and an absolute unadulterated pundit show. Shenker, Baliya, Bhagwan Das and one or two others had to stem the tide. The result of this action caused more gales to blow, so that Suraj Raina, Nand Lal Bakaya, Amar Chand, Vishnu Hakim and Tara Chand the motor-boat man made a league to fight for Isher Koul. We have had gay times. Nand Lal Bakaya has resigned and cheered me. The others are all on tenterhooks as they do not know what action I'm going to take. But the result of the kick up is they have left Balji alone and the young party is stronger than it was. The whole business is of course rotten but I have learnt more of the ways of the serpent. Had some sad days and amusing times and on the whole I think we have profited rather than lost. It will be quite a bit of interesting history which we will be able to relate by the time you return.

One especially interesting item the traitors, as I call them, went to Jaya Lal Kilam to ask his help to start a national school (the old game) but he sent them off with a flea in their ears, upbraiding them for being traitors.[23]

Traitors? Biscoe calls the staunch helpers of the Wular tragedy four months ago – Bakaya and Tara Chand – and Amar Chand traitors? This is extraordinary and suggests that he was seriously unwell. A month before writing those words he had suffered a bad fall from his horse at Nil Nag onto his head that had necessitated him being carried in a dandy (a kind of stretcher). Did he have concussion? Perhaps, except that these were not the only senior teachers that were targeted. In November Biscoe ordered the other Wular hero, Suraj Baliya, to resign from his headship because 'More than half the staff accused him of being a dictator and fearing him, only three spoke for him.'[24] This was the man who had been responsible two years before for overseeing the building of new classrooms and a swimming bath for the girls' school. Baliya provided the letter of resignation a week later but refused to acknowledge the charge. He must have been deeply offended by this treatment, especially as he is referred to in the earlier accusation as having helped Shenker Koul and Bagwan Das to 'stem the tide'.

From the distance of 80 years it is difficult to arrive at a just conclusion of these actions but it does seem that Biscoe in 1934 was behaving erratically and irrationally; or actions towards the staff that had worked for 40 years worked no longer. Men like his great friend Shenker Koul could see it and tried to let Eric know discretely that all was not well in Kashmir. The tone of Biscoe's letter about the so-called traitors and later Suraj Baliya indicates that he retained a deep-seated distrust of Kashmiri Hindus, as his term 'punditom' reflects. He readily acknowledged that he could not understand them and part of the reason was probably because he had never learnt to speak their language and only ever conversed in English; and he and Blanche never entertained them at home or visited them in their homes. In this they were typical of the English in India that Forster so deplored in *A Passage to India*. So long as the staff showed proper respect as subordinates all was well. But with the political winds blowing in India and recently in Kashmir, men of strong personality were no longer prepared to be bidden. To Biscoe, who had always commanded obedience, such men were insubordinate. Nand Lal Bakaya was a strong person who was not prepared to see his friend Isher Koul dismissed and when reprimanded by Biscoe chose to resign; likewise Suraj Baliya.

For Eric in England it must have been doubly disturbing; he had an enormous admiration for his father and what he had done in Kashmir but he also knew the players in this business far better than his father did. This was because he could speak their language and he and Phil entertained them in their home and went to theirs; these men were their friends, not their subordinates. He sent his father his assessments of some of the men mentioned:

Nand Lal Bakaya has never made any secret of the fact that he is a firmly believing Hindu. I call that a point in his favour. But consequent on that he has refused to send his daughter to school and excused himself behind his mother! Being a Hindu he will oppose any breaches such as the young men had made, and might throw in his lot with the orthodox pundits. When I had the rebellion of Muslim boys they all accused NL of partiality. His was the only name mentioned by them. As you know I refused to take any notice. When the pundits rebelled I remember having to reprove NL for not playing the game. I think I said that some of the staff were much stricter when Muslim boys were at fault and were letting things slide now that Hindu boys were fooling and NL began to argue about it. I did not take much notice at the time as I knew he was a keen Hindu. In his favour I will say that after the first communal fighting he was the only master who ever mentioned excesses by masters on Muslims.

Suraj Baliya. You know that he is a strong character. He has very definite likes and dislikes. I imagine he alienated Hindu sympathy for him over the case of the boy cribbing in the matric. That would tend to make him less orthodox. He is jealous of Vishnu Hakim. He dislikes Suraj Raina for some reason which I have never discovered. He has very definitely befriended Balji and some of the younger masters and has therefore made enemies. He pretends to laugh at Hindu orthodoxy but he observes some of its customs. I used to receive a good many anonymous letters accusing him of having swindled Muriel over building the Girls' School and that he never paid the carpenters and the masons. I finally brought the matter up at a staff meeting and said that in future if I received such letters they would go to the person about whom they were written to take what action he could to find out the writer. The result was that the letters ceased. Therefore someone on the staff was responsible. Though Baliya had never said any names, I am pretty sure he suspected NLB of having a hand in those letters.

In my own mind I think Baliya has been responsible for bringing off some private fights out of what started as a row between the progressives and the orthodox, eg Suraj Raina (and possibly Vishnu Hakim). I dare say NL is also free from any share in persecuting the junior staff, but I think he may now be trying to bring about the downfall of SB.

Vishnu Hakim. For some time I have felt uncertain of his trustworthiness – and I was not surprised when I heard you had had trouble with him. Curiously enough I was talking to Phil and I said to her I wonder whether it will end in Baliya's downfall for I know he dislikes Suraj Raina, Vishnu Hakim and Nand Lal Bakaya, and it seems curious that all those three should be in trouble. Fancy Suraj Raina playing false after all these years.

As I say, I think Baliya may have used this opportunity to pay off old scores, but even so I imagine that the orthodox pundits will do a good deal to put a stop to any break away by the more progressives and Baliya has been with them as their champion and a fairly open champion and I should date his break from hard and fast orthodoxy from the time of the Matric exam when he caught a boy cribbing. Also Baliya has never hesitated to investigate cases of sodomy and that does not make him popular.[25]

In England Eric showed a film of school activities and spoke at many venues about the work in Kashmir and promoted the endowment appeal. Most responses were favourable but some definitely were not. In Exeter Frank Lucey had sent out 1,400 notices but less than 200 turned up.[26] The Bishop of Exeter introduced Eric, knew nothing about him, talked for 25 minutes mostly about Africa and China and then left the meeting without seeing the film – too busy. He then wrote a highly critical letter to Lucey, which has not survived but can be deduced from Lucey's reply, written two weeks after the meeting and printed in the 1934 log:

> the English Raj is unpopular because of its contempt of the Hindu religion by such actions as forcing boys to play football and wear leather shoes; and missionary work is objectionable because their converts to Christianity are worthless.[27]

His views closely resemble those in Forster's 1920 review of Biscoe's book, discussed in Chapter 5, which is probably where he got his information. Lucey pointed out that:

> The story you read was referring to some 40 years ago. Kashmir then was a very backward State and I understand that any form of physical exercise was regarded as degrading by the Brahmin pandits, who consequently suffered from a complete lack of physical and moral stamina [...] Rightly or wrongly, I believe that in the early days some degree of physical persuasion was used to overcome that prejudice. I believe the Kashmiri would be the first today to thank Biscoe for breaking down that prejudice. I doubt whether it could have been broken down without such persuasion.[28]

Shortly after Biscoe read the Bishop's letter he was visiting one of those first footballers on his deathbed and told him how much the Bishop sympathised with the indignity he had suffered as a boy. The old boy thereupon wrote to the Bishop to say how thankful he was to Padre Biscoe who made them play the game of football and how this game had not only helped him to be a man but also many of his fellow countrymen.[29]

The response of the Hindu community in Srinagar to the Wular tragedy earlier in that year supports Lucey's comments.

Return of Eric and Phil, Reconciliation and Different Leadership

The beginning of 1935 saw Biscoe in bed for ten days with chest pains, as occurred nearly every winter. But this time Biscoe could not escape to the plains of India until Eric and Phil returned to Kashmir in February and resumed responsibility for the schools. He and Blanche left soon after for Jammu and Lahore. Biscoe wrote to Julian, 'It is all most difficult to belong to a missionary society as their ideas are not necessarily mine after years of experience.'[30] Eric and Phil were back in time for the April trip to the Wular Lake, exactly a year after the loss of the six masters; it was well attended and went without mishap but two quite different events marked this first anniversary.

Biscoe had been thinking of how to make the Wular Lake safer for Kashmiri craft and he now presented the Inspector of Police for the Wular district, who had been so helpful the year before, with a deck that could be fitted to a Kashmiri *shikara* to prevent it being swamped in a storm and so making it suitable as a lifeboat for rescue.[31]

A month later the British Resident in Kashmir in recognition of her years of service in Kashmir, bestowed on Blanche the Silver Jubilee Medal, commemorating the twenty-fifth year of the reign of King George and Queen Mary. I have no evidence of who nominated her for this but the most likely person would have been Ken Hadow, who had gone out to the Wular Lake two days after the tragedy, having probably learnt from Blanche about Biscoe's state of mind. I know that Ken admired her because ten years later when I, aged 14, expressed to him the common sentiment that my grandfather was a great man he replied: 'No, Hugh, it is your grandmother who is the really great one'. I was astonished then but now I understand why he said it.

How good relations with the staff was restored in 1935 from the low point in late 1934 is nowhere recorded; that it was can be gleaned from the presence in group photos of Nand Lal Bakaya in the 1935 log, of Isher Koul in July 1936 and of both of them in November 1936. Indeed, Bakaya was being offered to the Tanganyika Education Department in August 1935 by Biscoe.[32]

But Suraj Baliya fared worse; in November 1936 Biscoe, Eric and Jacob appeared in court against him.[33]

With Eric and Phil back, the annual climb of Mahadeo resumed in June and this time all carried their own gear. A month later the annual three mile swim across the Dal Lake took place, which over 100 boys completed. Phil was swimming with the first ten and was near the shore when the leading boy said to the others in Kashmiri 'take it easy and let the Memsahib come in first'. Phil heard this and shouted, 'if you do that I will stop and get into the boat'.[34] She was also very active in encouraging the girls to learn to swim in their swimming pool and two years later they were swimming in the Dal Lake.[35] However, the most important factor in restoring good relations was the start of the annual summer treks with the younger masters.

The Cashmere Climbing Club

In the summer holidays of 1935 about 20 teachers joined Eric, Phil and Fred Jacob for a week's trekking in the mountains, and so was founded the Cashmere Climbing Club (now known as the Jammu & Kashmir Mountaineering and Hiking Club). The following summer of 1936 a much more ambitious trek was organised at the instigation of Nand Lal Bakaya, now reinstated. They began from the Wular Lake and trekked up the Erin Nullah to the sacred Lake Gangabal under the massif of Mount Haramukh (16,872 feet). Nand Lal explained that the lake is sacred to Hindus because they believe it is the source of the River Ganges by an underground route that emerges in the plains of India at the confluence of it and the River Jumna at Allahabad, another very sacred site. For this reason Kashmiri Brahmins would carry the ashes of their deceased relatives to Lake Gangabal so that their spirits might be released into Mother Ganga. As a party carrying the ashes would arrive at a narrow part of the Erin valley called *Hamsa Dwar* (Swan Gate) they would cry out aloud for the benefit of the departed relative, 'We have arrived at Hamsa Dwar!'

When the Climbing Club party arrived at the lake they launched a collapsible canoe and invited reluctant local people to take rides in it. In one photo Isher Koul is happily paddling with his friend Samsar Chand,[36] so he must have been reappointed to the staff by then. As well as canoeing and bathing in the sacred lake most of the party climbed to the top of the low peak of Haramukh. Eight years later Nand Lal Bakaya climbed the main peak, as he describes in his book, *Holidaying and Trekking in Kashmir*.[37] He was only the third person to do that, being preceded by Ernest Neve and Geoffrey Millais in 1899[38] and C.G. Bruce in 1909.

In 1937 the Climbing Club trekked to another mountain lake, Konsanag, on the opposite side of the Kashmir Valley in the Pir Panjal Range. Once again they bathed in the icy waters and gave joy rides in the canoe to very surprised Gujars living nearby; and they climbed one of the three nearby Brahma Peaks – Brahma Shakri (14,500 feet) – also described in Bakaya's book. Bakaya relates the Kashmiri tradition that it was on these three peaks that Vishnu, Siva and Brahma survived the great deluge and saved the seeds of beings from destruction – the Hindu version of Noah's ark.

A special pleasure of these treks, as I remember from the trek of 1942, again to Lake Gangabal but from another direction, was the wide ranging discussions that took place as the party walked through the forest gorges, across the upland grassy meadows and sat around the evening camp fires; talk would range from the ancient history of Kashmir and Hindu mythology to contemporary politics and about the geology and natural history of the places the party passed through. Through these experiences Eric and Phil learnt much about Kashmir's ancient culture and the masters learnt much about the world beyond Kashmir that few of them had ever visited. Among their number was Samsar Chand Koul who was an enthusiastic naturalist and could regale them with the names of all the plants and birds they encountered. Like Bakaya he wrote about these trips in two books that he first published in these years and both went into three editions subsequently – *Birds of Kashmir* published in 1939,[39] 1956 and 1968, and *Beautiful Valleys of Kashmir and Ladakh* published in 1942,[40] 1963 and 1971. He used to joke that he was a graduate of the University of Hungry and Thirsty.

The Khillanmarg Avalanche

Across the valley from Srinagar city and 3,000 feet higher lies the popular holiday site of Gulmarg, much favoured by visitors for riding and golf; and 3,000 feet above it is the upland meadow of Khillanmarg above the permanent tree line. In winter it becomes a broad sloping snow field and in the early 1930s it was a popular place for skiing, and the local Ski Club of India built a timber lodge up there. Phil and Eric took a small party of boys there in 1930 to learn to ski and while sleeping there one night they heard a great roar nearby and discovered next morning that an avalanche had swept down a nearby gully. The club then built a new hut in a more secure position near a grove of large fir trees that had stood for many years and therefore was thought to be a site safe from avalanches.

On 2 March 1936,[41] three British army officers were based in the new hut with one Kashmiri caretaker when an immense avalanche totally engulfed the hut, the protecting trees and a large swathe of trees below the hut – the gap in the tree line could be seen across the valley for many years thereafter. The pressure wave of the avalanche was felt in Srinagar 30 miles away but its cause was not appreciated at the time. Three days later a relative of the caretaker arrived in the city to say that he had been up to Khillanmarg to see his relative and could find no trace of the hut. The news reached Eric at the hostel while he was celebrating Id with the boarders. He announced that he and Phil would form a search party immediately and all the hostel boys volunteered to join them. They chose five from Gilgit with much experience of mountain conditions – Mahbub Wali Khan, an old boy now in the Forest Department, Safdar Ali Khan, BM Gill, Fida Ali Khan and Ahmed Khan – and left that afternoon with Fred Bartlet, a retired Police Officer and Dr Marion Smyth from the Mission Hospital. They reached Gulmarg that night, where they had permission to open Nedou's Hotel, which was closed for the winter, and got a few hours sleep. Early next morning they reached the site where the hut had been but there was no sign of it in the wide expanse of avalanche debris. It was a beautiful clear day as Eric later wrote:

> We looked right across the Kashmir Valley at the vast expanse of mountains beyond. Among them were the familiar peaks of Haramukh, Mahadeo and Kolahoi. But towering up behind

them, like a cathedral among the roof tops, was Nanga Parbat with the sun coming up behind it, some 80 miles away.[42]

Soon they were joined by a large group of local men drafted by the State Government to assist but, as there was no one to organise them, the Mission School party assumed the role and began a systematic search by digging deep shafts at 30-foot intervals through the debris across the featureless site. It took until the afternoon before they found the remains of the hut by which time the Governor and a State Medical Officer had arrived. By the evening the bodies of the three skiers were found, frozen exactly as they had been at the moment the pressure wave reached them – two were sitting at the table having breakfast, one in the process of eating an egg, the third lying on a bunk. There was no sign that any had reacted to the pressure wave, which must have killed them instantly. The caretaker's body was not found until several days later some distance from the hut. Stretchers had been taken up to carry the bodies down to Gulmarg but by the time the last body was found the Governor's party had requisitioned the stretchers for themselves and had been carried down to the hotel on them! So makeshift stretchers had to be made from tree branches and the bodies slid down on the snow. The Mission School party again stayed in the hotel but late in the evening Eric discovered[43] that no arrangements had been made for cooked food and shelter for the village men who had been drafted to the task by the Governor. He decided that Willie Nedou, the owner of the hotel, would not object if he let them into the closed ball room. There they lit the big stoves and the exhausted men settled around them and cooked a meal of rice – the first time they had probably ever been inside the grand place.

Next day it started to snow hard and, as the State authorities had now taken full charge, the school party returned to Srinagar, much pleased with their joint efforts. What was remarkable about their effort was that the hostel boys were themselves the sons of chiefs from Gilgit and yet they had fully participated in the hard manual work, in marked contrast to the Kashmir Government officials. This was noted in an article on the event in the main Indian newspaper two weeks later:

The records of the CMS School at Srinagar shine with instances of heroism and self-sacrifice, and once again, in the Khillanmarg tragedy, boys and old boys of the School were in the forefront of the rescue operations [...] They carried loads, wielded shovels, and never complained, though hungry, cold and tired. The spirit infused into the students of the CMS School by the Biscoe family during many years of its existence shows itself in many and varied circumstances, but never more so than in an emergency of this nature.[44]

The regiments of the three officers who died subscribed money to be distributed among the village men, and Fred Bartlet personally gave a share to each man some weeks later; and, in recognition of their help, the mother of one of the officers presented the hostel with a wireless for the use of the boys – a considerable gift in 1936. The Ski Club of India presented the school with a trophy for the House showing the most interest in climbing and trekking each year, and Marion Smyth, Phil and Eric were made honorary life members. The Ski Club also asked the Mission School to design and build a new ski lodge that would withstand all avalanches, and this was completed within the year by the technical department.

The head of the technical department of the Mission School had been Nanak Chand Koul, until his tragic death at the Wular Lake in 1934. In the immediate aftermath of the Wular tragedy its future was uncertain but two months later a tall, gaunt and serious young man with a black beard appeared in Srinagar looking for work as a carpenter; Biscoe took him on, writing to Eric, 'I fancy you liked the fellow and if he is a good carpenter he should be really useful in the school workshop'.[45] Ralph Moan had trained as a carpenter and builder in Scotland and had come to Kashmir in 1928 under the auspices of the Central Asian Mission, a faith mission that did not support its adherents financially but expected 'the Lord to provide'. Ralph and another young man, George Sach, lived in very difficult circumstances in Baltistan for two years until first George and then Ralph became seriously ill with typhoid. They managed to get back to Srinagar where they slowly recovered at the Mission Hospital.[46] But their own mission abandoned them and by 1934 Ralph was destitute. Biscoe offered him Nanak Chand's job, which he took on with enthusiasm and competence for the next six years, until conscripted for war service in 1940.

For the Ski Club of India he began by making an exact scale model of the ski lodge he proposed to build and subjected it to extreme testing. From this he calculated that the final structure, made of whole tree logs bolted together and protected by a large ramp of earth above it would withstand 500 tons dead load or 150 feet of snow, 30 tons of avalanche thrust and a wind force of 60 tons. It was completed by the end of 1936[47] and remained the base for skiing at Khillanmarg for many years thereafter. In the next four years Ralph trained his students in woodwork and quite advanced metal work and he supervised the design and construction of four buildings for the Mission; a new Technical School building, extensions to the hostel and a new building for the Mission Hospital for Women at Rainawari. But by far the most ambitious was the design and construction of the large new building at Sheikh Bagh for assembly hall, classrooms and laboratories. In all these tasks Naranjan Nath Misri was the works manager. As described in Chapter 6, Misri had distinguished himself during the communal riots in 1932 and after a three year delay he received the Viceroy's Silver Medal for Gallantry. In 1935 he had been put in charge of the hostel.[48]

Hadow Memorial School Building

Ever since 1930 the schools had become increasingly difficult to maintain financially, as already mentioned. The endowment appeal in 1934 was not successful and the support of British people living in England was in decline, despite Biscoe's large correspondence; and support from the CMS continued to decline and ceased altogether in 1939. The day of reckoning was deferred for some years by the generosity of an American woman, Clarence Gasque, who came to live in Kashmir in 1938 and for the next seven years more than replaced the CMS annual grant. Looking to the future Eric believed that the schools could only survive if they became financially independent. While the support of the State was substantial and increasing each year, the only viable future for the institution was to raise the fees substantially and offer a higher standard of education with a strong emphasis on science and technical education; this would require an entirely new building on the Sheikh Bagh site. With the enlarged hostel and main playing field already at Sheikh Bagh, as well as the four houses of the missionaries and the original old building that had been the first church, now the Habba Kadal primary school, a large new building would inevitably move the centre of the enterprise away from the Central School at Fateh Kadal.

The Central School was where it had all begun 50 years before; here all visitors were taken to watch the whole school leave the building by poles in 20 seconds and perform gymnastics; here hung the honours boards in the main hall and here Biscoe's main interest remained. Building the new school block at Sheikh Bagh was symbolic of the changing of the guard and Eric putting his stamp on the place. This was made clear to the senior students a year later when Biscoe replied to their request that he visit the new school each week, 'Christ came to serve the poor not the rich. This school is essentially for the children of affluent parents and not for the poor. I am sorry, I love to work with poor and not with the rich'.[49]

The plans for the new building were approved by the Kashmir Government in September 1936[50] and the Biscoes left on their furlough six weeks later and did not return until the building was complete a year later.

For Kashmir the construction of the new building during April–November 1937 was ambitious and required novel skills from the technical department under the leadership of Ralph Moan; the large assembly hall on the ground floor was spanned by five large timber beams each reinforced by two steel trusses bolted to the beam at each end and incorporating two timber separating posts. These were designed by Moan to support the classrooms and science laboratory above the hall and as he wrote:

Our five truss beam reinforcements in the hall will delight the heart of any engineer for symmetry, straightness and perfectly forged joins. A perfect job supplied on the tick of the clock by semi-skilled apprentices [...] We would like to know of any other school in India that will forge 80 stirrup and vee irons and screw 328 three-quarter inch bolts, entirely by hand and fit same to queen post roof trusses in position 42 feet from the ground.[51]

In addition the eastern aspect of the building had an open veranda supported by ten arches of reinforced brick construction, a novelty for Srinagar in an earthquake-prone region. Each column was a box construction of brick inside which steel reinforcing rods were progressively embedded in concrete as the column rose and then continued into the associated arches. In October 1937, as the building neared completion, a moderately strong earthquake shook the city; Ralph and Eric ran out to the playing field to watch how the building fared and were relieved to see it unaffected. And in its 80 years since then it has withstood many more. A month later the school band welcomed Cecil and Blanche back and they were shown over the beautiful new school building by Eric, Ralph and Misri. Six months later Bishop George Barnes officially opened the new building and named it the Hadow Memorial High School in memory of Cecil Hadow, who had been Biscoe's strong friend since he first came to Kashmir and who had supported him through all the vicissitudes that beset him, especially the ever present financial worry of maintaining the schools. Part of his speech was quoted in Chapter 6.

On their furlough Cecil and Blanche spent several months in Africa with their son Julian, and the rest of the time in England, visiting relatives and old friends but doing much less deputation work for the CMS. Most remarkably, however, Biscoe did a television interview for the BBC in London. 'Met Blanche at BBC House, drove to Alexandra Park Palace. 12.30 rehearsal of questions, watched people televisioned. 4.30 my time, lights on face terrific! All staff most sahib like.'[52]

During this time, and especially on the sea voyages, Biscoe began the extraordinary task of transcribing into six exercise books selected parts of the diaries he had kept all his adult life, with contemporary comments.[53] In a way he was now re-living the past as he wanted it to be remembered, while Eric led the enterprise in new directions. The annual logs reflected this too; each one began with a lively recollection of past achievements and re-told stories by Biscoe while Eric and others provided the reports of current events.

Eric's Typhoid and the End of Succession

The goal of the Cashmere Climbing Club for the 1938 trek was to climb two other peaks in the Pir Panjal Range, Tatakuti and Sunset Peak. This was the first time that my sister Ann and I were allowed to join the party and I still remember the excitement of that first evening eating a Kashmiri meal around the camp fire and being told that the food tastes much better if eaten with the fingers rather than a spoon. But for us the experience was cut short; the next morning the party continued and achieved their goals but we had to return with our parents because Eric had become desperately ill with typhoid. He was carried back to Srinagar where he was not expected to live[54] – and Ralph Moan had the Technical School prepare an especially long coffin to accommodate his exceptional height.[55] This was before there was any antibiotic treatment for typhoid and survival was a matter of good nursing and a strong constitution. Eric remained in hospital for the next month and, like his father before him in 1894, slowly recovered but was not fit enough to resume school duties; Eric needed time to recuperate and an anonymous donor provided sufficient funds to enable him and Phil to take three months' sick leave. They decided to revisit New Zealand where they had first met in 1924 and in November left by sea. I was taken with them and when they returned in January 1939 was left at school there for the next two years.

Eric's near-fatal typhoid infection marked a subtle change in the relationship with his father. Through the thirties Eric had been the driving force in running the schools although his father remained officially the principal. This in itself was an unusual situation and would not have been tolerated by any other person; and indeed was not by the eventual successor, Phil Edmonds in 1946. When Eric returned in April 1939 he resumed his subordinate role until

October, when Biscoe was formally retired by the CMS.[56] But even then Eric was not appointed principal and in May 1940 Biscoe was re-confirmed as principal by the CMS until the end of 1940 when he would have completed 50 years in Kashmir.

With the outbreak of war, many British people working in India were reluctant to send their school-age children to Britain and there was a growing need for schools to cater for them in India. Also the CMS urged all missionaries that could do so to seek alternative employment because of the uncertainties of continued funding. Eric and Phil proposed to open a preparatory school at Sheikh Bagh for these children, sharing the grounds and facilities of the Mission School and continuing to contribute their time without salaries. This was approved by Miss Cocks, the CMS Secretary in Lahore. At the end of the summer term, a circular was sent out to some 50 people and Eric and Phil left on a week's trek with the Cashmere Climbing Club. When they returned they were overwhelmed with inquiries and even applications to enrol in the school that had not yet begun!

The school commenced with 30 pupils at the end of October 1940[57] and what became evident very soon was that running the new school was a full-time business and Eric could not continue as Vice Principal of the Mission Schools. Nevertheless, he was able to continue to occupy Barton House, which was converted into a dormitory building for the new school, and Muriel Mallinson also provided accommodation in her house on the Sheikh Bagh as a dormitory for the junior boys. At this remove it is not clear how this was organised between the CMS and the new school; nor is it clear what arrangements were made to use the Mission School facilities, such as the playing field, the swimming bath and the boatshed. Presumably the new school paid rent for the use of these facilities, and in this way alleviated some of the financial problems that were developing. With Eric unable to contribute to the management of the Mission Schools a new principal was appointed early in 1941 after Biscoe finally retired.

For Eric this was a transforming move. For more than ten years he had been the de facto Principal of the Mission Schools but never officially recognised as such. Years later he wrote to me:

During my years in Kashmir I felt at times a sense of inadequacy and frustration. Grandpa was such a giant and had made such an impression that there was nothing left for me to achieve. It was of course partly pride – a desire to be someone in my own right and to be worthy of some of the credit – but also it was a desire to prove to myself that I could achieve something [...] Eventually I got my chance to branch out on something of my own creation when Mum and I brought Sheikh Bagh into being – and it succeeded in satisfying that inner want of mine: for everything I planned I was enabled to carry through.[58]

When he wrote his memoirs he called them *Biskut Sahiban Nichu* which was what Kashmiris said when someone asked, *Suh kus chuh?* 'Who is that?' 'He is Biscoe Sahib's son.' When a Kashmiri once said to him that Canon Biscoe could talk Kashmiri perfectly, he replied that no, it was he and not his father who spoke Kashmiri and he then realised that now 'I and the Father are one'.

8

Two Kings on One Carpet: Final Years, 1940–49

The end of 1940 marked 50 years since Biscoe arrived in Srinagar to begin his life's work. Despite his age of 77, he was still officially the principal of the six boys' schools and one girls' school, although the main responsibility rested with his son Eric for the boys and Muriel Mallinson for the girls.

Europe was convulsed by the opening battles of World War II and Indian politicians were positioning themselves for a future of independence. Two of them visited Kashmir in May 1940 to assess its political status.[1] They were the Muslim leader Khan Abdul Gaffar Khan, known as the 'Frontier Gandhi' and Pandit Jawaharlal Nehru, a leading member of the Indian Congress. Nehru was very favourably impressed with Sheikh Abdullah, recognising him as a true national leader who possessed a broad political vision free from narrow communalism. They became firm friends, which would have huge significance seven years later when Nehru became the Prime Minister of the newly created Indian Union, and Sheikh Abdullah the Prime Minister of Jammu and Kashmir.

During their visit the Director of Education in Kashmir, Mr K.G. Saiyidain, invited several prominent educationists, including Biscoe, to meet them. Biscoe thought the Muslim leader had a kind face and was a gentleman but did not like Pandit Nehru, 'he gave me the impression of being a true Hindu – a dangerous, unscrupulous sort of man. The sort I would rather have as an enemy than a friend'.[2] This was a wholly predictable reaction from all his previous opinions of educated Indians, and of the independence movement that he had regarded for decades as woefully premature. When the partition of India occurred seven years later and terrible carnage followed, his worst fears for India were realised. But in 1940 the pattern of life in Kashmir seemed destined to continue indefinitely and a grand celebration of Biscoe's Jubilee was planned for the end of the year.

Fifty Year Jubilee Celebration

The 9th of October 1940 was a glorious autumn day in Kashmir and the spacious garden of the British Resident was resplendent under the great chenar trees: broad perfectly manicured lawns and herbaceous borders of well-tended foxgloves, zinnias, marigolds and sweet peas, gave quiet assurance of good taste, stability and authority, appropriate to the representative of the Government of India. The celebrations began when 900 boys in coloured uniforms representing the six schools and a small number from the girls' school, with bands playing and flags waving, marched from the school grounds to the Resident's garden. There the Resident, Colonel Denholm Fraser, presided over the large gathering headed by His Highness the Maharaja of Jammu and Kashmir, Brigadier-General Sir Hari Singh, the notables of the land – many of them old boys of the School – and British people working in Kashmir.

Conspicuously absent was Sheikh Abdullah, who would certainly not have been welcome at a gathering at which the Maharaja was present. After all, he had only recently been released from prison for publicly claiming that the Maharaja was illegitimate because his great grandfather had bought the country from the British who had no right to sell it,[3] and on his release had demanded complete responsible government for the State.[4]

The Resident spoke for the 1,700 well wishers from all over India and beyond who had paid tribute to Canon Biscoe for the revolution he had wrought in the minds and habits of the people of Kashmir.

He briefly alluded to the salient features of Biscoe's unconventional approaches to education and his emphasis on character building in preparation for a life of service:

> I am sure there is not a single Old Boy who would not testify and admit without hesitation that his life is now fuller, brighter and more enjoyable than was the life of his father or grandfather before him. It is not now a disgrace or ungentlemanly conduct to use a carpenter's tool, swim, kick a football, touch and tend wounded animals or do manual labour, but it was so 30 and more years ago.
>
> There are now nearly 1500 boys in the CMS [Church Missionary Society] schools and over 200 girls. There are 100 Indian and Kashmiri masters, nearly all Old Boys and hence imbued with the Biscoe spirit and fit custodians of the Biscoe tradition. But it is not numbers which count in the least, it is the spirit and influence for good which has now spread like leaven through so many walks of life in Kashmir whether in State service or in private business.
>
> For this remarkable transformation one man is responsible and that man is he whom we are honouring today. Associated with him during this long and arduous voyage is his devoted wife to whose inspiration he alone knows how much he owes. To her we also pay homage.[5]

Biscoe's achievement was indeed extraordinary; for 50 years he had promoted an idiosyncratic view about the central purpose of education and had held to it despite persistent opposition and discouragement from the missionary organisation that employed him. For much of the time he also had to contend with opposition from the Kashmiri establishment, particularly the State Government and the Hindu hierarchy, although this had recently softened after the Wular tragedy of April 1934.

What had buoyed him up from the very first years was the wholehearted support of his Kashmiri staff, both Hindu and Muslim, most of whom as time went on, had themselves been students in one of the six schools. It was they that were responsible for the truly unusual activities in social service and community actions that characterised the institution and filled the pages of the annual logs. By 1940, because of the initiative of the Kashmiri staff, over 400 people had been saved from drowning by boys and teachers of the schools, and over 500 young widows had been able to remarry and lead honourable lives.[6] Every year the school logs listed the numbers of occasions where teachers or students had helped at fires and saved the belongings of the distraught owners, rescued people marooned by flood waters, taken patients from the hospitals for trips on the lake and cared for sick or wounded animals. What other school anywhere could claim such a record of service? Many other schools did of course have Boy Scouts with the tradition of helping others but not as pervasive as the activities in the Kashmir schools, where these matters were central to every boy's school record.

The question often expressed in the school logs was whether the tradition of social service learnt at school persisted in later years. Biscoe always delighted in recording examples where an old boy was striving to maintain his reputation for honesty and generosity.

One example in the 1940 log was related by Eric when he was travelling incognito in a public bus and the driver was talking in Kashmiri to the passengers about his difficulties in observing all the various traffic laws.[7] Some one mentioned the name of an inspector who was an old boy. 'Ah there is a man now!' said the driver. 'Look out if you break the rules for you cannot square him! But so long as you keep the rules he does not trouble you. He is a fine man; he does his duty faithfully towards the Government and towards us.' Another name was mentioned and the driver said. 'Oh him! He has got a big stomach.' Meaning he takes bribes. What made this conversation even more interesting was that the man whom the driver so highly praised was of a different religion from himself, but the man whom he condemned was of the same religion.

Biscoe recalled in 1896 witnessing the trial at Kargil of a corrupt official, a member of a very wealthy and powerful Kashmiri family (see Chapter 2), and in 1940 was delighted to meet his son, an old boy, who was an official for social uplift.

Other examples were the work of an old boy in the police, Abdul Karim, in protecting Kashmiri girls from being abducted to India for prostitution, and the development of the Veterinary hospital, staffed by old boys.

Baptisms of Hindu Teachers

The important thing about all these examples of honest behaviour by old boys is that all of them were either Hindu or Muslim and were fully integrated members of Kashmir society. Biscoe had always been most chary of encouraging any of his people to become Christian because he knew that they would then be alienated from their own community and far less influential in their own society. In all his 50 years there had only been one true convert to the Christian faith, Samuel Bakkal, whose story has already been told.

But the lack of converts had been a constant reproach of the CMS against Biscoe from his first days; and since 1929 had been the main argument for progressively reducing the annual grant to the Kashmir schools until it ceased altogether in 1938. So, when in 1939 several of the younger teachers expressed the wish to become Christians the temptation to encourage them must have been very strong. It began when Chandra Pandit approached Eric and said that he wished to become a Christian. As a young Hindu orphan boy Chandra Pandit had been helped by the Biscoe family to stay at school by doing various jobs for them and now as a young adult he had been appointed boxing instructor and games master in the school. He was also very keen on climbing and, through an introduction from Ken Hadow, joined the 1939 American expedition to K2 as a liaison officer;[8] three years later he and Nand Lal Bakaya climbed Mount Kolahoi.[9] At the same time as Chandra approached Eric several other of the younger teachers, all Hindu, said they also wished to convert to Christianity; Eric encouraged them to seek baptism together so as to support each other, a decision he later came to deeply regret.

All of them were among the best of the second generation of Hindu teachers, who had grown up in the schools and participated fully in all the social work and outdoor activities; two of them had recently been promoted to be headmaster of branch schools on their own merit and another, Govind Razdan, had just been appointed to be headmaster of Islamabad High School to replace the retiring Shrida Butt. Now they sought to be baptised into the Christian faith, a momentous step for each of them, which would surely lead to rejection by their own family and community. They had been brought to this decision by their unbounded admiration for Biscoe's life. As one of them wrote:

> My conversion has been due to one man only and that man is Canon Biscoe and it has not been due to what Canon Biscoe has said but to what he is. I have been a student of Canon Biscoe's school for about 10 years and on his staff for the last 21 years. In all I should say that I have spent about three-quarters of my life in his close company. All this while I was taught to feel for others, and to be a healthy and helpful citizen [...] I wondered to see a man come from so distant a place into our land, and trying his best to uplift the people of this country socially, economically, politically and spiritually [...] his care and sorrow for women and children and especially his work in the cause of the Hindu widows; and also his achievements in the preventing of cruelty to animals. Many persons have been upset by his actions, as they did not think that a padre should be concerned with such matters. I venture to say that they were wrong and he was right.
>
> His actions touched my mind and changed the whole outlook of my life. I began to think of God as a kind and loving Father. I realised that Canon Biscoe was able to do all that he did because he had drunk from a certain Fountain; and it is 16 years back that I had started to quench my thirst at the same Fountain of immortality and life from which Canon Biscoe drank. I may convince you that it is neither books on religion nor the sermons preached by the preachers that have had any effect on my mind but the practical life of Canon Biscoe in Kashmir. Also I may point out that it is not the greed of money or any official pressure that can be held responsible for all this change in the outlook of my life.
>
> Some of our Staff members have been represented as very wicked men, liars and cheats [...] Among others our

Headmaster, Mr Shenker Koul and Munshi Nand Lal deserve special mention as our best friends and worthy of great honour and thanks for their efforts in making it possible for us to continue living in the City. It is they who have satisfied the public mind by pointing out that our conversions have been entirely at our will and not the result of any kind of pressure on the part of school authorities.[10]

The author of this was probably Govind Razdan, the oldest of the 12 men and two women who were baptised by Biscoe in 1939 and early 1940. There was no question that the desire of the others to embrace Christianity was as genuine as his; the tragedy was that Biscoe was no longer as cautious about the consequences that would follow for the converts as he had been years before when Samuel Bakkal had converted (see Chapter 4). It is also possible that the constant criticism levelled at him by the missionaries in Lahore, that the Kashmir schools were not fulfilling the mission purpose of making converts, worked its mischief.

The first baptisms took place in August 1939 at Nil Nag away from the city, although Kashi Nath said he would be baptised at Amira Kadal bridge if necessary![11] As well as Kashi Nath and his wife Indra, there was Sham Lal and his wife Tara Watti and Govind Razdan already mentioned. The only witnesses were foreign missionaries, no other Kashmiris were present.

What a contrast is this private, almost secret, affair with the momentous event 11 years before when the first Hindu widows were married in the presence of 200 Kashmiris, and no missionaries were present! Despite the secrecy, the news of the baptisms did get back to Srinagar because a month later the Prime Minister declined an invitation to attend the Old Boys Dinner at the Hadow School because of the baptisms.[12]

A year later again at Nil Nag nine more teachers were baptised by Biscoe in the presence only of missionaries and no other Kashmiris.[13] They were N.N. Fotidar, warden of the hostel; N.N. Misri, who had received the Silver Medal for Gallantry in 1934 and managed the construction of the Hadow School building in 1937; S.L. Mathew and his brother D.N. Mathew; Jiya Lal Dhar, headmaster of Ranawari Branch School; Radha Kishen Koul, headmaster of Nawa Kadal School; Chandra Pandit; Dina Nath Muttu and one Muslim Mustaffa from Islamabad. Biscoe wrote to Julian:

> Today is a red letter day as a party of nine of our school staff came here to join the Christian brotherhood. One Muslim and eight Brahmins and this morning I baptised them in the lake. It was a real joy as these men have for years been striving to follow our Master in service – not talk – giving the helping hand to every one in need including animals. They returned to Srinagar about midday. It will be interesting to see how the people will take this news. The ramparts of Hinduism are gradually giving way and the Brahmins are not able to work up mass opposition as they were able to do some years ago.[14]

Six months later the 'ramparts of Hinduism' responded when the recently baptised men were called before the Dharam Sabha to be cursed for their apostasy; and it was Shenker Koul, headmaster since 1906, who stood with them.[15] This was an unfortunate, although not unexpected, reversal of the better relations that had followed the Wular tragedy six years before when the President of the Dharam Sabha, Jia Lal Kilam, had supported Biscoe so warmly for what he had done for Kashmiris; and the very recent pronouncement by the Yuvak Sabha (the Young Brahmin Sanhedrin) that it is lawful for a Brahmin widow to remarry.[16]

In October 1940, just days before the Jubilee celebrations, the Bishop of Lahore, George Barnes, confirmed all the converts at St Luke's Church in Srinagar.[17] And now a further complication arose because St Luke's was attended by the small congregation of Indian Christians in Srinagar and they were not happy and did not welcome the newly confirmed fellow Christians. This was not really surprising because those from India were second or third generation Christians whose forbears had been low caste Hindus, whereas the newly converted Kashmiri Christians came from the highest caste of Hindus, the Brahmin. Christian missionaries might think this unimportant but it was not. Furthermore, Biscoe had made it abundantly clear that he preferred Hindu Kashmiris who lived a Christian life to professed Christians who may be didn't. Thus the newly confirmed Kashmiri Christians faced ostracism from their own people in Srinagar as well as from their new Christian brethren, which continued for the next five years.[18] Added to this the nationalism that was sweeping India and Kashmir, as described in Chapter 7, gave them the appearance of lackeys, who chose the religion of the foreign power over the established religions of India, in order to receive preferential treatment. Since the converts were among the most able of the young teachers, who could expect promotion on merit, their motives were further diminished in the eyes of their colleagues. Biscoe seemed oblivious to these complexities for he wrote to Julian expressing his joy at the outcome:

> We fortunately now have Kashmiri teachers whom we can trust and who work for the love of the work and for the uplift of their country so that the Schools run themselves more or less. The Headmasters of our two high schools, two middle schools and our primary school are all Kashmiri Christians and all have the ideal of our Master before them, so I sit back and cheer them on – not as in the days of old being continually after them with the stick.[19]

This is quite strange because it implies that all the work and loyalty of the older teachers, such as Shenker Koul, Nand Lal Munshi, Shrida Butt and Bagwan Dass – the leaders of all the social service in the schools and who championed the remarriage of widows – counted for nothing; only those that had been baptised could be trusted. If he really meant these words they are a dreadful commentary on his life's work and his lifetime friendship with Shenker Koul and his colleagues. Perhaps this is reading too much into a private letter to his son and does not signify more. At any rate his optimism was short-lived. There were no more conversions and the first recantations occurred a year later;[20] a body called the Kashmir Hindu League protested to the State Government that non-Christian staff were being discriminated against in the Mission

Schools and claimed that 'those persons who are alleged to have been converted to Christianity have denied this fact before a tribunal appointed by Kashmir Hindus and emphatically asserted that they were Brahmins and have been performing all Hindu religious ceremonies'.[21] Govind Razdan continued for some years but only Chandra Pandit remained a Christian for the rest of his life. It was a sorry mistake as Eric acknowledged much later:

> I grew to look back on this episode with a sense of shame. I had tried to hurry things on by appointing some of them to be headmasters of each of our six boys' schools. This of course laid them open to the charge of having changed their religion in order to get promotion. They received no support from the local Christian congregation, and were assailed by the Hindu community.
>
> It was this very largely, that caused me to decide not to remain on when the war came to an end. I knew quite well that baptism was not important to me, and that to expect people to accept the creed and liturgy and sacraments of our church was absurd. And I just could not go along with it any more. That group of young men were my friends. I had persuaded them to take a step I had never had to face myself; and I did not wish to become involved in this sort of thing any more. I cared not whether they were baptised or not, whether they called themselves Christians or not; it is not what you say, or what you profess to believe that matters. It is what you are, and how you treat others that matters.[22]

Happily, the episode of their ephemeral conversions did not affect their friendships with Eric and Phil in the long term, especially when they were welcomed back to Kashmir in 1960.

The Slow Decline and Eventual Succession

With Eric's resignation at the end of 1940, in order to run the Sheikh Bagh Preparatory School, the CMS sought a replacement and in March 1941 transferred Kenneth Jardine from Edwardes

College, Peshawar, to be the Principal of the Mission Schools in Kashmir. The Biscoes continued to live in the principal's house, which had been their home since 1894, and Biscoe continued to be an active presence in the schools; it is not clear where Jardine lived nor how much power he really exercised. At the end of 1941 while away in India Biscoe learnt that the CMS had ordered Jardine to hand over all school money to them.[23] Since by 1940 the CMS was providing no financial support for the Kashmir schools this was an extraordinary if not illegal demand. By then the main benefactor that enabled the Mission Schools to survive the war years, as mentioned in Chapter 7, was Clarence Gasque who came to live in Kashmir in 1938. For the next seven years she gave each year 5,000 rupees to support the Hadow School.[24] Two years later Biscoe received another substantial bequest for the schools and, on being asked to give some of it to the CMS, refused to do so.[25] He does not indicate whether he consulted Jardine in making this decision but it is clear that he still exercised considerable influence in school affairs.

For the first two years of his tenure, Jardine maintained the regular activities of the schools and the school logs for 1942 and 1943 report the usual events as well as incidents of social service. But unlike Biscoe he had much sympathy for the Indian Christian community in Srinagar and made it his task to build it up. He fostered the idea that Kashmir was moving from a mission-based stage to an indigenous church and he urged the Punjabi and Kashmiri Christians to sink their differences and work together. On Good Friday 1944 the congregation processed through the streets of Srinagar from St Luke's Church to the Hadow School Hall with Jardine and the Indian priest, Rev. John Paul, in full regalia, and a man carrying a cross in front of them. Biscoe was present in the Hall but did not participate; Sham Lal, one of the Kashmiri converts, read a lesson and Jardine and Paul preached. Two months later Sham Lal and Chandra took the Sunday service at St Lukes Church for the first time,[26] which indicated improved relations, but soon after Padre Paul was again preaching against the Kashmiri Christians. At about the same time Jardine resigned as principal and returned to Peshawar. Fred Jacob, who had worked voluntarily

Figure 24 The long partnership of Shenker Koul and Cecil Biscoe, 1906–46

since 1934, took over as Principal of the Mission Schools and as Biscoe wrote, 'Jacob has started discipline in the schools once more, wearing of badges, punctuality, silence etc'.[27] When Jacob asked Padre Paul why he was always late for his classes Paul promptly resigned. A month later Padre Paul was transferred from Kashmir to the Punjab, much to Biscoe's relief.[28]

Reading between the lines it is evident that there was a breakdown between Jardine and Biscoe; Jardine's main concern was to nurture the small Christian community while Biscoe was concerned at the decline of school discipline and social service activities, and abandonment of boxing and regattas. The appointment of Jacob began to restore these activities but it could only be a temporary arrangement because of his health, as indeed it proved to be, for he resigned five months later in February 1945. Bishop Barnes then established a Board of Governors to oversee the Kashmir schools with himself as Chairman and Bishop Woolmer, representing the CMS, Shenker Koul and N.N. Fotidar, representing the staff, and Biscoe, Eric, Muriel Mallinson and Ken Hadow, as members. Almost its first task was to accept Jacob's resignation on grounds of ill health – Jacob died a few months later. With no other option the Board reappointed Biscoe as principal at 82, and brought Shenker Koul out of retirement as Vice Principal at 65. Biscoe wrote to Julian:

> Did I tell you I am now back at my old job of Principal of the CMS Schools? It has made me feel twenty years younger as I can now stop the rot which had set in and back up the few honest and worthy men.[29]

It was fortunate that there were several very able younger men with experience who could be relied upon to keep the schools functioning. At the same time the finances of the institution were severely stretched and the second difficult decision for the Board was to close two branch schools and dismiss 30 teachers and four servants. The headmasters of these two schools were both Christians baptised five years before – Jaya Lal Dhar at Ranawari School and Radha Kishen Koul at Nawa Kadal School. However, within three weeks a group of 20 old boys had got together and offered to take over both schools, which they did. The two schools continued to be supported by Biscoe while he remained principal by letting them keep their boats in the school boathouse and participate in school regattas and long distance swims.

So, as the two theatres of war finally closed in May and August 1945, Biscoe's life's work seemed to be closing too. The new Government in Britain was determined that India should become independent as soon as possible so ongoing support for Mission Schools in Kashmir was unlikely and the prospect of finding a successor for Biscoe equally uncertain. The Sheikh Bagh School for British boys would soon close as its numbers fell but Eric was not in prospect because he had been offered the headship of a preparatory school in New Zealand and would leave Kashmir at the end of the year. When Biscoe distributed the school log for 1945, *It Can't Be Done, Then Do It*, in mid-1946 he wrote:

> I have now been Principal of the Schools again for the last twelve months, as no one has so far been found to relieve me. I have just passed my 83rd birthday [...] so I hope even in these days of stress some one may be found ready to tackle the

job of uplifting the youth of Kashmir [...] We in this land of India are just now sitting on a powder magazine. May God grant to our Viceroy and his Councillors the vision necessary in bringing through this most difficult business of 'Home Rule' without civil war.

When all seemed lost, Biscoe's wish was fulfilled; Phil Edmonds with his wife Belle and two sons, Lloyd and Phillip, visited Srinagar that summer and subsequently he accepted appointment as Principal of the Mission Schools and took over in October 1946. An Australian with a PhD in Political Science from London University, Edmonds was not a conventional missionary; he was not ordained and his religious beliefs might be described as agnostic humanist, or a modern version of Biscoe's own beliefs. However, he did not carry a prejudice against educated Indians like Biscoe did – perhaps because he was an Australian – and he was politically aware and engaged in the great events that were unfolding in India; he was the man for the time. Biscoe liked him and what was more important so did the school staff.

The finances, however, continued to be a big problem; Clarence Gasque had left Kashmir and so her support ceased, and Biscoe's supporters were falling away, despite the fact that he was still writing hundreds of letters to the diminishing number surviving.[30] Before Eric left at the end of 1946 he gave substantial help from the sale of the Sheikh Bagh School property. Edmonds wrote:

I must express some of the gratitude which I feel for the magnificence of your donation to the schools and I know how deep your affection is for them, but I must thank you for myself; it is thoughtful of you to give a beginner such an encouraging and substantial help over what will be the most difficult year of my life.[31]

And Govind Razdan from the Islamabad school wrote to Eric:

My kind Patron, I take this opportunity of expressing my sincere thanks to you for the generous gifts you so kindly gave

285

to the schools during the past week. You have all along your stay in Kashmir unhesitatingly given all that you had, your thought, energy, talent, money and above all your devotional service to promote and uplift the young Kashmiris both the teacher and the taught. You were a friend of the poor always. You are the true son of your worthy father and a sincere servant of the World's greatest Master, Jesus Christ.[32]

Two days later Eric farewelled his parents, leaving the succession to another man, and knew it was unlikely he would ever see them again because he and Phil were moving to New Zealand. Biscoe wrote in his diary, 'A crowd of staff and boys to see Eric off in bus at 7 am. A very sad farewell after years of faithful work for the youth of Kashmir'. And to Eric he wrote, 'Thank you for the thousand and one ways you have helped and strengthened me in the running of the CMS Schools'.[33] A week later, 28 December 1946 Biscoe wrote the last entry in his diary, 'Phil Edmonds said how happy he was in the school and with the staff'.

Arrival of Dr Phil Edmonds

Through the first half of 1947 as India became embroiled in the greatest movement of people ever seen and terrible massacres occurred, Kashmir remained calm and the schools accommodated to their new and energetic principal. Shenker Koul was initially upset that he lost his position as Vice Principal but a few months later wrote:

Our new Principal seems to be a very energetic man and makes every effort to keep up the efficiency of the schools. Beloved Canon has been keeping fit during the last severe and long winter and now he looks brighter and fitter comparatively than ever before.[34]

Relations between Biscoe and Edmonds remained good and Edmonds seemed to really appreciate him being around. He wrote to Eric in May:

Canon seems more active and happy than ever. I must say that the more I know him the more I admire and love him and it is a real pleasure to have him with us [...] If I had to begin to make the masters and boys so active and so habituated to hard work I would probably quail at the thought but now I put on the bold face and assume the most extraordinary feats as normality, the labour is Canon's and the harvest is mine [...] Hadow School is on the crest of a wave and it is pleasant to have so little to worry there.[35]

Nand Lal Bakaya was also very pleased that the traditional activities of Easter camp, Mahadeo climb and swimming and boating were continuing.

Under the guidance of Dr Edmonds the teaching is improving. We are very lucky in having him as he has a very keen eye. Nothing escapes his notice. He is determined to keep up the traditions of the school established by Canon Biscoe. He often says that his ambition is to make the schools the model schools for all India.[36]

Bakaya introduced Edmonds to the mountains where they climbed Tatakuti. 'It was a steep climb on loose rock on a cloudy day – a new experience for Dr Edmonds who was a bit nervous at places.'[37]

Two months later matters changed and the talk was of the Biscoes leaving Kashmir and going to live with Julian in Rhodesia. Edmonds wrote to Eric:

Your father and mother both seem very well and if it were not that Canon tires very, very easily I would say he is better than I have seen him in these twelve months. Actually the fuss about going to Africa has rather disturbed the well established routine of the house so that it's a bit difficult to form an opinion on their comfort. For myself I have grown so fond of Canon and he has always been so great a bulwark that I don't really want him to go but those that can take a less personal view, especially the Bishop, are convinced he should go rather than face the difficulties of another winter.[38]

It seems more likely that Bishop Barnes' concern was that there might be a repetition of the difficulties between Biscoe and Jardine, which could not be risked after the difficulty they had had in recruiting Edmonds, because Biscoe himself later wrote from exile:

> I personally had no wish to leave as long as I could be of some help to those Old Students who were honest men and were putting up a continual fight against the devil and all his beastly works in this fair land of Kashmir. But in certain quarters it was thought that my presence might cause difficulties for the new Principal of the CMS Schools as there should not be two kings on one carpet and Dr Phil Edmonds is a MAN and able to handle the disciples of the devil.[39]

The old teachers were very sad about this development and the idea grew that it was Edmonds that wanted him to leave. Bakaya wrote to Eric:

> Canon is packing and we are very sad to lose him for he, as you must know had decided to go to Africa and live there. Of course he must be also very sad for he is going away from his life's work. We can't help it in the same way as we could not help it when you decided to part from us.[40]

Nand Lal Munshi also wrote to Eric in similar words:

> Alas all our future plans have been frustrated by your deserting us. Now to our great disappointment Canon too is leaving us and it is a great shock to me who has been in close contact with you and Canon for the last twenty years.[41]

With the declaration of Indian independence on 14 August 1947 the British Resident in Srinagar closed the Residency and the Biscoes left on 9 October. By then the colossal movement of people and the terrible attendant massacres were occurring across the Punjab with little military or civil control. The Biscoe's son-in-law Colonel Richard McGill who had been in command of a regiment of Gurkhas throughout the recent war, was ordered to remain in command despite the departure of the British and he witnessed appalling scenes of carnage that his troops were unable to prevent.

Departure of the Biscoes from Kashmir

Into this maelstrom the old couple went. They left Srinagar in grand style, as 30 of the school staff hauled their car to the bus stand, preceded by the school band, and the road was lined for a quarter of a mile by the present scholars and old students. The first part of their travel was uneventful but after crossing the Jhelum River at Kohala they were in Pakistan where armed Muslims searched for any Hindu or Sikh traveller whom they dragged out and shot at sight; Rawalpindi, which they reached the next day, was absolutely cleared of all Hindus and Sikhs. Here Richard McGill was able to arrange their onward flight to Delhi and from there they travelled to Bombay and soon after sailed for Beira in Mozambique. The long train journey to Salisbury (now Harare) was too much for Blanche who died soon after arrival. Cecil lived on for another 20 months, following with growing anxiety the fate of his Kashmiri colleagues and friends as the civil war between Pakistan and India engulfed Kashmir. Indeed, it began a week after they had crossed the Jhelum River into Pakistan, as described by Nand Lal Munshi:

> Before the arrival of Indian army there was a very small number of Dogra sepoys here. They faced the raiders after retreating from Muzuffarabad to Uri where they suffered heavy loss and few survived. The colonel in charge sent a message of the situation to Maharaja and advised him to run away. That selfish fellow did so and collected all his valuables and sent them to Jammu and then scampered off along with Dogra officials throwing Kashmiris to wolves. At that juncture he asked the Indian Union for help and then made Sheikh Abdullah head of administration. He at once called for volunteers and they gathered around him. Each locality had to form a group who had to keep peace and order. This went on

successfully and is going on at present. One does not know whether it will last long. Emergency officers have been attached to Ministers for instance Sham Lal Saraf who took over Rainawari and Nawa Kadal schools is attached to Finance Minister and Director Civil Supplies. Mr Sadiq is in charge of Home Department. About half the boys at Hadow School have left so there is a fall in income. The Central and Habba Kadal are the same. We are unfortunate fellows deserted by you and Sahib. Alas! Alas![42]

Govind Razdan, from Islamabad wrote much the same:

Kashmir is under foreign raid. The country right from Kohala and Muzuffarabad up to Srinagar has been ruined. Men women and children killed houses burnt property looted. Regarding schools: Habba Kadal and Islamabad schools will be closed from April next.[43]

By the beginning of 1948 the immediate crisis of the invasion from Pakistan was over; the irregular raiders, encouraged if not actively supported by Pakistan, had been driven out of the valley of Kashmir as far as Kohala by the much more disciplined Indian army. The Maharaja fled Kashmir on 19 October 1947, as mentioned by Munshi, and soon after he opted for affiliation of Jammu and Kashmir with the Indian Union and abdicated. Sheikh Abdullah was released from prison and appointed as its Prime Minister, and many Old Boys of the Mission Schools were members of the new government.

Having survived the last months of 1947 the Edmonds were now faced with a severe financial crisis. The closure of the road to Pakistan meant that communication with Lahore and the CMS office there ceased – no mail came through and for Srinagar the main route for supplies had gone. For the Mission Hospital, all medical supplies ceased and the mission doctor, James Flower, had to make an emergency flight in an Indian Air force plane to Delhi to obtain essential medicines and surgical supplies. As Munshi mentioned, student numbers in all branches of the schools were down so that the financial situation was dire. Edmonds decided to close all branches except the Hadow School at Sheikh Bagh, which he did in April 1948; the girls' school, under the indefatigable Muriel Mallinson, however, continued at Fateh Kadal. This decision was a logical extension of the policy first introduced by Eric in 1938 with the opening of the Hadow School. With the funds from Biscoe's old supporters in steep decline, Edmonds decided to consolidate the effort entirely at Sheikh Bagh and offer a superior level of education for fee-paying students. Closing the Central School at Fateh Kadal was the symbolic end of the old order; and the old teachers still there recognised this and resisted it. They determined to continue the old school themselves, renaming it the Central High School. Edmonds agreed to hand it over to the staff as their joint property under a Board of Governors. The President of the Board was Miss Mahmuda Ahmad Ali Shah, a proud product of the CMS Girls' High School; Professor R.C. Pandita, the linguist and mathematician its Vice President, and Sri Nand Lal Kitroo its manager, with the headmaster, Sri D.N. Mattoo as its Secretary. When Biscoe heard about this development he was delighted and wrote to me:

The Girls' School goes strong and one of Muriel's girls – a MA BT – is the President of the Board of Governors which I call great. I know her to be of a wonderful strong character. But a girl head of men. They have gone further than we Britishers in honouring women, so utterly opposed to Eastern custom and ideals regarding women.[44]

Prior to the transfer, however, Edmonds removed most of the furniture, apparatus and books to the Hadow School. The honours boards from the main hall of the old Central School were also removed and re-erected in the Hadow School, which he renamed the Tyndale-Biscoe Memorial High School. Presumably his reason was that having them in the only remaining Mission School would help to ensure the continuity of the school's traditions – and they are still there today – but the core of old staff at Fateh Kadal felt grievously betrayed, especially as this all took place less than six months after the departure of the revered Canon. Relations between the Central High School and Edmonds remained poor, especially after he forbade them to use the racing *shikaras* and participate in the weekly regattas, unlike what Biscoe had done when the first two primary schools were closed two years earlier. Nevertheless, they battled on determined to maintain the old traditions of swimming, climbing and social service. The two retired teachers, Samsar Chand and Shenker Koul, encouraged this and each year the school produced a report, similar to the annual logs that Biscoe produced, with lists of good deeds done by the boys, accounts of the swim across Dal Lake and mountains climbed, and appeals for financial support. And they also maintained a close link with the girls' school next door with several of the older teachers helping with classes when necessary. In his last year in Rhodesia Biscoe supported them and encouraged them in what they were doing, including the provision of his list of supporters.

Each of his letters to Samsar Chand ended, 'My body is in Africa but my soul is in Kashmir. Your affectionate friend, C.E. Tyndale-Biscoe'.

My Body is in Africa But My Soul is in Kashmir

Cecil Tyndale-Biscoe died on 1 August 1949 and was buried beside his wife of 56 years in the cemetery near Salisbury Cathedral. His old friend Sir Henry Holland wrote:

> He stood by himself, a leader and maker of men [...] He was a great disciplinarian with a great sense of humour. Who can ever forget his cheery laugh? He was a man of amazing moral courage and of very deep affection. He was always the champion of the under dog. He had a great capacity for friendship and what a staunch friend he was, what a humble follower of Jesus Christ! [...] Dear old Biscoe, how we loved him, how we admired him.[45]

And his other good friend George Barnes, former Bishop of Lahore wrote:

His work for the country which has suffered so much and where fighting has only recently ceased is unique. There has been nothing like it in our diocese before. I doubt if there has ever been anything like it anywhere in the mission field. I think Cecil Tyndale-Biscoe would like the dying words of the Spaniard Giner[46] a hundred years ago:

> I want no mourning. Remember me by work.
> He who leaves work well done, is with us still.
> And he, who truly lived, lives on.
> Let anvils clash for me and bells be silent.[47]

9

Epilogue

Three years after he died, Biscoe's autobiography was published by Seeley Service, London. During the last years of his life Biscoe had not only transcribed all his diaries into six exercise books but had written an account of his life and took for its title the words of Joseph in Egypt to his brothers who had tried to kill him, *But God Meant it for Good*.[1] Julian edited the typescript for publication and, he or the publisher, changed the title to *Tyndale-Biscoe of Kashmir. An Autobiography*. It had four forewords by close friends: Earl Halifax a former Viceroy; Field Marshall Lord Birdwood; George Barnes the former Bishop of Lahore; and the Prime Minister of Kashmir, Sheikh Abdullah. The latter's final words sum up best what set Biscoe apart:

> He breathed his own idealism, purity of thought and action, and love of service into all his students, and made them models of uprightness, honesty and good character. He was a teacher in the real sense of the word. What makes his work all the more remarkable is the fact that elsewhere in India the gestures of foreigners, however friendly, were generally regarded with distrust and suspicion. But Canon Biscoe set an example of how true relationship between two peoples, seemingly quite alien to each other, could be built on equal and human terms. By sheer self-denial, courage and toil, he created for himself

goodwill and gratitude. He was regarded by the people of Kashmir as their friend and sympathizer.[2]

The question was whether his work would survive his death.

Transforming Kashmir

Profound changes were taking place in the social and economic conditions of Kashmiris that might make Biscoe's ideas seem archaic and irrelevant; certainly his views on British superiority and Indian incompetence would go but his emphasis on honesty and social service were qualities that remain relevant in all times. In the first decade after Biscoe's death the Mission Schools in Kashmir almost ceased to exist and the recovery that followed led to a very different kind of school that reflected the great changes that occurred in Kashmir, and India, during this time. At the same time remarkable changes took place in Kashmir in which Biscoe's influence could be discerned. When the Maharaja was obliged to relinquish power in October 1947 he appointed his nemesis, Sheikh Abdullah, the Prime Minister. He promptly set in train a transformation of Kashmir society that would benefit it for the next 40 years.[3] He appointed a Cabinet predominantly composed of old boys of the Mission School and introduced wide ranging reforms of land tenure and finance, the most important being that long-standing debts to money lenders were annulled if three times the capital had already been paid in interest. While Sheikh Abdullah had not been an old boy of the school his four successors were; most important of these were G.M. Bakshi (1953–63) and G.M. Sadiq, who was Chief Minister from 1963 to his death in 1972 and instituted many far reaching reforms and conducted a scrupulously honest administration.

What of the schools? Soon after Biscoe left Kashmir what had been six boys' schools were reduced to one and the total of boys on the roll fell from over 1,500 in 1944 to less than 400 ten years later. At this remove it is difficult to know what Dr Phil Edmonds accomplished in the eight years that he was Principal of the Tyndale-Biscoe High School; there is no record today because he ceased to produce an annual log of school activities. What did survive Biscoe's departure were the annual summer camps to Yus Marg and the climb of Tatakuti that he instituted, but swimming and boating declined as did the emphasis on social service that these activities were designed to support. Edmonds was certainly sympathetic to the reforms that Sheikh Abdullah's government introduced and, since he was closely associated with the leader, he suffered when in 1953 Sheikh Abdullah was removed from power for advocating a future for Kashmir independent from India. The position of Prime Minister was reduced to Chief Minister and Sheikh Abdullah was replaced by his former associate G.M. Bakshi who instituted closer federal integration of the country with India.[4] Since Edmonds' political sympathies lay with Pakistan and he favoured the incorporation of Kashmir into that State he progressively became *persona non grata* with the Indian Government, which was investing its armed forces and finances to retain Kashmir within the Indian Union. By late 1954 his time was up.

This became evident to me in that year after I wrote to ask Edmonds if I could join him in Kashmir. The year before I had graduated in Zoology from Canterbury University College, Christchurch and begun a career in the New Zealand Department of Scientific and Industrial Research, but was drawn back to my roots in Kashmir. His reply to my enquiry was to suggest I join him at Edwardes College in Peshawar:

> For several reasons the time has come for me to move on. For one thing it is most probable that professionally a man makes his greatest contribution in his first five or six years. I have been fortunate in Kashmir in taking over so fine a tradition to build on in a time of great vigour and change and to be able to make so great an impression on a country notoriously resistant to change. If I had stayed like your grandfather another forty years I would not make a much greater contribution than I already have made. Whatever decision had to be made has been precipitated by two events. The first is the too evident signs that the Government of India dislikes the almost legendary position which I have in the State today and is

reluctant to have me continue here. It is clearly only a matter of time before I shall be refused permission to stay and a decision will have to be made on that score alone. Secondly the very great mission college in Peshawar, Edwardes College, is about to be closed because there is no Principal available [...] The school here has reached a firm and stable position in the State, a high standard of scholastic achievement, a brilliant level of field work and mountain craft, a sound staff working loyally together it could be continued by a much less vigorous leadership (or so I hope).[5]

Decline of the Schools, 1955–59

The Edmonds moved to Peshawar early in 1955 and I joined them there some months later. Muriel Mallinson sent me a strong warning against the decision – but it proved to be a happy and very fulfilling three years for me. However, Phil Edmonds' assessment of the future of the Tyndale-Biscoe High School in Kashmir was much too optimistic. For the next year it had no principal and the local priest, Anthony Spurr, kept it together. In 1956 Victor Johnson became the principal and in his first report mentioned that school camps were run and 'large arrears of administrative, financial and legal business have been reduced to manageable proportions. The decade which followed the departure and death of Canon Tyndale-Biscoe was a troublous one for the school and State'.

Relations with the now independent Central High School at Fateh Kadal improved from the low point when Edmonds removed the honours boards and furniture in 1948, to cordiality under Johnson; and its enrolment was actually higher than the Tyndale-Biscoe Memorial High School.

Working in Peshawar in the fifties it was very difficult to have any communication with people in Srinagar because the border between Pakistan-controlled Kashmir and India-controlled Kashmir was closed. I did, however, meet several Biscoe old boys living in Pakistan. These were men who had lived in the hostel while at school in Srinagar and came from the northern areas of Chitral, Gilgit, Hunza and Nagir. Being mainly Muslim countries, their rulers had immediately opted to join Pakistan; but because the fate of the original State of Jammu and Kashmir remained undecided – and still is – they have remained in political limbo.[6] When I visited all these places I received a most friendly reception because of the affection these men still held for my parents and grandparents. Towards the end of my time in Peshawar I was finally able to get a permit to visit India-controlled Kashmir for two weeks in April 1958. It was a very moving and memorable time for me and significant for the future of the school, so I will quote excerpts from the letter I wrote to my parents as the visit unfolded:

12 April 1958. So the unbelievable has happened and I am back at Sheikh Bagh almost 13 years to the day since I left. We flew across the Pir Panjal and I tried to pick out Sunset Peak and Gulmarg and then in less than an hour we were circling down over the Kashmir aerodrome and out of the window I saw Haramukh, Mahadeo, Zabarwan, the Takht, the Fort and Srinagar; and then I was stepping down onto Kashmir soil again and hearing Kashmiri spoken all around. We drove through the villages where the mustard crop was in flower and the little irises were out and the large blue and white irises on the graves, then past the Silk Factory and the *maidan* near it. I was lost as we crossed the new bridge but felt right again as I saw the kuchus lined up against the banks of the River.

You can imagine how exciting it is and also how touching to find so much affection to greet one, which I receive as representative of the family. I feel very much as I did when I reached Gilgit; incredulous that it has happened and as happy as one can be – there is nothing else in the world like it; an experience which fills one with pride and humility and joy all at once.

13 April. The boathouse is as firm as ever but its contents looked very sad; few *shikaras* and the rowing boats quite decayed and only the 12 oar still afloat. There was a *doonga* moored beside the boathouse and inside I found all the present staff of the school – Radha Kishen Butt and R.K. Kau, whom I had met yesterday. Also in the boat were Salam ud Din, Arjan

Nath, Bulgi and S.M. Butt. I cannot hope to tell you all that I heard from them but the general theme seemed to be how much they all miss you and long for your return. On the whole they seem to be contented and I must say I haven't seen such a happy looking crowd for a long time. Mind you there were no Muslims there because of Ramzan and I guess the Hindus do prefer being a part of India. We had two real Kashmiri *khanas* in the *doonga*.

14 April. At 10 am I rode to the Girls' School with Muriel and was greeted by Isher Koul, looking as jolly and rotund as ever. As we were waiting for Assembly to start Shenker [Koul] arrived and we embraced. He is very bent but can see and hear well and has all his faculties with him. They say he is revered in the city as a saint now and many people go to his house to meet him. Muriel's girls looked very clean and neat and after prayers and a hymn I was introduced and had to speak a few words – regrettably in English but Isher Koul translated for me. Then I went with Isher Koul to the Central High School and met dear Samsar Chand – we were both nearly in tears! They got out the band and had the boys come out of the classrooms and do a short PT in the old style and then we went into the hall and I had to make my little speech again. Then Samsar Chand took me round – he showed me where the old honours boards had been taken away by Phil to Sheikh Bagh. It must have hurt them terribly to have so much taken away – boards, furniture, books and boats and I have a great admiration for the way they have continued notwithstanding. Muriel doesn't agree and she thinks they have behaved wrongly in keeping the name of the school and taking visitors down there. We came back to Sheikh Bagh for tea and afterwards I strolled around the gardens for the first time and saw the school. They showed me the busts of Grandpa and you, which were brought out of hiding after the Edmonds left. God knows what one can believe and what is said for flattery – they say Phil tried to get rid of anything tangible connected with the past, that Grandpa's bust with nose knocked off lay in a godown but was restored and replaced at a great ceremony when [Chief Minister G.M.] Bakshi unveiled it and said 'Everything I owe to this man.'

22 April. Victor Johnson and I went to an Id tea given by Bakshi. A huge crowd there, probably 2000 in the grounds of the new tourist centre. A distinguished Indian was there, Vishnu Sahi, Secretary in the Central Government for Kashmiri affairs. He said that the Indian Government approached CMS [Church Missionary Society] in 1955 to ask you to return to Kashmir – did you know that? I think there is little doubt that you would be welcomed back by everyone and would get as much support financially and otherwise as the Rainawari Hospital is getting. Incidentally Vishnu Sahi said that Phil was prevented from returning to Kashmir by the Kashmir and Indian Governments because of his political activities. On my return Muriel and I went to Munshi Nand Lal's house for dinner. Again it was a pleasant affair and his wife and daughter sat with us which was nice.[7]

Return of Eric and Phil Tyndale-Biscoe, 1960–62

This letter made a big impression on Eric and Phil. He wrote, 'I can't express adequately what joy it has given to [your Mother] and me. Ever since it arrived last Tuesday I have been thinking of it and of Kashmir'. Four months later when I returned to New Zealand we discussed the idea of them returning to Kashmir intensely; at the time they had an invalid friend living with them but the next year, after she died, Eric wrote to CMS in London offering to return for two years while a permanent principal was found. An Agreement was signed on 4 January 1960 for two years, to commence from the date they reached Srinagar. They were both 60 and in excellent health from seven years working a small dairy farm and were very excited about going back; they reached Srinagar on 24 April and for the next few weeks were overwhelmed with welcome from staff and friends at both the Central High School and the Tyndale-Biscoe Memorial High School.

In contrast to the wonderful welcome they received, however, the condition of the latter school was pitiful. There had been no principal for more than a year and Muriel Mallinson had tried to oversee it along with her other responsibilities. The buildings were in very poor condition with many bizarre alterations – illegal squatters had encroached on the grounds and were carrying on various businesses quite unrelated to the school – and in the school the former activities of boating, swimming and social service had ceased. On the positive side there was a general sense of optimism in the city, the economy was strong and parents much better off than before so that the former perennial problem of lack of funds to run the school no longer existed. Eric wrote:

The biggest change we notice is that Kashmiris are, for the first time in many centuries, in positions of authority in their own country. This has undoubtedly had an excellent psychological effect on everyone. I am continually struck by the difference in the way the ordinary folk walk about the streets with their heads held high. It is also quite obvious that the people are better off than they used to be: people are better dressed; in villages new well-built houses, instead of mud huts, are everywhere in evidence. Of course money is being poured into the country by the Indian Government and too much easy money is a temptation to those who are dishonest.

Another change which affects the School more closely is that many of our old boys hold important posts in the Government. This means that whereas in the old days our School was not regarded with any particular favour, now we have friends in high places. Also we have many sons and other relatives of these officials in the School.

The overwhelming desire for education, and especially for education in English, has quite altered our problems. In the old days, we used to canvass for pupils; and among certain types of schools there was a tendency to poach pupils from other schools! Now our problem is how to accommodate the numbers who wish to come here. In spite of charging what in old times would have been considered absolutely outrageous fees, we still have to turn boys away. Incidentally our financial worry is not what it used to be, when my father had to collect £2,000 every year. Our fees now more or less cover the running expenses of the School, and we are able to give generous concessions to deserving cases.[8]

By the end of 1960 a great deal had been achieved to restore the buildings and site to a workable condition and the traditional school activities had resumed with enthusiastic support of the staff and old boys. A high wall was built around the perimeter of the campus and all the squatters' material thrown outside by the senior boys – including by the son of one of the squatters! The classrooms were restored to their former size and purposes and the swimming bath, which had been unused for two years, was cleaned and refilled after a new pump was installed. The 12-oar cutter was restored by the old carpenter who had previously worked on it and was joyfully crewed by those older staff who remembered how to row. The racing *shikaras* were restored but it took longer to get them crewed because few of the boys could swim and none knew how to use a paddle. Eric continued:

> I suppose that what made this School famous in the past, and certainly what made it unique, was the emphasis my father placed on training the boys in service to others. Everything else was subservient to this. He felt that a Mission School which sets out to proclaim the Christian faith should put this faith into practice by 'doing unto others as ye would they should do unto you.' Though the School was also famous for having pioneered education in Kashmir, for having introduced the boys of this land to sports, swimming, climbing, camping and the like, these activities were only means to an end, never ends in themselves. The end was to fit oneself for service for others. Especially did my father hammer away at changing the age-old attitude towards the treatment of women.
>
> In old days it was a common sight to see women carrying heavy loads, and nobody offering to help them; women were always shouldered out of the way, that is if they were foolish enough to stand in the way of a man. Now when I return to Kashmir, where boys trained by my father, are in positions of authority, I have been delighted and wonder-struck to note that on all the government buses special seats are allotted for women. The conductors have orders to see that women, children and old people are allowed on and off first. With my

own eyes I have seen the miracle of a bus, on which I was travelling, stop to pick up a woman. Why was it a miracle? Firstly because the bus was quite full, and had already refused to pick up any more passengers, yet when the driver saw her, he said 'I must pick her up as she was waiting here on my outward journey.' Secondly the driver was a Muslim, and the woman was a Hindu. And thirdly the driver seeing she had some luggage, called to the conductor to go out and pick up her bundles for her. Such a change would never have come about but for the Mission School.

The most outstanding feature of the School in past times was the annual record of boys risking their lives to save others. Every boy had to learn to swim, so that he could be ready to save others. I was therefore distressed to find that, when we returned last year, there were hardly a hundred boys, out of close on a thousand who could swim. The swimming bath was in disrepair, and had not been used at all for two years. Of course boating had also suffered; in the past, boys had used their skill at boating to help in time of flood, and in taking sick patients from the hospitals for outings, and in many other ways.

No longer did boys go out with the dog ambulance to pick up wounded and diseased dogs. The dog ambulance, or rather its remains, I picked up out of a heap of scrap iron in a shed. No brave deeds in saving life, or deeds of kindness to animals had been recorded since the early fifties; in fact some of the honours boards on which these deeds had been recorded in the past, had been removed, and in their place were recorded the names and marks gained of those who had passed the matric examination.

But things were not as depressing as they might have been. I found the older members of the Staff, the Old Boys, and especially those who are parents of boys now in the school, only too happy to have the old traditions revived. In 1960 we put the swimming bath in working order again, and were able to teach over 100 boys to swim. This year we are already up to the 200 mark. Whereas, at the beginning of summer 1960, we could barely man four boat crews, we now have 12 crews out practicing every Tuesday afternoon. Once again, after 15 years, our boys are learning the joy that comes from giving patients from the Mission Hospital an outing on the Lake. Last month one of our boys, who had twice swum 3.5 miles across the Dal Lake, saved a boy from drowning in the River. The old ruin of the dog ambulance has been put in working order again, and is in constant use. Boys see dogs that have had legs broken by traffic on their way to and from School; they fetch the ambulance, go out and pick up the dog, and take it to the veterinary hospital, as their fathers used to do before them.

The New Order: John Ray and Premi Gergan

As Eric and Phil restored the spirit of the boys' school through 1960–61 its future was still uncertain because no one had been found to succeed them as principal. Then John and Catherine Ray offered themselves and were accepted. John had worked for some time at Lawrence College, Muree in Pakistan and Catherine had recently graduated in medicine from Edinburgh University so they had the right background for this unusual task. It was in fact Phil Edmonds who in 1959 suggested to John that he consider the task. Early in February 1962 John and Catherine Ray arrived in Srinagar to understudy the job from Eric and Phil and take over six months later. This was a very successful appointment; John Ray fully supported the ideals of the school, which grew in size and influence through the 25 years of his leadership. John recalled his first impressions years later:

> On arriving in Srinagar I found that the heads of nine government departments were Old Boys. Six out of seven Chief Ministers in the succeeding 25 years were either Old Boys or parents of children in the School, or both. More than this, their wives in most cases were Old Girls of Miss Mallinson's school. Given that many of our teachers, who were often private tutors in ministers' homes, were also former students and that everyone, it seemed, wanted admission, the position of Principal of the Biscoe School was one of some influence.

This could be uncomfortable, as when Mr Sadiq, Chief Minister in 1965, rebuked me in front of five thousand people for planning to demolish Canon Biscoe's house – a rat infested barn by that time – 'the house of the founder of modern Kashmir.' I was to learn how this one school had such an influence on the development of society.[9]

Not only was the boys' school in dire straights in 1960, but so was the girls' school at Fateh Kadal. Muriel Mallinson had kept it going on her own through the political crises of 1947–49 and the subsequent transformation of Kashmir under independent government but it had taken a toll on her resilience. She had not liked the changes that the Edmonds introduced to the boys' school and, when Eric and Phil returned it was clear to them that she was exhausted. She was then 65 so there was an urgent need for succession as in the boys' school but so far no one had been found. While the future of the school was most uncertain, the demand for a good girls' school was great and the place for it was with the Boys' School at Sheikh Bagh. If the new Government would agree to make over the whole site in perpetuity there was sufficient space to build the necessary accommodation for both schools. Together with Muriel, Eric and Phil planned how it could be achieved but all attempts to meet Prime Minister Bakshi to present their ideas failed. Then towards the end of 1960 another old boy, G.M. Sadiq, who had been very prominent in the movement for independence with Sheikh Abdullah, was appointed Minister for Education and he strongly supported the proposal and early in 1962 he gave the school a 40-year lease at an annual rent of 1 rupee, so that it could begin. In April 1962 the whole of the girls' school moved from Fateh Kadal to Sheikh Bagh where it was temporarily accommodated in Barton House, but there was still uncertainty as to who would succeed Muriel; John Ray certainly did not envisage that as part of his task. Muriel retired, most reluctantly, in October 1962 and for a short time the school had no principal so perforce, John Ray assumed the task. His first challenge was the inadequacy of the staff for a modern girls' school; none of the staff were trained teachers and enrolments were insufficient to maintain it. John had to retire several of the old teachers and this proved difficult because they had grown up with Muriel Mallinson and appealed to their class mates, the wife of the Minister for Education and, when that failed, to the wife of the Chief Minister. John continued:

> Bakshi Sahib called me, 'Mr Ray, you have sent away these seven sisters and they are very unhappy. I advise you to take them back.' I said (in a very Kashmiri manner) 'Sir, if you advise me, I will do so but we have no money.' Bakshi gave us ten thousand rupees to get started, and things steadily took off. In October he came as our Chief Guest on Parents' Day. Bluff but friendly, his advice was, 'Build or close; build or bust.'[10]

They took his advice and also found a very suitable successor as principal in 1964. Premi Gergan was the daughter of Skyabalden Gergan and niece of Chimed Gergan. They were members of the Ladakhi family whose connection with the Mission Schools went back to the early days of Biscoe's time when Premi's grandfather, Joseph, was the first boy to be accommodated in the hostel and later returned to Leh as the Christian pastor there. Premi remained principal of the newly named Mallinson Girls' School for the next 17 years, working closely with John Ray, and oversaw its development into a modern school accommodated in its own modern buildings.

In September 1980 the Tyndale-Biscoe and Mallinson Schools celebrated the centenary of Christian education in Kashmir.[11] Eric and Phil were invited back as guests of honour; Muriel had died in England a few months earlier or she would also have been invited. Many old students recalled the influence of the schools on their lives. Eric renewed his friendship with Sheikh Abdullah, restored to Chief Minister of Kashmir in 1974 after 11 years imprisonment by the Indian Government for advocating political independence of the State that Eric had also supported.

It was at that time that I encountered the doctor when the taxi driver died, and his remark that 'Canon Biscoe taught us to help other people' inspired me to explore the story of his life.

Figure 25 Eric Tyndale-Biscoe and Sheikh Abdullah, September 1980

Kashmiri Succession: Parwez and Joyce Koul

In October 1986 after 25 years, John Ray retired and Samuel Parwez Koul was appointed principal, the first Kashmiri in over 100 years of the school's existence! With his wife, Joyce Koul, who succeeded Premi Gergan as principal of the Mallinson Girls' School, they have led the combined institution to the present day (2018).

They were in charge when Eric made his last visit to Kashmir in 1987 and hoped to die there. It was not to be; but when he was back in New Zealand he expressed to me the wish that his ashes be taken to Kashmir and scattered at Nil Nag. After he died in March 1988 his ashes remained on my desk for ten years while Kashmir was convulsed by terrible ethnic, religious and political upheaval. Most of the minority Hindu population fled or was encouraged to leave the valley, several radical Islamic groups, supported by Pakistan, attempted to seize political control by violent intimidation of the rural population and the Indian armed forces responded with equal ferocity. Throughout this time Parwez and Joyce continued to keep the schools open, although it was impossible to maintain any of the traditional boating and other outdoor activities. By 1998 the country was slowly returning to normality and, when I wrote to Parwez about Eric's last wish he saw it as an opportunity to help restore normal school activities and encouraged us to visit Kashmir.

On our second day in Kashmir we were asked to come early to the combined Mallinson Girls' School and Tyndale-Biscoe Boys' School at Sheikh Bagh. Four very well dressed students, two girls and two boys, took us there, where we found an enormous welcome parade. On the old playing field were 4,000 boys and girls in school colours and a huge banner 'Welcome to Marina and Hugh'. In his introduction Parwez said that I was bringing back to Kashmir the mortal remains of Mr Eric to be cast into Nil Nag. In the *Kashmir Times* the next day there was an article about my father and how appropriate it was that his ashes should be brought back to Kashmir.[12] Some days later a party of students and staff accompanied us to Buzgu village, where I explained to the villagers Eric's wish and sought their approval. They gave approval and accompanied us to the lake where I paddled out on a couple of logs and shook the ashes into the waters of the lake. Subsequently the villagers put up a stone on the shore inscribed with his name and the date.

On our return through Jammu we met several of the Hindu staff who had fled Kashmir in 1990 and one of them said to me, 'we Hindus believe that the soul is not liberated until the ashes are cast into sacred water, so what you have done is very good'. It is fortunate that Nil Nag is fed from a sacred spring.

And so the Tyndale-Biscoe link with Kashmir ended in the lake that had refreshed Cecil Tyndale-Biscoe and his family since 1892; and, despite great tribulation, the enterprises he devoted his life to now flourish as never before, and under Kashmiri leadership.

Notes

Several unpublished sources that are referred to frequently are abbreviated as follows:

CMSAnnletters   Annual letters by missionaries of the Church Missionary Society, held in the Theological College, Bangalore

CMSArch.   Archives of the Church Missionary Society, University of Birmingham

CTB   Cecil Tyndale-Biscoe

CTBDiary   Diary of Cecil Tyndale-Biscoe, transcribed from his original daily diaries between 1937 and 1947, with later comments, and bound in five volumes

ETB   Eric Tyndale-Biscoe

ETBMem.   Unpublished autobiography of Eric Tyndale-Biscoe, entitled *Biskut Sahiban Nichu*

GMG   Typescript of Cecil Tyndale-Biscoe's autobiography entitled *God Meant It for Good*

IOR   India Office Records, Residency of Jammu and Kashmir, British Library, London

(Year) Log (*title*)   Refer to the 51 Annual Reports of the activities of the Kashmir Mission Schools from 1892 to 1946

These records (or copies), along with all other papers of Cecil Tyndale-Biscoe, are held in the Archives of Jesus College, Cambridge.

Chapter 1 Breaking Up and Building, 1890–95

1 CTBDiary, May 1892.

2 Clara Louise Warren, 22 November 1890. First letter home from Karachi. See email from Edward Nicholl (emn@enicholl.com).

3 For full description, see 1922 Log, *A School in Action*, p. 7.

4 P.N.K. Bamzai, *A History of Kashmir: Political, Social, Cultural* (Delhi, 1962), p. 636.

5 Kashmiri cedar, *Cedrus libani deodara*; W.R. Lawrence, *The Valley of Kashmir* (London, 1895), p. 79.

6 Letter ETB to HTB, 11 April 1968, 'Amar Chand was the first Kashmiri Pandit to greet Dad when he arrived at Sopor in 1890 and had arranged a *doonga* for him to travel the rest of the journey because there was no road any further at that time. Later Amar Chand was taken on as a teacher.'

7 1932 Log, *Riding the Storms in Kashmir*, p. 5.

8 Common Pariah Kite, *Milvus govinda*; Lawrence, *Valley of Kashmir*, p. 134.

9 W. Wakefield, *The Happy Valley* (London, 1879), pp. 163–8.

10 J.H. Knowles, *Folk Tales of Kashmir* (London, 1887), p. 419.

11 CMSArch. 111, 12 February 1890, A. Neve to H. Gray.

12 IOR, 4 May 1886. Memo from Colonel Sir O. St John, Resident in Kashmir.

13 E.F. Neve, A Review of Fifty Years Work and Witness in Kashmir. *Church Missionary Review* 65 (1914), pp. 420–4.

14 CMSArch. 423, 10 October 1890, R. Clark to Gray, London.

15 A. Lamb, *Kashmir, a Disputed Legacy, 1846–1990* (Karachi, 1991), pp. 23–7, 46.

16 1935 Log, *Digging Foundations in Kashmir*, p. 7.

17 *Capra falconeri*. See W.S. Burke, *The Indian Field Shikar Book* (Calcutta, 1920), p. 83.

18 F. Popham Young. See CTBDiary, 23 May 1912.

19 Bamzai, *A History of Kashmir*, p. 638.

20 CMSArch. 162, 13 March 1891, CTB to Gray.

21 Probably Pallas. Sea Eagle, *Haliaetus leucoryphus*, Lawrence, *Valley of Kashmir*, p. 134.

22 CTB handwritten letter, 16 April 1891.

23 CMS Annual report 1895, p. 184.

24 CMSArch. 162, 13 March 1891, CTB to Gray.

25 *Ibid.*

26 W. Irvine, *Apes Angels and Victorians* (London, 1956), p. 11.

27 W.R. Lawrence, *The India We Served* (London, 1928), p. 13.
28 E.F. Knight, *Where Three Empires Meet* (London, 1897), pp. 71–83.
29 S.A. Qadri, *Biscoe in Kashmir* (Srinagar, 1998), pp. 140–2.
30 R. Thorp, *Cashmere Misgovernment* (London, 1870), p. 80.
31 IOR, 15 May 1880. F. Henvey, Officer on Special Duty in Kashmir. The Famine in Kashmir 1877–80, p. 45.
32 IOR, 20 January 1884. Sir Oliver St John, Officer on Special Duty in Kashmir. Extract of Memorandum.
33 Lawrence, *The India We Served*, pp. 130–3.
34 1921 Log, *Straighter Steering in Kashmir*, p. 9.
35 CMSArch. 296, 2 July 1891, Munshi Bagh, CTB to Gray.
36 GMG, p. 40.
37 *Ibid.*
38 Knight, *Where Three Empires Meet,* p. 528.
39 CTBDiary, 18 January 1892.
40 C.E. Tyndale-Biscoe, *Kashmir in Sunlight and Shade* (London, 1922), pp. 276–80.
41 *Ibid.*, pp. 282–3.
42 *Ibid.*, p. 286.
43 CTBDiary, 8 May 1892.
44 *The Punjab Mission News,* August 1892.
45 Lawrence, *The Valley of Kashmir*, pp. 218–20.
46 CTBDiary, July 1892, insert.
47 CTBDiary, 25 August 1892, insert.
48 CTBDiary, May 1892.
49 CMS Extracts from Annual Letters 1892, p. 26.
50 C.E. Tyndale-Biscoe, *Tyndale-Biscoe of Kashmir* (London, 1950), pp. 166–7.
51 CMSArch. 20, 20 December 1892, Annual letter of CTB.
52 CMSArch. 85, 28 January 1893, Minutes CC, Lahore.
53 CMSArch. 136, 1 March 1893, Knowles to Gray.
54 CMSArch. 255, 13 April 1893, Srinagar, CTB to R. Clark.
55 CMSArch. 273, 13 April 1893, CTB to R. Clark.
56 H.M. Clark, *Robert Clark of the Panjab* (London, 1907), pp. 342–7.
57 CMSArch. 272, 20 May 1893, Dalhousie, R. Clark to Rev. W. Gray, London.
58 CMSArch. 294b, 6 June 1893, Kashmir, CTB to R. Clark.
59 1893 Log, *Tacking* p.5; C.E. Tyndale-Biscoe, *Kashmir in Sunlight and Shade* (London, 1922), pp. 183–6.
60 *Ibid.*
61 J. Duke, *Kashmir Handbook* (Calcutta, 1903), pp. 250–1.

62 CTBDiary, 2 August 1893.

63 1893 Log, p. 1.

64 CMSArch. 20, 31 October 1893, A. Neve to R. Clark.

65 CMSArch. 110, 24 January 1894, Kashmir, Knowles to Gray.

66 Elizabeth Newman had to return to England to care for her mother but did return to Kashmir seven years later.

67 CMSArch. 222, 9 April 1894, Kashmir, CTB to Gray.

68 CTBDiary, May 1894.

69 A. Carus-Wilson, *Irene Petrie* (London, 1901), p. 164.

Chapter 2 Now is the Day of Small Things, 1895–99

1   Annual accounts for 1895: outlay Rs 4,716; receipts from, CMS 1,800, Perkins 50, Neve brothers 90, TB family 380, fees 8, balance from Kashmir residents and some English donors.

2   G.J. and F. Younghusband, *The Relief of Chitral* (London, 1896).

3   G. Tyndale-Biscoe, Diary.

4   1920 Log, *Still Pegging Away in Kashmir*, p. 8.

5   G.T. Vigne, *Travels in Kashmir*, Vol. 2 (London, 1842), pp. 203–4.

6   A. Neve, *Tourist's Guide to Kashmir, Ladakh, Skardu etc.* (Lahore, 1918), p. 170.

7   K. Mason, *Abode of Snow* (London, 1955), p. 108; A.F. Mummery, *My Climbs in the Alps and Caucasus* (London, 1946), pp. xiv – xxiii.

8   Vigne, *Travels in Kashmir*, p. 239.

9   A. Neve, *Thirty Years in Kashmir* (London, 1913), p. 92.

10 W. Kick, 'The people of Arandu and their Chogo Lungma Glacier', *The Mountain World* (1956–7), pp. 163–72.

11 With porters at 4d. (= 5 annas) a day it is not necessary to limit one's baggage. The ordinary labourer earns about 5 rupees a month (= 3 annas per day). Neve, *Tourist's Guide to Kashmir, Ladakh, Skardu etc.*, p. 88.

12 3 July 1892 from Hispar Glacier to Arandu by Bruce, Eckenstein two Gurkhas and eight Nagiris; by Zurbriggen and Roudebush on 13 July and returned on 18 July (see Mason, *Abode of Snow*, pp. 103–4); C.G. Bruce, *Himalayan Wanderer* (London, 1934), pp. 94–6.

13 A. Carus-Wilson, *Irene Petrie* (London, 1901), p. 252.

14 1895 Log, *Coaching in Kashmir*, p. 4.

15 *Ibid.*

16 Letter CTB to Julian Tyndale-Biscoe, 22 January 1944.

17 A. Carus-Wilson, *Irene Petrie* (London 1901), p. 258.

18 Carus-Wilson, *Irene Petrie*, pp. 259–61.

19 E. Neve, *Beyond the Pir Panjal* (London, 1912), pp. 170–202; C.E. Tyndale-Biscoe, *Kashmir in Sunlight and Shade* (London, 1922), pp. 197–233, and CTBDiary, May to August 1896.

20 Captain Godfrey bought the superbly embroidered Kashmir Shawl, depicting in great detail the city of Srinagar, which was specially made for the Royal visit of the Prince of Wales in 1870. When the visit did not eventuate the shawl remained with the Kashmir Government until offered for sale in September 1896. It was presented by the Godfrey family to the National Gallery of Australia in 1992.

21 A. Walker, *Aurel Stein. Pioneer of the Silk Road* (London, 1995), p. 45.

22 J. Mirsky, *Sir Aurel Stein: Archaeological Explorer* (Chicago, 1977), p. 63.

23 Neve, *Beyond the Pir Panjal*, pp. 188–9.

24 A.H. Francke, *A History of Western Tibet* (London, 1907), pp. 175–6.

25 1909 Log, *Character Building in Kashmir*, p. 5. Arjan Nath Mujoo recalled this in July 1998 in Jammu.

26 CMSArch. 531, 6 August 1896, Kashmir, CTB to Clark.

27 CMSArch. 234, 24 May 1897, R. Clark to G.B. Durrant.

28 The white swan (or goose) in Hindu mythology represents purity and truth and in this context indicates that knowledge must be acquired and applied for the good of mankind.

29 1896 Log, *Coxing in Kashmir*, p. 14.

30 A. Neve, *Picturesque Kashmir* (London, 1900), p. 105 et seq., and *Thirty Years in Kashmir*, pp. 191–218, the latter being a fuller account of the former but with much of the same wording; also T.G. Longstaff, 'Obituary: Arthur Neve'. *The Geographical Journal* 54 (1919), pp. 396–8.

31 A. Neve, 'Journeys in the Himalayas and some factors of Himalayan erosion', *The Geographical Journal* 38 (1911), pp. 345–62.

32 A. Neve, *Thirty Years in Kashmir*, p. 242.

33 I Corinthians XV 58.

34 CMSArch. 482, 20/21 December 1897. CTB to Durrant.

35 CMSArch. 194, 28 May 1899, Kashmir. CTB to Durrant.

36 CMSArch. 262, 26 July 1899, Simla. Clark to Durrant.

37 ETBMem. Chapter 5.

38 *Ibid.*

39 J.W. Kaye, *Christianity in India* (London, 1859), pp. 475–506.

40 23 August 1948, letter CTB to HTB.

41 W. Moorcroft and G. Trebeck, *Travels in the Himalayan Provinces of Hindustan and the Panjab* (New Delhi, 1971 reprint) Vol. 2, pp. 290–9.

42 V. Jacquemont, *Letters from India*, Vol. 2 (Karachi, 1979 reprint), pp. 54–159.

Chapter 3 The Challenge, 1900–05

1 CMSAnnletters, 1900–1, pp. 301–5.
2 *Ibid.*, Mission Hospital report.
3 W.H. McNeill, *Plagues and Peoples* (Oxford, 1976), p. 273.
4 CTBDiary, 10 September 1900. Footnote: 'later deaths ran up to 500 to 700 per day'.
5 Neve, *Beyond the Pir Panjal*, p. 272.
6 1900 Log, *Steering in Kashmir*, pp. 9–10.
7 CMSAnnletters, 1901, pp. 549–51.
8 CTBDiary insert, October 1894.
9 1901 Log, *Punting in Kashmir*, p. 17.
10 A. Taylor, *Annie Besant: a Biography* (Oxford, 1992), pp. 279–80.
11 GMG, p. 69.
12 *Central Hindu College Magazine* Vol.1, pp. 28–9. Referred by Taylor, *Annie Besant: a Biography*, pp. 278–9.
13 M. Bevir, 'Mothering India', *History Today* (2006), pp. 19–25.
14 CTBDiary, 6 June 1901.
15 CTBDiary, 1 February 1902, 1 July 1902.
16 A.M. Pennell, *Pennell of the Afghan Frontier* (London, 1923), p. 158.
17 Taylor, *Annie Besant: a Biography*, p. 272.
18 1901 Log, p. 27.
19 Pennell, *Pennell of the Afghan Frontier*, pp. 159–60.
20 1901 Log, pp. 20–2.
21 GMG, p. 70.
22 CTBDiary, 1 July 1902.
23 CMS Annual Report 1903, 24 November 1902 to 17 March 1903.
24 CTB Letter to Blanche, 15 January 1903.
25 CTB Letter to Blanche, 30 January 1903.
26 CTB Letter to Blanche. Mandalay, 8 February 1903.
27 *Ibid.*
28 H.M. Hyde, *Famous Trials 7: Oscar Wilde* (London, 1962), p. 316.
29 GMG, p. 89.
30 CMSArch. 4, August 1903, CTB to Durrant.
31 Note that the subscription list for 1901 raised 3,702 rupees of which 1,095 rupees (30 per cent) was contributed by members of the Tyndale-Biscoe family. Other income was CMS 5,640 rupees, Kashmir State 2,400 rupees, Fees etc. 1,711 rupees.
32 CMSArch. 226, 24 June 1903. CTB to H.U. Weitbrecht.
33 CMSArch. 29, June 1903. Weitbrecht to CTB.
34 CMSArch. 248, 4 August 1903, CTB to Durrant, Permanent Secretary, London.

35 CMSArch., 9 December 1904, Durrant to T. Wade.

36 CMSArch., February 1905, Durrant to Wade.

37 CMSArch. 91, 2 March 1905, Lahore, Wade to Durrant.

38 CMSArch. 93, 18 March 1905, Brighton, A. Neve to Durrant.

39 M. Rosenthal, *The Character Factory* (London, 1986), pp. 52–87.

40 *Ibid.*

41 E.T. Seton, *The Red Book or How to Play Indian* (Philadelphia, 1904).

42 Rosenthal, *The Character Factory*, p. 68.

43 CTBDiary, 18 January 1905.

44 D. Tyndale-Biscoe, *Sailor Soldier* (2004), p. 175.

45 C.E. Tyndale-Biscoe, *Character Building in Kashmir* (London, 1920), p. 95.

46 C. Allen, *Plain Tales from the Raj* (London, 2007), pp. 64–72.

47 1905 Log, *Plugging Again Kashmir*, pp. 1–2.

48 P. French, *Younghusband* (London, 1994), p. 270.

Chapter 4 Exceedingly a Bad Man, 1905–10

1 French, *Younghusband*, p. 467.

2 *Ibid.*, pp. 268–9.

3 M. Gilbert, *Servant of India* (London, 1966), p. 25; Sir Bampfylde Fuller, *Studies of Indian Life and Sentiment* (London, 1910), pp. 316–9.

4 J.S. Hoyland, *The Man India Loved: C.F. Andrews* (London, 1944), p. 5.

5 B. Chaturvedi and M. Sykes, *Charles Freer Andrews. A Narrative* (London, 1949), p. 49.

6 H. Tinker, *A New System of Slavery: The Export of Indian Labour Overseas, 1830–1920* (London, 1974), pp. 35–6.

7 T. Pennell, *The Civil and Military Gazette*, 12 October 1906.

8 Chaturvedi and Sykes, *Charles Freer Andrews*, pp. 49–51; Tinker, *A New System of Slavery*, pp. 36–7.

9 French, *Younghusband*, p. 269.

10 Bamzai, *A History of Kashmir*, p. 652.

11 *Punjab Mission News*, 15 November 1906.

12 CTBDiary, 5 May 1907.

13 Chaturvedi and Sykes, *Charles Freer Andrews*, p. 51; S. Razi Wasti, *Lord Minto and the Indian Nationalist Movement, 1905 to 1910* (Oxford, 1964), pp. 97–9.

14 CTBDiary, 6 November 1906.

15 1912 Log, *Scouts in the Making in Kashmir*, p. 10.

16 C.F. Andrews, *North India* (London, 1908).

17 1906 Log, *Training in Kashmir*, p. 6.

18 GMG, p. 65–6.

19 1908 Log, *More Odds and Ends of School Life in Kashmir*, p. 12.

20 1906 Log, p. 13.

21 1931 Log, *Pile Driving in Kashmir*, p. 16.

22 1906 Log, p. 8.

23 *Ibid*, p. 6.

24 A movement based in north India, especially in Punjab and the districts around Delhi, which did not attempt to absorb or assimilate Christian precepts or practices into Hinduism; instead they launched a direct challenge both to Christianity and Islam – Tinker, *A New System of Slavery*, p. 20.

25 28 November 1908. CTB Annual Letter, p. 351.

26 GMG, pp. 98–9.

27 CTBDiary, 17 July 1906.

28 CTBDiary, 7 September 1907.

29 CMSArch. 266a, 24 June 1908, Srinagar CTB to Ireland Jones.

30 1906 Log, p. 9.

31 1909 Log, *Character Building in Kashmir*, p. 23.

32 1907 Log, *Odds and Ends of School Life in Kashmir*, pp. 5–6.

33 CTBDiary, August 1907.

34 CMSArch., Outgoing letter Durrant to GWTB, 4 October 1906. Letter book 8, p. 481.

35 CTBDiary, 13 October 1907.

36 28 November 1908. CTB Annual Letter, p. 351.

37 C.E. Tyndale-Biscoe, *A Valiant Man of Kashmir* (London, 1933), p. 14.

38 CTBDiary, February 1907.

39 CTBDiary, 19 September 1908.The first hydro-electric power house below Baramula was nearing completion and would soon be opened by the Maharaja to provide power for the dredges operating below the Wular Lake and soon after to bring electric light to the city.

40 CMSArch. 266a, 24 June 1908, Srinagar CTB to Ireland Jones.

41 CTBDiary, 26 June 1908.

42 CTBDiary, 25 March 1909.

43 CTBDiary, 23 June 1909.

44 Bamzai, *A History of Kashmir*, p. 659.

45 1908 Log, pp. 13–14; 28 November 1908. CTB Annual Letter, p. 351.

46 Local clothing, i.e. *shalwar* and *pheran*.

47 CTBDiary, 15 July 1908.

48 1937 Log, *Against the Current in Kashmir*, p. 7; GMG, pp. 49, 174.

49 CMSArch. 104, 22 March 1905, London Interview of Dr Elliott with Dr M. Gomery.

50 CMSArch. 4, May 1905, Lahore, Ireland Jones to Durrant.
51 CMS Annual Letters, pp. 227-8. November 1905. Kate Knowles, Islamabad.
52 CMSArch. 17, March 1906, Lahore, Ireland Jones to K. Knowles.
53 CMSArch. 280, 7 July 1906, Islamabad, Gomery to Ireland Jones.
54 CMSArch. 281, 8 July 1906, Islamabad, K. Knowles to Ireland Jones.
55 CMSArch. 263, 10 July 1906, Kohala Dak Bungalow, Ireland Jones to Durrant.
56 CMSArch. 108, 9 April 1907, London, Medical Committee.
57 CMSArch. 163, 30 May 1907, Lahore, Ireland Jones to Durrant.
58 CMSArch. 205, 2 July 1907, Srinagar, Weitbrecht to Durrant.
59 ETB to HTB, excerpt from letter 7 June 1976.
60 CMSArch. 332, 7 November 1907, Srinagar, CTB to Ireland Jones.
61 CMSArch. 100, 8 February 1908, Srinagar, K. Knowles to Durrant.
62 CMSArch. 108a, 7 February 1908, Srinagar, CTB to Ireland Jones.
63 CMSArch. 141, 6 March 1908, Proceedings Punjab Corresponding Medical Committee, Lahore.
64 CMSArch. 287, 6 July 1908, Proceedings of Kashmir District Medical Committee, Srinagar.
65 CTBDiary, 17 October 1908.
66 1908 Log, pp. 3-7.
67 CTBDiary, 18, 19 September 1908.
68 CTBDiary, 1 August 1909.
69 CMSArch., 30 March 1910, Proceedings Punjab Corresponding Medical Committee, Lahore.
70 5 November 1930. *Sydney Morning Herald*.
71 CTBDiary, 18 March 1923. An anonymous gift of £400 arrives in registered envelope from Australia.
72 R.R. Sturrock, 'The Anatomy Department at University College, Dundee, 1888-1954', *Medical History* 21 (1977), p. 314.

Chapter 5 War Years and the Aftermath, 1911-22

1 R.K. Massie, *Dreadnought, Britain, Germany, and the Coming of the Great War* (New York, 1991), pp. 623-5.
2 CTBDiary, 19 March 1911.
3 CMSArch. 175, 22 September 1913. A. Neve to Canon Waller.
4 *Ibid.*, 173, 16 October 1913. Waller to F.E. Wigram, London.
5 CTBDiary, 28 July 1911, to 21 August 1911.
6 1913 Log, *Jerry Building in Kashmir*, p. 26.
7 CTBDiary, 20 July 1914.
8 CMSArch. 96, 26 May 1914. Wigram to Waller.

9 CTBDiary, 17 December 1914.

10 CTBDiary, 11 March 1916.

11 J. Tyndale-Biscoe, *Gunner Subaltern 1914–1918* (London, 1971), pp. 95–101.

12 CTBDiary, 29 September 1916.

13 CTBDiary, 4 October 1916.

14 CTBDiary, 2 July 1910.

15 M. Rosenthal, *The Character Factory* (London, 1986), p. 185.

16 *Ibid.*, pp. 264–5.

17 *Civil and Military Gazette*, 28 May 1912.

18 1911 Log, *Scouting in Kashmir*, p. 20.

19 1912 Log, *Scouts in the Making in Kashmir*, p. 19.

20 1913 Log, p. 21.

21 1914 Log, *Men in the Making*, p. 14.

22 *Ibid.*, pp. 18–19.

23 1911 Log, p. 21.

24 1916 Log, *Rock Shifting in Kashmir*, p. 13.

25 CTBDiary, 30 March 1911.

26 CTBDiary, 6 April 1911.

27 CTBDiary, 7 April 1911.

28 CTBDiary, 10 April 1911.

29 CTBDiary, 1 September 1911; 1913 Log, pp. 20–1.

30 CTBDiary, 25 May 1911.

31 See photo in 1913 Log, p. 22.

32 CTBDiary, 20 March 1912.

33 CTBDiary, 29 January 1914.

34 14 November 1914, CTB testimonial for Salama carpenter in 1900–10 file.

35 1912 Log, p. 21.

36 CTBDiary, 22 June 1911.

37 Kairoo, Kashmiri for Himalayan Blue Pine, Pinus excelsa.

38 CTBDiary, 24 January 1912.

39 1911 Log, p. 26.

40 CTBDiary, 27 March 1914.

41 1917 Log, *Forging up Stream in Kashmir*, pp. 19–20.

42 1918 Log, *A School in Being*, p. 17.

43 CTBDiary, 25 May 1918.

44 CTBDiary, 9 August 1918.

45 CTBDiary, 13 October 1918.

46 CTBDiary, 30 October 1918.

47 CTBDiary, 6 November 1918.

48 1918 Log, p. 17.
49 CTBDiary, 12 January 1919.
50 CTBDiary, 10 September 1918.
51 CTBDiary, 18 July 1919. England.
52 French, *Younghusband*, p. 270.
53 CTBDiary, 27 March 1920. Marseilles. Embarked on SS Nankeen P&O.
54 CTBDiary, 5 December 1924.
55 CTBDiary, 3 June 1920; 1920 Log, *Still Pegging Away in Kashmir*, p. 17.
56 CMSArch. 71, 4 February 1921, Srinagar CTB to Wigram.
57 1921 Log, *Straighter Steering in Kashmir*, pp. 10–11.
58 CMSArch. 126, 27 June 1921, Srinagar, CTB to Wigram; CTBDiary, 1 July 1921.
59 CTBDiary, 31 August 1921.
60 This was the last time this was done; on Lord Reading's next visit in 1924 Biscoe's son Eric persuaded him that it was too dangerous and they arranged instead for a large banner to be unfurled on the school balcony with many heads poking through it.
61 CTBDiary, 15 October 1921.
62 CTBDiary, 5 December 1921.
63 CTBDiary, 9 December 1921.
64 1921 Log, p. 12.
65 CMSArch. 142, 6 September 1919, Srinagar, H.T. Holland to Wigram.
66 E.M. Forster, 'Missionaries' The Athenaeum, 22 October 1920, pp. 545–7.
67 E.M. Forster, *A Passage to India* (London, 1924), p. 335.
68 Forster, 'Missionaries', pp. 545–7.
69 D. Galgut, *Arctic Summer* (London, 2014), p. 355.
70 1923 Log, *Knight Errantry in Kashmir*, back cover.
71 G.K. Das, *E.M. Forster's India* (London, 1977), p. 170.
72 A.S.N. Wadia, *In the Land of Lala Rookh* (London, 1921), pp. 221–5.
73 Mangan, J.A., *The Games Ethic and Imperialism* (London, 1985).
74 1912 Log, p. 12.
75 Lord Hardinge, *My Indian Years* (London, 1948), p. 130.
76 CTBDiary, 3 March 1916.
77 CTBDiary, 16 October 1917; 1917 Log, p. 20.
78 CTB Letter to Blanche, 23 September 1917.
79 G. Studdert-Kennedy, 'Canon Cecil Earle Tyndale-Biscoe', in H.C.G. Matthew, ed., *New Dictionary of National Biography* (Oxford, 2014).
80 G. Studdert-Kennedy, *Providence and the Raj* (New Delhi, 1998), pp. 194–7.

81 A. Draper, *Amritsar, the Massacre That Ended the Raj* (London, 1981), p. 35.
82 H. Tinker, *The Ordeal of Love* (Oxford, 1979), p. 152.
83 CTBDiary, 26 January 1919. Lahore.
84 CMSArch. 68, 21 April 1919, Lahore, Gough to CMS London.
85 CMSArch. 72, 11 May 1920, Tarn Taran. Guildford to Wigram.
86 Draper, Amritsar, pp. 174–7.
87 CTBDiary, 9 June 1920.

Chapter 6 Succession and Success, 1923–33

1 Letter to Julian, 21 October 1941.
2 CMSArch. 21, 29 March 1922, Lahore, Gough to Wigram on retirement of CTB on attaining age 60 on 9 February 1923.
3 CMSArch. 27, 10 February 1924, CTB to Wigram.
4 CTBDiary, 2 October 1919, Julian entered for the Indian Civil Service exam and passed but refused because he might find himself under the command of an Indian Commissioner.
5 A. Barnes, *You May Keep Your Own Horse. The Story of What Happened to Phyllis Long When She Went to New Zealand in 1923* (Canberra, 2013), p. 216.
6 CMSArch. 90, 11 August 1927, Lahore, Force Jones to Wigram.
7 CMSArch. 98, 29 July 1924, Srinagar, Force Jones to Wigram.
8 1928 Log, *Crusaders in Kashmir*, pp. 17–20.
9 CTBDiary, 1 December 1927. Sam Bakkal passes from us great grief. Also C.E. Tyndale-Biscoe, *A Valiant Man of Kashmir* (London, 1933), p. 14.
10 CTBDiary, 20 June 1929; C.E. Tyndale-Biscoe, *Tyndale-Biscoe of Kashmir. An Autobiography* (London, 1951), pp. 219–23.
11 *Saussurea lappa*, see B.O. Coventry, *Wild Flowers of Kashmir*, Vol. 1 (London, 1923), pp. 51–3.
12 CTBDiary, 29 October 1935. Arranged for brass tablets on the goal posts for Sam Bakkal and Chimed. The goal posts are two mulberry trees.
13 CMSArch. 126, 12 July 1928, Srinagar, ETB to Wigram.
14 ETBMem. Chapter 28, 5–6; CMS Newsletter 1931, pp. 3–5.
15 1929 Log, *Grinding Grit into Kashmir*, p. 15; ETBMem. Chapter 28.
16 CTBDiary, 12 December 1929. Cecil Hugh christened. School holiday in his honour. Church full with friends and school staff. At home to all afterwards.
17 CTBDiary, 24–6 June 1933. Weekend camp at Nil Nagh of Hindu and Muslim teachers with Eric and Phil, all eating together.

18 CMSArch. 93b, 4 October 1932, Bromley, Wigram to Treanor. Comments on Douglas Barton's letter.

19 CMSArch. 93, 9 August 1932, Quetta, Annual letter, Douglas E. Barton.

20 E.M. Forster, 'Missionaries' pp. 545–7.

21 CMSArch. 50, 13–16 April 1929, Amritsar. 25th Church and Mission Central Council Meeting.

22 CMSArch. 115, 3 October 1929, Lahore, Force Jones to Treanor.

23 CMSArch. 127, 24 October 1929, Lahore, Force Jones to Treanor.

24 CTBDiary, 1 February 1932.

25 CMSArch. 62, 15 June 1932, Lahore, Punjab Corresponding Medical Committee, Estimates 1933. Educational grants.

26 CMSArch. 75, 2 July 1932, Srinagar, CTB to Wigram.

27 CMSArch. 74, 21 July 1932, Lahore, Wigram to Treanor, Kashmir schools.

28 CTBDiary, 5 August 1932. Canon Hares lets the cat out of the bag at Gulmarg, re the wicked Canon being made to toe the line and his son like his father.

29 CTBDiary, 27 July 1932. Letter from Wigram.

30 CTBDiary, 1 October 1932.

31 CTBDiary, 2 November 1932.

32 CMSArch. 108, 2 November 1932, Lahore.

33 1938 Log, *With Pick and Shovel in Kashmir*, p. 9.

34 K. Mayo, *Mother India* (London, 1927), p. 110.

35 CTBDiary, 17 April 1929. Insert in Newspaper letter by CTB. '"Truth": The Child Wives of India'.

36 Earthenware fire pot encased in a wicker basket.

37 Letter to Julian 14 January 1934. 'When you think 12 years ago (1922) when they let down the weir at the Seventh Bridge every month the bag was usually about 200 baby corpses.'

38 Lawrence, *Valley of Kashmir*, pp. 224–8.

39 K. Knowles, 'Osteomalacia in Kashmir', *British Medical Journal Supplement* 1914, pp. 62–3.

40 K. Vaughan, 'Osteomalacia in Kashmir', *British Medical Journal* 6 March 1926, 1, pp. 413–5.

41 L. Starr-Underhill, *The Rights of Woman in 1926* (Government Printer, Peshawar, c.1926) p. 8.; 4 July 1926, letter CTB to Julian TB.

42 CTBDiary, 26 February 1923.

43 Starr-Underhill, *The Rights of Woman in 1926*, p. 8.

44 July 1927. Comment by CTB in Underhill pamphlet. Also in 1927 Log, *Amphibious Scouts in Kashmir*, p. 21.

45 1928 Log, p. 10; CTBDiary, 27 April 1928. (Note: entry in CTBDiary is for 1927 but this is incorrect. See letter to Julian 28 May 1928.)

46 Mayo, *Mother India*, p. 391.

47 C.F. Andrews, *The True India. A Plea for Understanding* (London, 1939), p. 251.

48 1924 Log, *Social Service in Kashmir*, p. 12.

49 CTBDiary, 12 May 1918; Tyndale-Biscoe, *Autobiography*, pp. 181–3.

50 CTBDiary, 20 September 1923.

51 1922 Log, *A School in Action*, p. 14.

52 1928 Log, pp. 10–11; Letter CTB to Julian TB 21 May 1928; Tyndale-Biscoe, *Autobiography*, pp. 97–8.

53 CTBDiary, 20 May 1928.

54 1928 Log, p. 11.

55 28 May 1928. Letter CTB to Julian TB.

56 1929 Log, p. 16.

57 1933 Log, *Hewing Timber in Kashmir*, p. 10.

58 1938 Log, p. 7.

59 1931 Log, *Pile Driving in Kashmir,* inserted circular letter by ETB, *Some Sidelights on the Kashmir Disturbances.*

60 CTBDiary, 20 January 1903; letter CTB to Blanche.

61 1917 Log, *Forging Up Stream in Kashmir*, p. 24.

62 CMSArch. 21, 8 January 1921, Srinagar. CTB to Gough.

63 CMS Arch. 126, 27 June 1921, Srinagar, CTB to Wigram.

64 CTBDiary, 19 October 1922.

65 Excerpt from 1962, 50-year anniversary account by ETB.

66 1930 Log, *Steeple-Chasing in Kashmir*, p.18.

67 L. Starr-Underhill, *The Rights of Woman in 1926.*

68 1930 Log, p. 17.

69 1931 Log, p. 18.

70 1932 Log, *Riding the Storms in Kashmir*, p. 23.

71 1934 Log, *Victory after Defeat,* photo, p. 18.

72 Letter CTB to ETB 2 September 1934, Srinagar.

73 CTBDiary, 2 September 1933.

74 ETB circular letter. Srinagar, Kashmir. May 1962.

75 ETBMem. Chapter 27.

76 Lamb, *Kashmir,* p. 87.

77 CTBDiary, 9 September 1929; CTB circular letter not for publication, January 1930.

78 See Lamb, *Kashmir,* p. 88.

79 G.E.C. Wakefield, *Recollections, 50 years in the Service of India* (Lahore, 1942), pp. 203–4.

80 H. Jaisingh, *Kashmir. A Tale of Shame* (New Delhi, 1996), p. 50; Lamb, *Kashmir*, p. 57.

81 CTBDiary, 12 March 1931, London. Tea with Sir Walter Lawrence and son.

82 1931 Log, p. 8.

83 Jaisingh, *Kashmir,* p. 52.

84 P. French, *Liberty or Death* (London, 1997), pp. 78–80.

85 1930 Log, p. 8.

86 S. Gupta, *Kashmir. A Study in India–Pakistan Relations* (Bombay, 1966), p. 51.

87 Lamb, *Kashmir,* p. 91.

88 1931 Log, inserted circular letter by ETB, *Some Sidelights on the Kashmir Disturbances.*

89 ETBMem, 27, pp. 5–6.

90 Letter CTB to ETB. 5 June 1934, Srinagar. 'Yesterday at the Residency Garden Party a member of H.H.'s Council was telling me of the riots of two years ago and expressed his admiration of your brave action at the time.'

91 1931 Log, inserted letter by ETB, *Some Sidelights on the Kashmir Disturbances.*

92 ETBMem, 27, p. 8.

93 *Ibid.*

94 Lamb, *Kashmir,* p. 90.

95 24 September 1931. Second arrest of Sheikh Abdullah. See M.J. Akbar, *Kashmir Behind the Vale* (New Delhi, 1991), pp. 72–7.

96 1931 Log, inserted letter by ETB, *Some Sidelights on the Kashmir Disturbances.*

97 CTBDiary, 3 November 1931. Left Lahore at 8 am. Trouble at Jammu, British troops in charge; CTBDiary, 3 February 1932. The people of Poonch rebel, troops sent there, also British troops sent to Kashmir.

98 1934 Log, p. 6.

99 CTBDiary, 28 November 1931.

100 Letter from Sheikh Abdullah to CTB, 23 September 1933.

101 CTBDiary, 31 March 1932.

102 CTBDiary, 1 March 1932.

103 CTBDiary, 22 September 1932.

104 1932 Log, pp. 9–10.

105 CTBDiary, 23 September 1932.

106 CTBDiary, 24 September 1932.

107 CTBDiary, 28 September 1932.

108 CTBDiary, 28 September 1935.

109 1931 Log, p. 16.
110 1932 Log, p. 11.
111 *Ibid.*, p. 15.
112 Letter from Sheikh Abdullah to CTB, 11 February 1934.

Chapter 7 Victory After Defeat, 1934–39

1 Genesis Ch. 50, v. 20.
2 21 January 1934, Srinagar, CTB to ETB.
3 CMSArch. 23, February 1934. Mortimore, CEZMS to London. CEZMS General Committee discussed their work in Kashmir and asked CMS to take over the educational and medical work.
4 28 January 1934, Srinagar, CTB to ETB.
5 CTBDiary, 12 April 1923.
6 Singhara nut from the aquatic plant, *Trapa bispinosa*. See Lawrence, *Valley of Kashmir*, pp. 72, 355.
7 T. Nath Zalpuri, 'The Tragedy of Wular Lake 11 April 1934 – an eye witness account'. *Neelamatam* 2(1) (July 2004) pp. 1–30.
8 *Ibid.*
9 1928 Log, *Crusaders in Kashmir*, p. 13.
10 1934 Log, *Victory After Defeat*, p. 17.
11 1934 Log, pp. 6–7.
12 *Ibid.*; CTB letter to ETB 30 April 1934.
13 Nath Zalpuri, 'The Tragedy of Wular Lake 11 April 1934'.
14 24 April and 6 May 1934, Srinagar. CTB to ETB.
15 23 May 1934, Cambridge. ETB to CTB.
16 15 May 1934, Srinagar. CTB to ETB.
17 CTBDiary, 13 July 1934.
18 19 September 1934, Srinagar. CTB to ETB.
19 1934 Log, p. 7.
20 24 June 1934, Srinagar. CTB to ETB Your parcel containing the lorry and shirt for NK's child arrived.
21 17 July 1934, Malsis Hall, Keighley. ETB to CTB.
22 1 August 1934, Worth Matravens, Dorset. ETB to CTB.
23 12 August 1934, Nil Nag. CTB to ETB.
24 CTBDiary, 21 November 1934.
25 12 December 1934, Shalford.ETB to CTB.
26 27 November 1934, Keston Park. ETB to CTB.
27 1934 Log, pp. 14–5.
28 *Ibid.*
29 1945 Log, *It Can't Be Done, Then Do It*, p. 4.

30 9 April 1935. Letter CTB to Julian TB.

31 CTBDiary, 21 April 1935.

32 25 August 1935. Letter CTB to Julian TB.

33 CTBDiary, 17 November 1936.

34 11 July 1935. Letter CTB to Julian TB.

35 1937 Log, *Against the Current in Kashmir*, pp. 15–18.

36 S. Chand Koul, *Beautiful Valleys of Kashmir* (Srinagar, 1971), p. 95.

37 N.L. Bakaya, *Holidaying and Trekking in Kashmir* (Srinagar, 1966), p. 159.

38 E.F. Neve, *Beyond the Pir Panjal*, pp. 51–2.

39 S.C. Koul, *Birds of Kashmir* (Srinagar, 1939), p. 103.

40 S.C. Koul, *Beautiful Valleys of Kashmir and Ladakh* (Srinagar, 1942), p. 149.

41 1935 Log, *Digging Foundations in Kashmir*, p. 21.

42 ETBMem. Chapter 29 p. 7.

43 *Ibid.*, 9.

44 *The Statesman*, Delhi, 17 March 1936.

45 24 June 1934, Srinagar. CTB to ETB; CTBDiary, 3 July 1934, 'Ralph Moan arrived from Calcutta to run our technical department'.

46 G.R. Moan, *The Long Long Trail Awinding* (Unpublished memoir, 1982).

47 1936 Log, *Driving the Djinns out of Kashmir*, pp. 15–6.

48 CTBDiary, 15 July 1935. N.N. Misri in charge of hostel.

49 Letter from S.L. Mathu to ETB 23 July 1983. Biscoe School 55 Years ago.

50 CTBDiary, 11 September 1936. Visited Wajayat Hussein re plan for school building on hostel ground. He had signed the plan.

51 1937 Log, *Against the Current in Kashmir*. Insert by G.R. Moan, *Three Years Hard Labour*. CMS Technical School, pp. 13–20.

52 CTBDiary, 30 June 1937.

53 CTBDiary 20 April and May 1937. Notes in diary for 1921 with comment 'not to this date' presumably indicating that he was re-writing his original diaries in 1937 and earlier.

54 CTBDiary 4 August 1938.

55 A year later an exceptionally tall Englishman died suddenly in Srinagar. At the funeral Eric asked Ralph Moan did he stock coffins in all sizes, to which he replied, 'that is the coffin I made for you last year!'

56 14 October 1939. Letter CTB to Julian TB. 'I have today received a letter from the CMS London saying that I am retired but may continue to live and work here.'

57 E.D. Tyndale-Biscoe, *The Story of Sheikh Bagh* (Mysore, 1946), p. 58.

58 27 April 1958. Ruby Bay, New Zealand. Letter ETB to HTB.

Chapter 8 Two Kings on One Carpet. Final Years, 1940–49

1 Lamb, *Kashmir*, pp. 95–6.

2 CTBDiary, 31 May 1940; 1 June 1940. Letter CTB to Julian TB.

3 IOR23JK, 31 August 1938. Resident's fortnightly resume. S.M. Abdullah and six others were sentenced to 6 months imprisonment.

4 IOR23JK 498, 8 January 1939. Office of the All India States Peoples' Conference. The National Demand, signed by S.M. Abdullah.

5 1940 Log, *Fifty Years Steeple Chase in Kashmir*, p. 8.

6 1944 Log, *Tackling the Impossible*, p. 1.

7 1940 Log, p. 9.

8 A.J. Kaufman and W.L. Putnam, *K2, the 1939 Tragedy* (Seattle, 1992), p. 55.

9 1942 Log, *A Tree in Truth*, p. 2.

10 1939 Log, *Still carrying on in Kashmir*, inserted anonymous pamphlet.

11 CTBDiary, 12 August 1939.

12 CTBDiary, 25 September 1939.

13 CTBDiary, 18 August 1940.

14 18 August 1940. Letter CTB to Julian TB.

15 CTBDiary, 13 March 1941.

16 1941 Log, *Working for Victory in Kashmir*, p. 2.

17 CTBDiary, 6 October 1940. School Sunday. Bishop of Lahore preached in All Saints and then to St Luke's Confirmation Service. N.N. Fotidar, N.N. Misri, Chandra, Jaya Lal, Sham Lal, Gopi Nath Mattoo, his brother Matthew, Kashi Nath Mattoo, Radha Kishen and Mustaffa were confirmed.

18 CTBDiary, 21 February 1943. Padre John Paul preached against our Christian masters which naturally upset them.

19 14 December 1940. Letter CTB to Julian TB.

20 CTBDiary, 12 September 1942. N.N. Misri renounces Christianity and joined the Hindu fold.

21 28 August 1942. Press note from office of Kashmir Hindu League, Srinagar.

22 ETBMem. Chapter 30. Concluding paragraph.

23 CTBDiary, 25 December 1941. Agra. 'A letter from Fred Jacob'.

24 See statement of accounts in logs for 1939–1942 and 1945.

25 CTBDiary, 29 May 1944.

26 CTBDiary, 23 July 1944.

27 CTBDiary, 13 September 1944.

28 CTBDiary, 30 October 1944. Good news, Rev John Paul has been transferred to TarnTarn.

29 21 March 1945. Letter CTB to Julian TB.
30 24 August 1946. Letter CTB to HTB.
31 15 December 1946. Letter Phil Edmonds to ETB.
32 17 December 1946. Anantnag. Letter from Govind Razdan to ETB.
33 22 December 1946. Srinagar. Letter CTB to ETB.
34 9 May 1947. Srinagar. Letter Shenker Koul to HTB.
35 30 May 1947. Srinagar. Letter Phil Edmonds to ETB.
36 16 June 1947. Srinagar. Letter N.L. Bakaya to ETB.
37 *Ibid.*
38 21 July 1947. Nil Nag. Letter Phil Edmonds to ETB.
39 9 October 1947. CTB Circular letter, Salisbury, Rhodesia.
40 28 September 1947. Letter Nand Lal Bakaya to ETB, Srinagar.
41 21 July 1947. Letter Nand Lal Munshi to ETB, Srinagar.
42 12 December 1947. Srinagar. Letter N.L. Munshi to ETB.
43 15 December 1947. Anatnag. Letter Govind Razdan to ETB.
44 14 October 1948, Salisbury, letter CTB to HTB.
45 19 August 1949, The Guardian.
46 Francisco Giner de los Rios, Spanish philosopher, 1839–1915.
47 18 August 1949, The Times of London; 21 September 1949, The Guardian.

Chapter 9 Epilogue

1 Genesis 50, 20.
2 C.E. Tyndale-Biscoe, *Tyndale-Biscoe of Kashmir. An Autobiography* (London, 1952), p. 8.
3 J. Ray, 'Kashmir 1962 to 1986: A Footnote to History' *Journal of the Royal Society for Asian Affairs* (2000) 195–205.
4 N. Chadha Behera, *Demystifying Kashmir* (Washington, 2007), pp. 40–1.
5 28 December 1954. Letter from Srinagar, Phil Edmonds to HTB.
6 Behera, *Demystifying Kashmir*, p. 170.
7 13 April 1958. Letter from Srinagar, HTB to ETB.
8 September 1961. ETB. Second Circular letter from Srinagar.
9 John Ray, Twenty Five Years in Kashmir (Delhi, 2018), p. 13.
10 Ibid p. 67–8
11 J.M. Ray (Ed.) *A Century of CMS Schools 1880–1980* (Srinagar, 1980), p. 62.
12 *The Kashmir Times,* Jammu, 23 July 1998, pp. 1, 7.

Bibliography

Akbar, M.J. *Kashmir: Behind the Vale* (Delhi, 1991).

Allen, C. *Kipling Sahib. India and the Making of Rudyard Kipling* (London, 2007).

Andrews, C.F. *North India* (London, 1908).

Andrews, C.F. *The True India, a Plea for Understanding* (London, 1939).

Bakaya, N.L. *Holidaying and Trekking in Kashmir* (Srinagar, 1966).

Bamzai, P.N.K. *History of Kashmir: Political, Social, Cultural. From the Earliest Times to the Present Day* (Delhi, 1974).

Barnes, A. *You May Keep Your Own Horse. The Story of What Happened to Phyllis Long When She Went to New Zealand in 1923* (Canberra, 2013).

Bates, C.E. *A Gazetteer of Kashmir and the Adjacent Districts* (New Delhi, 1980).

Behera, N.C. *Demystifying Kashmir* (Washington, 2007).

Bevir, M. 'Mothering India', *History Today* (2006), pp. 19–25.

Bruce, C.G. *Himalayan Wanderer* (London, 1914).

Burke, W.S. *The Indian Field Shikar Book* (Calcutta, 1920).

Carus-Wilson, A. *Irene Petrie* (London, 1900).

Chaturvedi, B. and Sykes, M. *Charles Freer Andrews. A Narrative* (London, 1949).

Clark, H.M. *Robert Clark of the Panjab. Pioneer and Missionary Statesman* (London, 1907).

Coventry, B.O. *Wild Flowers of Kashmir* (London, 1923).

Das, G.K. *E.M. Forster's India* (London, 1977).

Draper, A. *Amritsar. The Massacre That Ended the Raj* (London, 1981).

Duke, J. *Kashmir Handbook* (Calcutta, 1903).

Forster, E.M. 'Missionaries'. *The Nation and the Athanaeum*, 22 October 1920, pp. 545–7.

Forster, E.M. *A Passage to India* (London, 1924).

Francke, A.H. *A History of Western Tibet, One of the Unknown Empires* (London, 1907).

French, P. *Younghusband: the Last Great Imperial Adventurer* (Glasgow, 1994).

French, P. *Liberty or Death. India's Journey to Independence and Division* (London, 1997).

Fuller, Sir Bampfylde, *Studies of Indian Life and Sentiment* (London, 1910).

Galgut, D. *Arctic Summer* (London, 2014).

Gilbert, M. *Servant of India. A study of Imperial Rule from 1905 to 1910 as Told Through the Correspondence and Diaries of Sir James Dunlop Smith* (London, 1966).

Gupta, S. *Kashmir. A Study in India–Pakistan Relations* (Bombay, 1966).

Hardinge of Penshurst, Lord *My Indian Years. Memoirs of the Viceroy from 1910–1916* (London, 1948).

Hoyland, J.S. *The Man India Loved, C.F. Andrews* (London, 1944).

Hyde, H.M. *Famous Trials 7: Oscar Wilde* (Harmondsworth, 1962).

Irvine, W. *Apes Angels and Victorians* (London, 1956).

Jacquemont, V. *Letters from India: Describing a Journey in the British Dominions of India, Tibet, Lahore and Cashmere, During the Years 1828–1831* (Karachi, 1979 reprint).

Jaisingh, H. *Kashmir. A Tale of Shame* (New Delhi, 1996).

Kaufman, A.J. and Putnam, W.L. *K2, the 1939 Tragedy* (Seattle, 1992).

Kaye, J.W. *Christianity in India: an Historical Narrative* (London, 1859).

Knight, E.F. *Where Three Empires Meet* (London, 1897).

Knowles, J.H. *Folk Tales of Kashmir* (Srinagar, 1996 reprint).

Knowles, K. 'Osteomalacia in Kashmir', *British Medical Journal Supplement* 1914, pp. 62–63.

Koul, S.C. *Birds of Kashmir* (Srinagar, 1939).

Koul, S.C. *Beautiful Valleys of Kashmir* (Srinagar, 1942).

Lamb, A. *Kashmir, a Disputed Legacy, 1846–1990* (Karachi, 1991).

Lawrence, W.R. *The Valley of Kashmir* (London, 1895).

Lawrence, Sir W.R. *The India We Served* (London, 1928).

Mangan, J.A. *The Games Ethic and Imperialism* (London, 1985).

Mason, K. *Abode of Snow. A History of Himalayan Exploration and Mountaineering* (London, 1955).

Massie, R.K. *Dreadnought, Britain, Germany, and the Coming of the Great War* (New York, 1991).

Mayo, K. *Mother India* (London, 1927).

McNeill, W.H. *Plagues and People* (Oxford, 1976).

Mirsky, J. *Sir Aurel Stein – Archaeological Explorer* (Chicago, 1998 reprint).

Moorcroft, W. and Trebeck, G. *Travels in the Himalayan Provinces of Hindustan and the Panjab; in Ladakh and Kashmir; in Peshawar, Kabul, Kunduz, and Bokhara, from 1819 to 1825* (New Delhi, 1971 reprint).

Mummery, A.F. *My Climbs in the Alps and Caucasus* (Oxford, 1946).

Neve, A. *Picturesque Kashmir* (London, 1900).

Neve, A. 'Journeys in the Himalayas and some factors of Himalayan erosion', *The Geographical Journal* 38 (1911) pp. 346–62.

Neve, A. *Thirty Years in Kashmir* (London, 1913).

Neve, A. *The Tourist's Guide to Kashmir, Ladakh, Skardo, etc.* (Lahore, 1918).

Neve, E.F. *Beyond the Pir Panjal. Life and Missionary Enterprise in Kashmir* (London, 1912).

Pennell, A.M. *Pennell of the Afghan Frontier. The Life of Theodore Leighton Pennell* (London, 1923).

Qadri, S.A. *Biscoe in Kashmir* (Srinagar 1998).

Ray, J. 'Kashmir 1962 to 1986: a footnote to history'. *Journal of the Royal Society for Asian Affairs* (2002), pp. 194–205.

Ray, John *Twenty Five Years in Kashmir* (Delhi, 2018).

Rosenthal, M. *The Character Factory. Baden-Powell and the origins of the Boy Scout Movement* (London, 1986).

Starr-Underhill, Lilian A. *To the British Visitors in Kashmir. For Women Only. The Rights of Woman – 1926* (Peshawar, 1926).

Studdert-Kennedy, G. *Providence and the Raj: Imperial Mission and Missionary Imperialism* (New Delhi, 1998).

Studdert-Kennedy, G. 'Canon Cecil Earle Tyndale-Biscoe', in H.C.G. Matthew, ed., *New Dictionary of National Biography* (Oxford, 1999).

Sturrock, R.R. 'The Anatomy Department at University College, Dundee, 1888–1954', *Medical History* 21 (1977) pp. 310–15.

Taylor, A. *Annie Besant: a Biography* (Oxford, 1992).

Thorp, R. *Cashmere Misgovernment. An Account of the Economic and Political Oppression of the People of Cashmere by the Maharaja's Government* (London, 1870).

Tinker, H. *A New System of Slavery: The Export of Indian Labour Overseas, 1830–1920* (London, 1974).

Tinker, H. *The Ordeal of Love: C.F. Andrews and India* (Oxford, 1979).

Tyndale-Biscoe, C.E. *Character Building in Kashmir* (London, 1920).

Tyndale-Biscoe, C.E. *Arthur Neve, FRCS. Missionary, Physician and Mountaineer* (London, 1920).

Tyndale-Biscoe, C.E. *Kashmir in Sunlight and Shade* (London, 1922).

Tyndale-Biscoe, C.E. *Elizabeth May Newman 1855–32. The Florence Nightingale of Kashmir* (London, 1933).

Tyndale-Biscoe, C.E. *A Valiant Man of Kashmir* (London, 1933).

Tyndale-Biscoe, C.E. *Tyndale-Biscoe of Kashmir: An Autobiography* (London, 1951).

Tyndale-Biscoe, E.D. *Fifty Years Against the Stream. The Story of a School in Kashmir 1880–1930* (Mysore, 1930).

Tyndale-Biscoe, E.D. *The Story of Sheikh Bagh* (Madras, 1947).

Tyndale-Biscoe, J. *Gunner Subaltern 1914–1918* (London, 1971).

Vaughan, K. 'Osteomalacia in Kashmir', *British Medical Journal* (6 March 1926), 1, pp. 413–15.

Vigne, G.T. *Travels in Kashmir, Ladak, Iskardo, the Countries Adjoining the Mountain-Course of the Indus and the Himalaya, North of the Punjab* (New Delhi, 1981 reprint).

Wadia, A.S. *In the Land of Lalla Roukh. Being the Impressions of a Thousand Miles Tramp Through the Vale of Cashmere* (London, 1921).

Wakefield, G.E.C. *Recollections of Fifty Years in the Service of India* (Lahore, 1942 reprint).

Wakefield, W. *The Happy Valley: Sketches of Kashmir and the Kashmiris* (London, 1879).

Walker, A. *Aurel Stein. Pioneer of the Silk Road* (London, 1995).

Wasti, S.R. *Lord Minto and the Indian Nationalist Movement, 1905 to 1910* (Oxford, 1964).

Younghusband, Captain G.J. and Younghusband, Colonel Sir F. *The Relief of Chitral* (London, 1895).

Zalpuri, T.N. 'The Tragedy of Wular Lake April 11 1934 – an eye witness account', *Neelamatam* 2 (July 2004), pp. 1–30 (Journal of Nityanand Shastri Kashmir Research Institute).

Index

Publications, figures and vernacular words in italics.
Abbreviations: CTB, Cecil Tyndale-Biscoe; HS, High School; J&K, Jammu and Kashmir State; PS, Primary School
Special endnotes shown as n. after locator